The Complete

Instant Pot

Cookbook

for Beginners

1800+ Days of Easy, Delicious, and Time-Saving Recipes to Transform Your Everyday Cooking—From Comforting Dinners to Quick Breakfasts

Clyde E. Payne

Table of Contents

INTRODUCTION

Welcome to the World of Instant Pot Cooking

In today's fast-paced world, finding time to prepare healthy, delicious meals can be a challenge. We often rely on convenience foods or takeout, sacrificing nutrition for speed. But what if you could have both? Imagine preparing wholesome, mouth-watering meals in a fraction of the time, with minimal effort and maximum flavor. The Instant Pot makes this possible, revolutionizing the way we cook at home.

This cookbook is your gateway to discovering the incredible potential of the Instant Pot. Whether you're a beginner who's just unboxing your Instant Pot for the first time or a seasoned pro looking for fresh ideas, you'll find a wealth of recipes designed to simplify your life and elevate your cooking. From hearty breakfasts to comforting dinners, light snacks to decadent desserts, this book has it all.

What Makes the Instant Pot So Special?

The Instant Pot has taken the culinary world by storm, and for good reason. It's not just a pressure cooker — it's a multi-cooker that combines several kitchen appliances into one convenient device. With functions like sautéing, steaming, slow cooking, rice cooking, and yogurt making, the Instant Pot does it all. This versatility makes it an invaluable tool for any home cook, whether you're preparing a quick weeknight dinner or an elaborate holiday feast.

The magic of the Instant Pot lies in its ability to cook food quickly and efficiently while preserving its flavors and nutrients. Traditional cooking methods can take hours, especially for dishes like stews, braised meats, or soups. The Instant Pot cuts down on cooking time significantly, thanks to its pressure-cooking function. This means you can enjoy slow-cooked flavors in a fraction of the time, without compromising on taste or texture.

Why Choose This Cookbook?

This cookbook is designed to help you make the most out of your Instant Pot. Inside, you'll find a wide variety of recipes tailored to suit every palate and dietary preference. We've included options for meat lovers, vegetarians, vegans, and those following low-carb or gluten-free diets. The recipes are carefully curated to ensure they are easy to follow, delicious, and make full use of the Instant Pot's capabilities.

We understand that the Instant Pot can be intimidating at first. That's why we've structured this cookbook to guide you step-by-step, from understanding the different settings and functions to mastering basic cooking techniques. Each recipe comes with clear instructions, cooking times, and tips to help you get the best results every time. Whether you want to whip up a quick breakfast, prepare a nutritious lunch, or indulge in a comforting dinner, this book has got you covered.

Healthier Cooking, Made Easy

One of the greatest advantages of the Instant Pot is its ability to prepare healthier meals with ease. By cooking with pressure, the Instant Pot locks in flavors and nutrients, meaning you can use less oil, salt, and seasoning without sacrificing taste. This makes it perfect for those looking to eat healthier or manage their weight.

The recipes in this cookbook are designed with health in mind. You'll find plenty of dishes that are low in fat, high in fiber, and packed with fresh, wholesome ingredients. From vegetable-packed soups and stews to lean proteins and whole grains, these recipes will help you create balanced meals that nourish your body and delight your taste buds.

A Recipe for Every Occasion

The Instant Pot is versatile enough to handle just about any recipe you throw at it. This cookbook reflects that versatility with a wide range of dishes for every meal and occasion:

Breakfasts: Start your day with energy-boosting breakfasts like steel-cut oats, frittatas, or yogurt made from scratch.

Soups and Stews: Enjoy a comforting bowl of soup or stew, from classic chicken noodle to exotic Thai coconut curry.

Main Dishes: Savor hearty main dishes like pulled pork, chicken tikka masala, or vegetarian chili.

Sides: Complement your meals with flavorful sides such as garlic mashed potatoes, quinoa pilaf, or steamed vegetables.

Desserts: Indulge in sweet treats like creamy rice pudding, molten chocolate cake, or fruity cobbler.

Each chapter includes a mix of familiar favorites and innovative new dishes, ensuring there's something for everyone. Whether you're cooking for a crowd or just for yourself, you'll find recipes that are easy to scale up or down.

Tips for Mastering the Instant Pot

To help you get the most out of your Instant Pot, we've included a chapter full of tips and tricks. You'll learn how to adjust cooking times based on your ingredients, how to properly use the sauté function, and how to safely release pressure. We'll also provide troubleshooting advice for common issues, such as the dreaded "burn" warning or undercooked beans.

In addition, we've included tips on meal prepping with the Instant Pot, so you can make the most of your time and ingredients. You'll find advice on freezing leftovers, batch cooking, and making double-duty recipes that can be repurposed for multiple meals.

Why You'll Love Cooking with the Instant Pot

Cooking with the Instant Pot is not just about saving time — it's about enhancing the entire cooking experience. The Instant Pot is perfect for busy professionals, parents juggling hectic schedules, and anyone who wants to eat well without spending hours in the kitchen. It takes the guesswork out of cooking and allows you to create meals that are both quick and impressive.

By incorporating the Instant Pot into your routine, you'll find yourself experimenting more, trying new ingredients, and expanding your culinary horizons. The ease of use and reliability of the Instant Pot give you the confidence to cook more often, making home-cooked meals a regular part of your life.

Your Instant Pot Journey Starts Here

This cookbook is your companion on a journey to mastering the Instant Pot. With every recipe, you'll gain new skills and insights, building confidence in your cooking abilities. You'll discover how easy it is to prepare meals that are both nourishing and delicious, and you'll fall in love with the process of cooking all over again.

So, let's get started! Whether you're a beginner or an experienced cook, this book will help you unlock the full potential of your Instant Pot, transforming your cooking routine and bringing joy back into your kitchen. Happy cooking!

Chapter 1

Breakfasts

Spicy Pulled Pork Skillet

Prep time: 10 minutes | Cook time: 15 minutes | Serves 4

- 4 eggs
- 10 ounces (283 g) pulled pork, shredded
- 1 teaspoon coconut oil
- 1 teaspoon red pepper
- 1 teaspoon chopped fresh cilantro
- 1 tomato, chopped
- ¼ cup water

1. Melt the coconut oil in the instant pot on Sauté mode. 2. Then add pulled pork, red pepper, cilantro, water, and chopped tomato. 3. Cook the ingredients for 5 minutes. 4. Then stir it well with the help of the spatula and crack the eggs over it. 5. Close the lid. 6. Cook the meal on Manual mode (High Pressure) for 7 minutes. Then make a quick pressure release.

Egg Bites with Sausage and Peppers

Prep time: 5 minutes | Cook time: 15 minutes | Serves 7

- 4 large eggs
- ¼ cup vegan cream cheese (such as Tofutti brand) or cream cheese
- ¼ teaspoon fine sea salt
- ¼ teaspoon freshly ground black pepper
- 3 ounces lean turkey sausage, cooked and crumbled, or 1 vegetarian sausage (such as Beyond
- Meat brand), cooked and diced
- ½ red bell pepper, seeded and chopped
- 2 green onions, white and green parts, minced, plus more for garnish (optional)
- ¼ cup vegan cheese shreds or shredded sharp Cheddar cheese

1. Begin by blending together eggs, cream cheese, salt, and pepper in a blender. Blend at medium speed for roughly 20 seconds until everything is well mixed. Next, add in the sausage, bell pepper, and green onions, pulsing the mixture for about 1 second once or twice to incorporate the solid ingredients without fully chopping them up.2. Next, pour 1 cup of water into the Instant Pot. Generously grease a 7-cup egg-bite mold or seven 2-ounce silicone cups with butter or coconut oil, ensuring each cup is coated thoroughly. Position the prepared mold or cups on a silicone steam rack with a long handle. (If you don't have a long-handled steam rack, you can use a wire metal steam rack along with a homemade sling.)3. Fill each prepared mold or cup with ¼ cup of the egg mixture. Carefully lower the egg bites into the pot by holding onto the steam rack handles.4. Lock the lid in place and adjust the Pressure Release valve to Sealing.

Select the Steam setting, setting the timer to 8 minutes on low pressure. (It will take about 5 minutes for the pot to reach pressure before the cooking begins.)5. Once the cooking time is up, allow the pressure to release naturally for 5 minutes, then turn the Pressure Release to Venting to let out any remaining steam. Open the pot carefully. The egg muffins will have puffed up significantly during cooking but will shrink back as they cool. Use heat-resistant mitts to grasp the steam rack handles and lift the egg bites gently from the pot. Sprinkle cheese on top of the egg bites and let them cool for approximately 5 minutes until the cheese melts completely, allowing you to handle the mold or cups comfortably.6. Carefully detach the sides of the egg mold or cups from the egg bites. If needed, run a butter knife around the edge of each bite to loosen them. Move the egg bites to plates, adding extra green onions for garnish if desired, and serve warm. To store leftovers, let them cool to room temperature, then place them in an airtight container and refrigerate for up to 3 days. Reheat gently in the microwave for about 1 minute before serving.

Southwest Avocado Frittata

Prep time: 5 minutes | Cook time: 20 minutes | Serves 4

- 2 tablespoons coconut oil
- ¼ cup diced onion
- ¼ cup diced green chilies
- ½ green bell pepper, diced
- 8 eggs
- 1 teaspoon salt
- ½ teaspoon chili powder
- ¼ teaspoon garlic powder
- ¼ teaspoon pepper
- ¼ cup heavy cream
- 4 tablespoons melted butter
- ½ cup shredded Cheddar cheese
- 1 cup water
- 2 avocados
- ¼ cup sour cream

1. Press the Sauté button and add coconut oil to Instant Pot. Add onion, chilies, and bell pepper. Sauté until onion is translucent and peppers begin to soften, approximately 3 minutes. While sautéing, whisk eggs, seasoning, heavy cream, and butter in large bowl. Pour into 7-inch round baking pan. 2. Press the Cancel button. Add onion and pepper mixture to egg mixture. Mix in Cheddar. Cover pan with aluminum foil. 3. Pour water into Instant Pot, and scrape bottom of pot if necessary to remove any stuck-on food. Place steam rack into pot and put in baking dish with eggs on top. Click lid closed. 4. Press the Manual button and set time for 25 minutes. 5. While food is cooking, cut avocados in half, remove pit, scoop out of shell and slice thinly. When timer beeps, quick-release the pressure. Serve with avocado slices and a spoonful of sour cream.

Breakfast Farro with Berries and Walnuts

Prep time: 8 minutes | Cook time: 10 minutes | Serves 6

- 1 cup farro, rinsed and drained
- 1 cup unsweetened almond milk
- ¼ teaspoon kosher salt
- ½ teaspoon pure vanilla extract
- 1 teaspoon ground cinnamon
- 1 tablespoon pure maple syrup
- 1½ cups fresh blueberries, raspberries, or strawberries (or a combination)
- 6 tablespoons chopped walnuts

1. Start by adding farro, almond milk, 1 cup of water, salt, vanilla extract, cinnamon, and maple syrup into your electric pressure cooker.2. Secure the lid tightly and set the valve to the sealing position.3. Select the high-pressure cooking option and set the timer for 10 minutes.4. After the cooking cycle is finished, let the pressure release naturally for 10 minutes before using the quick release method for any remaining pressure. Press Cancel to stop the cooking process.5. When the pressure pin drops, carefully unlock and remove the lid.6. Give the farro a good stir. Serve it in bowls and garnish each portion with ¼ cup of fresh berries and 1 tablespoon of walnuts for added crunch.

Cynthia's Homemade Greek Yogurt

Prep time: 10 minutes | Cook time: 8 hours | Serves 16

- 1 gallon low-fat milk
- ¼ cup low-fat plain
- yogurt with active cultures

1. Pour milk into the inner pot of the Instant Pot. 2. Lock lid, move vent to sealing, and press the yogurt button. Press Adjust till it reads "boil." 3. When boil cycle is complete (about 1 hour), check the temperature. It should be at 185°F. If it's not, use the Sauté function to warm to 185. 4. After it reaches 185°F, unplug Instant Pot, remove inner pot, and cool. You can place on cooling rack and let it slowly cool. If in a hurry, submerge the base of the pot in cool water. Cool milk to 110°F. 5. When mixture reaches 110, stir in the ¼ cup of yogurt. Lock the lid in place and move vent to sealing. 6. Press Yogurt. Use the Adjust button until the screen says 8:00. This will now incubate for 8 hours. 7. After 8 hours (when the cycle is finished), chill yogurt, or go immediately to straining in step 8. 8. After chilling, or following the 8 hours, strain the yogurt using a nut milk bag. This will give it the consistency of Greek yogurt.

Pork and Quill Egg Cups

Prep time: 15 minutes | Cook time: 15 minutes | Serves 4

- 10 ounces (283 g) ground pork
- 1 jalapeño pepper, chopped
- 1 tablespoon butter,
- softened
- 1 teaspoon dried dill
- ½ teaspoon salt
- 1 cup water
- 4 quill eggs

1. In a mixing bowl, combine all the ingredients, leaving out the quail eggs and water. Once mixed, transfer the meat mixture into silicone muffin molds, pressing down gently on the surface to pack it well.2. Pour water into the Instant Pot and place the trivet inside. Position the filled muffin molds on the trivet.3. Carefully crack the quail eggs over the meat mixture in each mold.4. Secure the lid and choose the Manual setting, adjusting the cooking time to 15 minutes at High Pressure. When the timer signals, perform a quick release of the pressure. Gently open the lid afterward.5. Serve the meat cups warm, ready to enjoy!

Nutty Coconut Breakfast Bowl

Prep time: 5 minutes | Cook time: 4 minutes | Serves 4

- 2 tablespoons coconut oil
- 1 cup full-fat coconut milk
- 1 cup heavy whipping cream
- ½ cup macadamia nuts
- ½ cup chopped pecans
- ⅓ cup Swerve, or more
- to taste
- ¼ cup unsweetened coconut flakes
- 2 tablespoons chopped hazelnuts
- 2 tablespoons chia seeds
- ½ teaspoon ground cinnamon

1. Before you get started, soak the chia seeds for about 5 to 10 minutes (can be up to 20, if desired) in 1 cup of filtered water. After soaking, set the Instant Pot to Sauté and add the coconut oil. Once melted, pour in the milk, whipping cream, and 1 cup of filtered water. Then add the macadamia nuts, pecans, Swerve, coconut flakes, hazelnuts, chia seeds, and cinnamon. Mix thoroughly inside the Instant Pot. 2. Close the lid, set the pressure release to Sealing, and hit Cancel to stop the current program. Select Manual, set the Instant Pot to 4 minutes on High Pressure, and let cook. 3. Once cooked, carefully switch the pressure release to Venting. 4. Open the Instant Pot, serve, and enjoy!

Spicy Mexican Beef Chili Breakfast

Prep time: 5 minutes | Cook time: 45 minutes | Serves 4

- 2 tablespoons coconut oil
- 1 pound (454 g) ground grass-fed beef
- 1 (14-ounce / 397-g) can sugar-free or low-sugar diced tomatoes
- ½ cup shredded full-fat Cheddar cheese (optional)
- 1 teaspoon hot sauce
- ½ teaspoon chili powder
- ½ teaspoon crushed red pepper
- ½ teaspoon ground cumin
- ½ teaspoon kosher salt
- ½ teaspoon freshly ground black pepper

1. Set the Instant Pot to Sauté and melt the oil. 2. Pour in ½ cup of filtered water, then add the beef, tomatoes, cheese, hot sauce, chili powder, red pepper, cumin, salt, and black pepper to the Instant Pot, stirring thoroughly. 3. Close the lid, set the pressure release to Sealing, and hit Cancel to stop the current program. Select Manual, set the Instant Pot to 45 minutes on High Pressure and let cook. 4. Once cooked, let the pressure naturally disperse from the Instant Pot for about 10 minutes, then carefully switch the pressure release to Venting. 5. Open the Instant Pot, serve, and enjoy!

Pumpkin Mug Muffin

Prep time: 5 minutes | Cook time: 9 minutes | Serves 1

- ½ cup Swerve
- ½ cup blanched almond flour
- 2 tablespoons organic pumpkin purée
- 1 teaspoon sugar-free chocolate chips
- 1 tablespoon organic coconut flour
- 1 egg
- 1 tablespoon coconut oil
- ½ teaspoon pumpkin pie spice
- ½ teaspoon ground nutmeg
- ½ teaspoon ground cinnamon
- ⅛ teaspoon baking soda

1. In a large mixing bowl, combine Swerve, almond flour, pumpkin purée, chocolate chips, coconut flour, egg, melted coconut oil, pumpkin pie spice, nutmeg, cinnamon, and baking soda until well blended. Pour this mixture into a greased mug suitable for the Instant Pot.2. Add 1 cup of filtered water to the inner pot of the Instant Pot, and place the trivet inside. Cover the mug with aluminum foil and set it on top of the trivet.3. Secure the lid, adjust the pressure release valve to Sealing, and select the Manual setting. Set the cooking time to 9 minutes at High Pressure.4. After the cooking cycle finishes, quickly release the pressure by switching the valve to Venting. Check if the muffin is fully cooked by inserting a toothpick into the center; it should come out clean, as cooking times may differ.5. Carefully remove the mug from the pot and enjoy your delicious treat!

Mediterranean Kale and Feta Frittata

Prep time: 5 minutes | Cook time: 45 minutes | Serves 6

- 8 large eggs
- ½ cup plain 2 percent Greek yogurt
- Fine sea salt
- Freshly ground black pepper
- 2 cups firmly packed finely shredded kale or baby kale leaves
- One 12-ounce jar roasted red peppers, drained and cut into ¼ by 2-inch strips
- 2 green onions, white and green parts, thinly sliced
- 1 tablespoon chopped fresh dill
- ⅓ cup crumbled feta cheese
- 6 cups loosely packed mixed baby greens
- ¾ cup cherry or grape tomatoes, halved
- 2 tablespoons extra-virgin olive oil

1. Pour 1½ cups water into the Instant Pot. Lightly butter a 7-cup round heatproof glass dish or coat with nonstick cooking spray. 2. In a bowl, whisk together the eggs, yogurt, ¼ teaspoon salt, and ¼ teaspoon pepper until well blended, then stir in the kale, roasted peppers, green onions, dill, and feta cheese. 3. Pour the egg mixture into the prepared dish and cover tightly with aluminum foil. Place the dish on a long-handled silicone steam rack, then, holding the handles of the steam rack, lower it into the Instant Pot. (If you don't have the long-handled rack, use the wire metal steam rack and a homemade sling) 4. Secure the lid and set the Pressure Release to Sealing. Select the Pressure Cook or Manual setting and set the cooking time for 30 minutes at high pressure. (The pot will take about 15 minutes to come up to pressure before the cooking program begins.) 5. When the cooking program ends, let the pressure release naturally for 10 minutes, then move the Pressure Release to Venting to release any remaining steam. Open the pot and let the frittata sit for a minute or two, until it deflates and settles into its dish. Then, wearing heat-resistant mitts, grasp the handles of the steam rack and lift it out of the pot. Uncover the dish, taking care not to get burned by the steam or to drip condensation onto the frittata. Let the frittata sit for 10 minutes, giving it time to reabsorb any liquid and set up. 6. In a medium bowl, toss together the mixed greens, tomatoes, and olive oil. Taste and adjust the seasoning with salt and pepper, if needed. 7. Cut the frittata into six wedges and serve warm, with the salad alongside.

Bacon Cheddar Bites

Prep time: 15 minutes | Cook time: 3 minutes | Serves 2

- 2 tablespoons coconut flour
- ½ cup shredded Cheddar cheese
- 2 teaspoons coconut
- cream
- 2 bacon slices, cooked
- ½ teaspoon dried parsley
- 1 cup water, for cooking

1. In a mixing bowl, combine coconut flour, shredded Cheddar cheese, coconut cream, and dried parsley until evenly mixed.2. Next, chop the cooked bacon into small pieces and add it to the mixture.3. Mix everything thoroughly until well combined.4. Pour water into the Instant Pot and place the trivet inside.5. Line the trivet with baking paper to prevent sticking.6. Form small balls (bites) from the cheese mixture and arrange them on the prepared trivet.7. Set the Instant Pot to Manual mode and cook for 3 minutes at High Pressure.8. After cooking, perform a quick pressure release and allow the bites to cool down before serving.

Hearty Sausage and Cauliflower Breakfast Bake

Prep time: 5 minutes | Cook time: 10 minutes | Serves 6

- 1 cup water
- ½ head cauliflower, chopped into bite-sized pieces
- 4 slices bacon
- 1 pound (454 g) breakfast sausage
- 4 tablespoons melted butter
- 10 eggs
- ⅓ cup heavy cream
- 2 teaspoons salt
- 1 teaspoon pepper
- 2 tablespoons hot sauce
- 2 stalks green onion
- 1 cup shredded sharp Cheddar cheese

1. Pour water into Instant Pot and place steamer basket in bottom. Add cauliflower. Click lid closed. 2. Press the Steam button and adjust time for 1 minute. When timer beeps, quick-release the pressure and place cauliflower to the side in medium bowl. 3. Drain water from Instant Pot, clean, and replace. Press the Sauté button. Press the Adjust button to set heat to Less. Cook bacon until crispy. Once fully cooked, set aside on paper towels. Add breakfast sausage to pot and brown (still using the Sauté function). 4. While sausage is cooking, whisk butter, eggs, heavy cream, salt, pepper, and hot sauce. 5. When sausage is fully cooked, pour egg mixture into Instant Pot. Gently stir using silicone spatula until eggs are completely cooked and fluffy. Press the Cancel button. Slice green onions. Sprinkle green onions, bacon, and cheese over mixture and let melt. Serve warm.

Baked Eggs

Prep time: 15 minutes | Cook time: 20 minutes | Serves 8

- 1 cup water
- 2 tablespoons no-trans-fat tub margarine, melted
- 1 cup reduced-fat buttermilk baking mix
- 1½ cups fat-free cottage cheese
- 2 teaspoons chopped
- onion
- 1 teaspoon dried parsley
- ½ cup grated reduced-fat cheddar cheese
- 1 egg, slightly beaten
- 1¼ cups egg substitute
- 1 cup fat-free milk

1. Begin by placing the steaming rack at the bottom of the inner pot and adding 1 cup of water.2. Grease a round springform pan that fits comfortably inside the Instant Pot.3. Pour melted margarine into the greased springform pan.4. In a large mixing bowl, combine buttermilk baking mix, cottage cheese, chopped onion, parsley, cheese, egg, egg substitute, and milk, mixing until well blended.5. Carefully pour the mixture over the melted margarine in the springform pan, stirring gently to incorporate the margarine throughout.6. Set the springform pan on the steaming rack, close the lid, and secure it in the locked position, ensuring the vent is set to sealing. Cook for 20 minutes on Manual at high pressure.7. Once cooking is complete, allow the pressure to release naturally.8. Use the handles of the steaming rack to carefully lift the springform pan from the pot, letting it stand for 10 minutes before cutting and serving.

Mini Spinach Quiche Cup

Prep time: 5 minutes | Cook time: 15 minutes | Serves 1

- 2 eggs
- 1 tablespoon heavy cream
- 1 tablespoon diced green pepper
- 1 tablespoon diced red onion
- ¼ cup chopped fresh spinach
- ½ teaspoon salt
- ¼ teaspoon pepper
- 1 cup water

1. In medium bowl whisk together all ingredients except water. Pour into 4-inch ramekin. Generally, if the ramekin is oven-safe, it is also safe to use in pressure cooking. 2. Pour water into Instant Pot. Place steam rack into pot. Carefully place ramekin onto steam rack. Click lid closed. Press the Manual button and set time for 15 minutes. When timer beeps, quick-release the pressure. Serve warm.

Chocolate Chip Pancake

Prep time: 5 minutes | Cook time: 37 minutes | Serves 5 to 6

- 4 tablespoons salted grass-fed butter, softened
- 2 cups blanched almond flour
- ½ cup Swerve, or more to taste
- 1¼ cups full-fat coconut milk
- ¼ cup sugar-free chocolate chips
- ¼ cup organic coconut flour
- 2 eggs
- 1 tablespoon chopped walnuts
- ¼ teaspoon baking soda
- ½ teaspoon salt
- ½ cup dark berries, for serving (optional)

1. Generously grease the bottom and sides of your Instant Pot with butter, ensuring a thick coating for easy release.2. In a large mixing bowl, combine almond flour, Swerve, milk, chocolate chips, coconut flour, eggs, walnuts, baking soda, and salt, stirring until well blended. Pour this mixture into the Instant Pot. Close the lid, set the pressure release valve to Sealing, and select the Multigrain option. Adjust the cooking time to 37 minutes on Low Pressure and start the cooking process.3. Once the cooking time is complete, switch the pressure release to Venting and carefully open the Instant Pot. Check to ensure your pancake is fully cooked, then use a spatula to gently lift it out. Serve with berries if desired, and enjoy your delicious creation!

Cheesy Spinach Breakfast Frittata

Prep time: 5 minutes | Cook time: 20 minutes | Serves 4 to 5

- 6 eggs
- 1 cup chopped spinach
- 1 cup shredded full-fat Cheddar cheese
- 1 cup shredded full-fat Monterey Jack cheese (optional)
- 2 tablespoons coconut oil
- 1 cup chopped bell
- peppers
- ½ teaspoon dried parsley
- ½ teaspoon dried basil
- ½ teaspoon ground turmeric
- ½ teaspoon freshly ground black pepper
- ½ teaspoon kosher salt

1. Pour 1 cup of filtered water into the inner pot of the Instant Pot, then insert the trivet. 2. In a large bowl, combine the eggs, spinach, Cheddar cheese, Monterey Jack cheese, coconut oil, bell peppers, parsley, basil, turmeric, black pepper, and salt, and stir thoroughly. Transfer this mixture into a well-greased Instant Pot-friendly dish. 3. Using a sling if desired, place the dish onto the trivet, and cover loosely with aluminum foil. Close the lid, set the pressure release to Sealing, and select Manual. Set the Instant Pot to 20 minutes on High Pressure, and let cook. 4. Once cooked, let the pressure naturally disperse from the Instant Pot for about 10 minutes, then carefully switch the pressure release to Venting. 5. Open the Instant Pot, serve, and enjoy!

Keto Cabbage Hash Browns

Prep time: 5 minutes | Cook time: 8 minutes | Serves 3

- 1 cup shredded white cabbage
- 3 eggs, beaten
- ½ teaspoon ground nutmeg
- ½ teaspoon salt
- ½ teaspoon onion powder
- ½ zucchini, grated
- 1 tablespoon coconut oil

1. In a bowl, combine all the ingredients, reserving the coconut oil for cooking. Shape the cabbage mixture into medium-sized hash browns.2. Activate the Sauté function on the Instant Pot and add the coconut oil to heat it up.3. Carefully place the hash browns into the hot coconut oil. Cook for about 4 minutes on each side, or until they are golden brown and crispy.4. Once cooked, transfer the hash browns to a plate and serve them warm for a delicious side dish.

Bacon Potato Omelet Bake

Prep time: 15 minutes | Cook time: 20 minutes | Serves 6

- 3 slices bacon, cooked and crumbled
- 2 cups shredded cooked potatoes
- ¼ cup minced onion
- ¼ cup minced green bell pepper
- 1 cup egg substitute
- ¼ cup fat-free milk
- ¼ teaspoon salt
- ⅛ teaspoon black pepper
- 1 cup 75%-less-fat shredded cheddar cheese
- 1 cup water

1. With nonstick cooking spray, spray the inside of a round baking dish that will fit in your Instant Pot inner pot. 2. Sprinkle the bacon, potatoes, onion, and bell pepper around the bottom of the baking dish. 3. Mix together the egg substitute, milk, salt, and pepper in mixing bowl. Pour over potato mixture. 4. Top with cheese. 5. Add water, place the steaming rack into the bottom of the inner pot and then place the round baking dish on top. 6. Close the lid and secure to the locking position. Be sure the vent is turned to sealing. Set for 20 minutes on Manual at high pressure. 7. Let the pressure release naturally. 8. Carefully remove the baking dish with the handles of the steaming rack and allow to stand 10 minutes before cutting and serving.

Bacon Egg Cups

Prep time: 5 minutes | Cook time: 7 minutes | Serves 4

- 6 large eggs
- 2 strips cooked bacon, sliced in ¼-inch wide pieces
- ½ cup Cheddar cheese, divided
- ¼ teaspoon sea salt
- ¼ teaspoon black pepper
- 1 cup water
- 1 tablespoon chopped fresh flat leaf parsley

1. In a small bowl, whisk the eggs until well beaten. Mix in the cooked bacon, ¼ cup of cheese, sea salt, and pepper until fully combined. Distribute the egg mixture evenly into four ramekins, then loosely cover each with aluminum foil.2. Pour water into the Instant Pot and place the trivet inside. Arrange two ramekins on the trivet and stack the remaining two on top of them.3. Secure the lid in place. Choose the Manual mode and set the cooking time for 7 minutes at High Pressure. Once the timer finishes, allow for a natural pressure release for 10 minutes before releasing any leftover pressure. Carefully open the lid.4. Sprinkle the remaining ¼ cup of cheese on top of each ramekin. Lock the lid back in place and melt the cheese for an additional 2 minutes. Garnish with chopped parsley and serve immediately for a delightful dish.

Cinnamon French Toast

Prep time: 10 minutes | Cook time: 20 minutes | Serves 8

- 3 eggs
- 2 cups low-fat milk
- 2 tablespoons maple syrup
- 15 drops liquid stevia
- 2 teaspoons vanilla extract
- 2 teaspoons cinnamon
- Pinch salt
- 16 ounces whole wheat bread, cubed and left out overnight to go stale
- 1½ cups water

1. In a medium bowl, beat together the eggs, milk, maple syrup, Stevia, vanilla extract, cinnamon, and salt until well combined. Gently fold in the cubes of whole wheat bread.2. Prepare a 7-inch round baking pan by spraying the inside with nonstick spray. Pour the bread mixture into the greased pan.3. Place the trivet at the bottom of the inner pot and pour in the water.4. Create a foil sling and place it on the trivet. Carefully position the 7-inch pan on top of the foil sling and trivet.5. Lock the lid in place, ensuring the vent is set to sealing.6. Press the Manual button and adjust the timer to 20 minutes using the "+/-" buttons.7. Once the cooking time is finished, allow the Instant Pot to release pressure naturally for 5 minutes, then perform a quick release for any

remaining pressure.

Southwest Cheesy Egg Bake

Prep time: 10 minutes | Cook time: 20 minutes | Serves 12

- 1 cup water
- 2½ cups egg substitute
- ½ cup flour
- 1 teaspoon baking powder
- ⅛ teaspoon salt
- ⅛ teaspoon pepper
- 2 cups fat-free cottage cheese
- 1½ cups shredded 75%-less-fat sharp cheddar cheese
- ¼ cup no-trans-fat tub margarine, melted
- 2 (4-ounce) cans chopped green chilies

1. Place the steaming rack into the bottom of the inner pot and pour in 1 cup of water. 2. Grease a round springform pan that will fit into the inner pot of the Instant Pot. 3. Combine the egg substitute, flour, baking powder, salt and pepper in a mixing bowl. It will be lumpy. 4. Stir in the cheese, margarine, and green chilies then pour into the springform pan. 5. Place the springform pan onto the steaming rack, close the lid, and secure to the locking position. Be sure the vent is turned to sealing. Set for 20 minutes on Manual at high pressure. 6. Let the pressure release naturally. 7. Carefully remove the springform pan with the handles of the steaming rack and allow to stand 10 minutes before cutting and serving.

Kale Omelet

Prep time: 5 minutes | Cook time: 10 minutes | Serves 2

- 2 eggs
- 1 cup chopped kale
- 1 teaspoon heavy cream
- ⅔ teaspoon white pepper
- ½ teaspoon butter

1. Begin by generously greasing the Instant Pot pan with butter to ensure easy removal later.2. In a separate bowl, crack the eggs and whisk them thoroughly until well beaten.3. Next, incorporate heavy cream and white pepper into the eggs, stirring gently to combine.4. Place the chopped kale in the greased pan, then pour the whisked egg mixture over the kale, ensuring it's evenly distributed.5. Add 1 cup of water to the Instant Pot to create steam for cooking.6. Position the trivet inside the Instant Pot and carefully place the pan containing the egg mixture on top of the trivet.7. Secure the lid of the Instant Pot and select the Manual (High Pressure) setting, adjusting the time to 5 minutes for cooking the frittata. Allow the pressure to release naturally for 5 minutes once cooking is complete.

Nutty Strawberry Millet Breakfast Bowl

Prep time: 0 minutes | Cook time: 30 minutes | Serves 8

- 2 tablespoons coconut oil or unsalted butter
- 1½ cups millet
- 2⅔ cups water
- ½ teaspoon fine sea salt
- 1 cup unsweetened
- almond milk or other nondairy milk
- 1 cup chopped toasted pecans, almonds, or peanuts
- 4 cups sliced strawberries

1. Select the Sauté setting on the Instant Pot and melt the oil. Add the millet and cook for 4 minutes, until aromatic. Stir in the water and salt, making sure all of the grains are submerged in the liquid. 2. Secure the lid and set the Pressure Release to Sealing. Press the Cancel button to reset the cooking program, then select the Porridge, Pressure Cook, or Manual setting and set the cooking time for 12 minutes at high pressure. (The pot will take about 10 minutes to come up to pressure before the cooking program begins.) 3. When the cooking program ends, let the pressure release naturally for 10 minutes, then move the Pressure Release to Venting to release any remaining steam. Open the pot and use a fork to fluff and stir the millet. 4. Spoon the millet into bowls and top each serving with 2 tablespoons of the almond milk, then sprinkle with the nuts and top with the strawberries. Serve warm.

Bacon and Spinach Eggs

Prep time: 5 minutes | Cook time: 9 minutes | Serves 4

- 2 tablespoons unsalted butter, divided
- ½ cup diced bacon
- ⅓ cup finely diced shallots
- ⅓ cup chopped spinach, leaves only
- Pinch of sea salt
- Pinch of black pepper
- ½ cup water
- ¼ cup heavy whipping cream
- 8 large eggs
- 1 tablespoon chopped fresh chives, for garnish

1. Start by setting the Instant Pot to Sauté mode and melting 1 tablespoon of butter. Add the bacon and sauté for about 4 minutes, or until it becomes crispy. Use a slotted spoon to transfer the bacon to a bowl and set it aside. 2. Next, add the remaining 1 tablespoon of butter along with the shallots to the pot. Sauté for about 2 minutes, or until the shallots are tender. Then, add the spinach leaves and sauté for an additional minute until wilted. Season the mixture with sea salt and black pepper, stirring well, and transfer the spinach to a separate bowl. 3. Drain the excess oil from the pot into a bowl. Pour in the water and place the trivet inside the pot. 4. Using a paper towel, grease four ramekins with the reserved bacon grease. In each ramekin, add 1 tablespoon of heavy whipping cream, the reserved bacon bits, and the sautéed spinach. Crack two eggs into each ramekin, being careful not to break the yolks. Cover the ramekins with aluminum foil and place two on the trivet, stacking the other two on top. 5. Lock the lid in place. Select the Manual mode and set the cooking time for 2 minutes at Low Pressure. When the timer finishes, allow for a natural pressure release for 5 minutes, then release any remaining pressure. Carefully open the lid. 6. Gently remove the ramekins from the pot and serve, garnished with fresh chives for added flavor.

Blueberry Oat Mini Muffins

Prep time: 12 minutes | Cook time: 10 minutes | Serves 7

- ½ cup rolled oats
- ¼ cup whole wheat pastry flour or white whole wheat flour
- ½ tablespoon baking powder
- ½ teaspoon ground cardamom or ground cinnamon
- ⅛ teaspoon kosher salt
- 2 large eggs
- ½ cup plain Greek yogurt
- 2 tablespoons pure maple syrup
- 2 teaspoons extra-virgin olive oil
- ½ teaspoon vanilla extract
- ½ cup frozen blueberries (preferably small wild blueberries)

1. In a large bowl, combine the oats, flour, baking powder, cardamom, and salt, mixing thoroughly. 2. In a separate medium bowl, whisk together the eggs, yogurt, maple syrup, oil, and vanilla extract until well blended. 3. Pour the egg mixture into the oat mixture and stir until just combined. Carefully fold in the blueberries to avoid crushing them. 4. Distribute the batter evenly into each cup of the egg bite mold. 5. Add 1 cup of water to the electric pressure cooker. Place the egg bite mold on the wire rack and gently lower it into the pot. 6. Secure the lid of the pressure cooker and set the valve to the sealing position. 7. Cook at high pressure for 10 minutes. 8. After the cooking time is up, allow the pressure to release naturally for 10 minutes, then use a quick release for any remaining pressure. Press Cancel to stop the cooking cycle. 9. Carefully lift the wire rack out of the pot and set it on a cooling rack for 5 minutes. Invert the mold onto the cooling rack to gently release the muffins. 10. Enjoy the muffins warm, or store them in the refrigerator or freezer for later use.

Gouda Egg Casserole with Canadian Bacon

Prep time: 12 minutes | Cook time: 20 minutes | Serves 4

- Nonstick cooking spray
- 1 slice whole grain bread, toasted
- ½ cup shredded smoked Gouda cheese
- 3 slices Canadian bacon, chopped
- 6 large eggs
- ¼ cup half-and-half
- ¼ teaspoon kosher salt
- ¼ teaspoon freshly ground black pepper
- ¼ teaspoon dry mustard

1. Begin by spraying a 6-inch cake pan with cooking spray, or skip this step if your pan is nonstick. If you don't have a 6-inch cake pan, any bowl or pan that fits inside your pressure cooker will work just fine.2. Crumble the toast and place it at the bottom of the pan. Evenly sprinkle the cheese and Canadian bacon over the crumbled toast.3. In a medium bowl, whisk together the eggs, half-and-half, salt, pepper, and dry mustard until well combined.4. Pour the egg mixture over the ingredients in the pan, then loosely cover the pan with aluminum foil.5. Pour 1½ cups of water into the electric pressure cooker and insert a wire rack or trivet. Position the covered pan on top of the rack.6. Securely close and lock the lid of the pressure cooker, ensuring the valve is set to sealing.7. Set the cooker to high pressure and cook for 20 minutes.8. Once cooking is complete, press Cancel and perform a quick release of the pressure.9. After the pressure pin drops, carefully unlock and remove the lid.10. Gently transfer the pan from the pressure cooker to a cooling rack and let it sit for 5 minutes.11. Slice into 4 wedges and serve warm for a delicious meal.

Bacon Avocado Egg Sandwich

Prep time: 5 minutes | Cook time: 15 minutes | Serves 1

- 2 slices bacon
- 2 eggs
- 1 avocado

1. Press the Sauté button. Press the Adjust button to set heat to Low. Add bacon to Instant Pot and cook until crispy. Remove and set aside. 2. Crack egg over Instant Pot slowly, into bacon grease. Repeat with second egg. When edges become golden, after 2 to 3 minutes, flip. Press the Cancel button. 3. Cut avocado in half and scoop out half without seed. Place in small bowl and mash with fork. Spread on one egg. Place bacon on top and top with second egg. Let cool 5 minutes before eating.

Chicken and Egg Sandwich

Prep time: 5 minutes | Cook time: 15 minutes | Serves 1

- 1 (6-ounce / 170-g) boneless, skinless chicken breast
- ¼ teaspoon salt
- ⅛ teaspoon pepper
- ¼ teaspoon garlic powder
- 2 tablespoons coconut oil, divided
- 1 egg
- 1 cup water
- ¼ avocado
- 2 tablespoons mayonnaise
- ¼ cup shredded white Cheddar
- Salt and pepper, to taste

1. Begin by slicing the chicken breast in half lengthwise. Use a meat tenderizer to pound the chicken until it's thin. Season with salt, pepper, and garlic powder, and set aside.2. Add 1 tablespoon of coconut oil to the Instant Pot. Press the Sauté button, then use the Adjust button to set the temperature to Less. Once the oil is heated, fry an egg until cooked, then remove it from the pot and set aside. Press the Cancel button. Next, press the Sauté button again and set the temperature to Normal. Add the second tablespoon of coconut oil to the pot and sear the chicken for 3 to 4 minutes on each side, or until golden brown.3. Press the Manual button and set the cooking time for 8 minutes. While the chicken cooks, use a fork to mash the avocado and mix it with the mayo. Once the timer goes off, perform a quick release of the pressure. Remove the chicken from the pot and pat it dry with a paper towel.4. Assemble the sandwich using the chicken pieces, topped with the fried egg, cheese, and avocado mayo. Season lightly with salt and pepper to taste.

Cheesy Egg Bites

Prep time: 5 minutes | Cook time: 10 minutes | Serves 6

- 4 eggs
- 2 tablespoons heavy cream
- ¼ teaspoon salt
- ⅛ teaspoon pepper
- ⅓ cup shredded Cheddar cheese
- 1 cup water

1. In a large bowl, whisk eggs and heavy cream. Add salt and pepper. 2. Pour mixture into 6 silicone cupcake baking molds. Sprinkle cheese into each cup. 3. Pour water into Instant Pot and place steam rack in bottom of pot. Carefully set filled silicone molds steadily on steam rack. If all do not fit, separate into two batches. 4. Click lid closed. Press the Manual button and adjust time for 10 minutes. When timer beeps, allow a quick release and remove lid. Egg bites will look puffy at first, but will become smaller once they begin to cool. Serve warm.

Salmon and Asparagus Quiche Bites

Prep time: 15 minutes | Cook time: 15 minutes | Serves 2

- Nonstick cooking spray
- 4 asparagus spears, cut into ½-inch pieces
- 2 tablespoons finely chopped onion
- 3 ounces (85 g) smoked salmon (skinless and boneless), chopped
- 3 large eggs
- 2 tablespoons 2% milk
- ¼ teaspoon dried dill
- Pinch ground white pepper

1. Pour 1½ cups of water into the electric pressure cooker and insert a wire rack or trivet. 2. Lightly spray the bottom and sides of the ramekins with nonstick cooking spray. Divide the asparagus, onion, and salmon between the ramekins. 3. In a measuring cup with a spout, whisk together the eggs, milk, dill, and white pepper. Pour half of the egg mixture into each ramekin. Loosely cover the ramekins with aluminum foil. 4. Carefully place the ramekins inside the pot on the rack. 5. Close and lock the lid of the pressure cooker. Set the valve to sealing. 6. Cook on high pressure for 15 minutes. 7. When the cooking is complete, hit Cancel and quick release the pressure. 8. Once the pin drops, unlock and remove the lid. 9. Carefully remove the ramekins from the pot. Cool, covered, for 5 minutes. 10. Run a small silicone spatula or a knife around the edge of each ramekin. Invert each quiche onto a small plate and serve.

Cauliflower Nutty Porridge

Prep time: 40 minutes | Cook time: 5 minutes | Serves 4

- 2½ cups water, divided
- ½ cup raw cashews
- ½ cup almond slivers
- ¼ cup raw pumpkin seeds
- ¼ head cauliflower, chopped
- Sea salt, to taste
- ¼ cup heavy whipping cream
- Topping:
- ¼ cup hemp seeds
- ¼ cup chia seeds
- 1 tablespoon cinnamon

1. In a small bowl, combine 2 cups of water with the cashews, almonds, and pumpkin seeds. Allow them to soak for 30 minutes, then drain and set aside. Reserve a handful of nuts and pumpkin seeds in a separate bowl for garnish later.2. Pour the remaining ½ cup of water into the Instant Pot, then add the soaked nut mixture along with the cauliflower and sea salt.3. Secure the lid on the Instant Pot and select Manual mode, setting the cooking time to 5 minutes at High Pressure. Once the timer goes off, let the pressure release naturally for 10 minutes before releasing any remaining pressure. Carefully remove the lid.4. Transfer the cauliflower and nut mixture to a food processor. Add the heavy cream and blend until smooth.5. Taste and adjust seasoning with a pinch of sea salt if needed. Garnish with the reserved nuts, pumpkin seeds, hemp seeds, and chia seeds, then sprinkle with cinnamon. Serve immediately for a delicious and nutritious dish.

Mini Chocolate Chip Almond Muffins

Prep time: 5 minutes | Cook time: 20 minutes | Serves 7

- 1 cup blanched almond flour
- 2 eggs
- ¾ cup sugar-free chocolate chips
- 1 tablespoon vanilla extract
- ½ cup Swerve, or more to taste
- 2 tablespoons salted grass-fed butter, softened
- ½ teaspoon salt
- ¼ teaspoon baking soda

1. Pour 1 cup of filtered water into the inner pot of the Instant Pot, then insert the trivet. Using an electric mixer, combine flour, eggs, chocolate chips, vanilla, Swerve, butter, salt, and baking soda. Mix thoroughly. Transfer this mixture into a well-greased Instant Pot-friendly muffin (or egg bites) mold. 2. Using a sling if desired, place the pan onto the trivet and cover loosely with aluminum foil. Close the lid, set the pressure release to Sealing, and select Manual. Set the Instant Pot to 20 minutes on High Pressure and let cook. 3. Once cooked, let the pressure naturally disperse from the Instant Pot for about 10 minutes, then carefully switch the pressure release to Venting. 4. Open the Instant Pot and remove the pan. Let cool, serve, and enjoy!

Boiled Eggs

Prep time: 10 minutes | Cook time: 5 minutes | Serves 7

- 1 cup water
- 6 to 8 eggs

1. Pour the water into the inner pot. Place the eggs in a steamer basket or rack that came with pot. 2. Close the lid and secure to the locking position. Be sure the vent is turned to sealing. Set for 5 minutes on Manual at high pressure. (It takes about 5 minutes for pressure to build and then 5 minutes to cook.) 3. Let pressure naturally release for 5 minutes, then do quick pressure release. 4. Place hot eggs into cool water to halt cooking process. You can peel cooled eggs immediately or refrigerate unpeeled.

Perfect Instant Pot Hard-Asparagus Gruyère Frittata Delight

Prep time: 10 minutes | Cook time: 22 minutes | Serves 6

- 6 eggs
- 6 tablespoons heavy cream
- ½ teaspoon salt
- ½ teaspoon black pepper
- 1 tablespoon butter
- 2½ ounces (71 g) asparagus, chopped
- 1 clove garlic, minced
- 1¼ cup shredded Gruyère cheese, divided
- Cooking spray
- 3 ounces (85 g) halved cherry tomatoes
- ½ cup water

1. In a large bowl, stir together the eggs, cream, salt, and pepper. 2. Set the Instant Pot on the Sauté mode and melt the butter. Add the asparagus and garlic to the pot and sauté for 2 minutes, or until the garlic is fragrant. The asparagus should still be crisp. 3. Transfer the asparagus and garlic to the bowl with the egg mixture. Stir in 1 cup of the cheese. Clean the pot. 4. Spritz a baking pan with cooking spray. Spread the tomatoes in a single layer in the pan. Pour the egg mixture on top of the tomatoes and sprinkle with the remaining ¼ cup of the cheese. Cover the pan tightly with aluminum foil. 5. Pour the water in the Instant Pot and insert the trivet. Place the pan on the trivet. 6. Set the lid in place. Select the Manual mode and set the cooking time for 20 minutes on High Pressure. When the timer goes off, perform a quick pressure release. Carefully open the lid. 7. Remove the pan from the pot and remove the foil. Blot off any excess moisture with a paper towel. Let the frittata cool for 5 to 10 minutes before transferring onto a plate.

Breakfast Burrito Bowls

Prep time: 10 minutes | Cook time: 15 minutes | Serves 4

- 6 eggs
- 3 tablespoons melted butter
- 1 teaspoon salt
- ¼ teaspoon pepper
- ½ pound (227 g) cooked breakfast sausage
- ½ cup shredded sharp Cheddar cheese
- ½ cup salsa
- ½ cup sour cream
- 1 avocado, cubed
- ¼ cup diced green onion

1. In a large bowl, combine the eggs, melted butter, salt, and pepper. Next, press the Sauté button on the Instant Pot, then use the Adjust button to set the heat to Less.2. Pour the egg mixture into the Instant Pot and cook for 5 to 7 minutes, gently stirring with a rubber spatula. As the eggs start to firm up, add the cooked breakfast sausage and cheese, continuing to cook until the eggs are fully set. Press the Cancel button to stop cooking.3. Once cooked, divide the eggs among four bowls and top each serving with salsa, sour cream, avocado, and green onion for a delicious finish.

Fluffy Almond Flour Pancakes

Prep time: 10 minutes | Cook time: 15 minutes per batch | Serves 6

- 4 eggs, beaten
- 2 cups almond flour
- ½ cup butter, melted
- 2 tablespoons granulated erythritol
- 1 tablespoon avocado oil
- 1 teaspoon baking powder
- 1 teaspoon vanilla extract
- Pinch of salt
- ¾ cup water, divided

1. In a blender, combine all the ingredients, except for the ½ cup of the water. Pulse until fully combined and smooth. Let the batter rest for 5 minutes before cooking. 2. Fill each cup with 2 tablespoons of the batter, about two-thirds of the way full. Cover the cups with aluminum foil. 3. Pour the remaining ½ cup of the water and insert the trivet in the Instant Pot. Place the cups on the trivet. 4. Set the lid in place. Select the Manual mode and set the cooking time for 15 minutes on High Pressure. When the timer goes off, do a quick pressure release. Carefully open the lid. 5. Repeat with the remaining batter, until all the batter is used. Add more water to the pot before cooking each batch, if needed. 6. Serve warm.

Eggs Benedict

Prep time: 5 minutes | Cook time: 1 minute | Serves 3

- 1 teaspoon butter
- 3 eggs
- ¼ teaspoon salt
- ½ teaspoon ground black
- pepper
- 1 cup water
- 3 turkey bacon slices, fried

1. Begin by greasing the egg molds with butter, then crack the eggs into each mold. Season them with salt and ground black pepper.2. Pour water into the Instant Pot and place the trivet inside. Position the egg molds on the trivet.3. Secure the lid in place, select the Manual mode, and set the cooking time to 1 minute on High Pressure. Once the timer goes off, perform a quick release of the pressure. Carefully open the lid.4. Gently transfer the eggs onto a plate and top them with crispy fried bacon slices for added flavor.

Egg-Stuffed Bell Pepper Boats

Prep time: 5 minutes | Cook time: 14 minutes | Serves 2

- 2 eggs, beaten
- 1 tablespoon coconut cream
- ¼ teaspoon dried oregano
- ¼ teaspoon salt
- 1 large bell pepper, cut into halves and deseeded
- 1 cup water

1. In a bowl, stir together the eggs, coconut cream, oregano and salt. 2. Pour the egg mixture in the pepper halves. 3. Pour the water and insert the trivet in the Instant Pot. Put the stuffed pepper halves on the trivet. 4. Set the lid in place. Select the Manual mode and set the cooking time for 14 minutes on High Pressure. When the timer goes off, do a quick pressure release. Carefully open the lid. 5. Serve warm.

Breakfast Cereal

Prep time: 5 minutes | Cook time: 5 minutes | Serves 4

- 2 tablespoons coconut oil
- 1 cup full-fat coconut milk
- ½ cup chopped cashews
- ½ cup heavy whipping cream
- ½ cup chopped pecans
- ⅓ cup Swerve
- ¼ cup unsweetened coconut flakes
- 2 tablespoons flax seeds
- 2 tablespoons chopped hazelnuts
- 2 tablespoons chopped macadamia nuts
- ½ teaspoon ground cinnamon
- ½ teaspoon ground nutmeg
- ½ teaspoon ground turmeric

1. Begin by setting the Instant Pot to Sauté mode and melting the coconut oil. Once melted, pour in the coconut milk.2. Add the cashews, whipping cream, pecans, Swerve, coconut flakes, flax seeds, hazelnuts, macadamia nuts, cinnamon, nutmeg, and turmeric to the Instant Pot. Mix everything together thoroughly.3. Close the lid securely, set the pressure release valve to Sealing, and press Cancel to stop the current program. Select Manual, adjust the cooking time to 5 minutes on High Pressure, and start the cooking process.4. After cooking, allow the pressure to naturally release for about 10 minutes, then carefully switch the pressure release valve to Venting.5. Once the Instant Pot is safe to open, carefully remove the lid, serve the mixture, and enjoy your delicious creation!

Lettuce Wrapped Chicken Sandwich

Prep time: 10 minutes | Cook time: 15 minutes | Serves 4

- 1 tablespoon butter
- 3 ounces (85 g) scallions, chopped
- 2 cups ground chicken
- ½ teaspoon ground nutmeg
- 1 tablespoon coconut flour
- 1 teaspoon salt
- 1 cup lettuce

1. Start by pressing the Sauté button on the Instant Pot and melting the butter. Once melted, add the chopped scallions, ground chicken, and ground nutmeg to the pot, sautéing for about 4 minutes. Next, sprinkle in the coconut flour and salt, continuing to sauté the mixture for an additional 10 minutes.2. Once the chicken mixture is cooked, spoon it into the lettuce leaves, creating wraps. Transfer the filled lettuce wraps to a plate and serve immediately for a fresh and flavorful dish.

Chapter 2

Poultry

Tangy Meatballs

Prep time: 10 minutes | Cook time: 10 minutes | Makes 20 meatballs

- 1 pound (454 g) ground chicken
- 1 egg, lightly beaten
- ½ medium onion, diced
- 1 teaspoon garlic powder
- 1 teaspoon pepper
- 1 teaspoon salt
- 1 cup water
- Sauce:
- 2 teaspoons erythritol
- 1 teaspoon rice vinegar
- ½ teaspoon sriracha

1. In a large bowl, combine the ground chicken, beaten egg, onion, garlic powder, salt, and pepper. Mix well and shape the mixture into bite-sized balls using your hands.2. Pour water into the Instant Pot and insert a steamer basket. Place the meatballs into the basket.3. Secure the lid on the Instant Pot. Select Manual mode and set the cooking time for 10 minutes at High Pressure.4. While the meatballs are cooking, whisk together all the ingredients for the sauce in a separate bowl until well combined.5. Once the cooking time is complete, perform a quick release of the pressure. Carefully open the lid.6. Toss the cooked meatballs in the prepared sauce and serve immediately for a delicious meal.

Chicken with Tomatoes and Spinach

Prep time: 5 minutes | Cook time: 18 minutes | Serves 4

- 4 boneless, skinless chicken breasts (about 2 pounds / 907 g)
- 2½ ounces (71 g) sun-dried tomatoes, coarsely chopped (about 2 tablespoons)
- ¼ cup chicken broth
- 2 tablespoons creamy, no-sugar-added balsamic
- vinegar dressing
- 1 tablespoon whole-grain mustard
- 2 cloves garlic, minced
- 1 teaspoon salt
- 8 ounces (227 g) fresh spinach
- ¼ cup sour cream
- 1 ounce (28 g) cream cheese, softened

1. Begin by placing the chicken breasts into the Instant Pot. Add the diced tomatoes, broth, and dressing over the chicken.2. Secure the lid and seal the vent. Cook on High Pressure for 10 minutes, then perform a quick release of the steam. Press Cancel to stop the cooking process.3. Carefully remove the chicken from the pot and transfer it to a plate. Cover the chicken with aluminum foil to keep it warm while you prepare the sauce.4. Switch the Instant Pot to Sauté mode. Whisk in the mustard, garlic, and salt, then add the spinach. Stir the spinach continuously for about 2 to 3 minutes until fully wilted. The spinach will absorb the sauce initially but will release it as it cooks down further.5. Once the spinach is wilted, add the sour cream and cream cheese to the pot. Whisk everything together until fully incorporated.6. Allow the sauce to simmer, thickening and reducing by about one-third for approximately 5 minutes. Stir occasionally to avoid burning, then press Cancel.7. Pour the creamy sauce over the chicken breasts and serve immediately for a delicious meal.

Creamy Butter Chicken

Prep time: 15 minutes | Cook time: 15 minutes | Serves 4

- 1 (14½-ounce / 411-g) can diced tomatoes, undrained
- 5 or 6 garlic cloves, minced
- 1 tablespoon minced fresh ginger
- 1 teaspoon ground turmeric
- 1 teaspoon cayenne
- 1 teaspoon smoked paprika
- 2 teaspoons garam masala, divided
- 1 teaspoon ground cumin
- 1 teaspoon salt
- 1 pound (454 g) boneless, skinless chicken breasts or thighs
- ½ cup unsalted butter, cut into cubes, or ½ cup coconut oil
- ½ cup heavy (whipping) cream or full-fat coconut milk
- ¼ to ½ cup chopped fresh cilantro
- 4 cups cauliflower rice or cucumber noodles

1. Put the tomatoes, garlic, ginger, turmeric, cayenne, paprika, 1 teaspoon of garam masala, cumin, and salt in the inner cooking pot of the Instant Pot. Mix thoroughly, then place the chicken pieces on top of the sauce. 2. Lock the lid into place. Select Manual and adjust the pressure to High. Cook for 10 minutes. When the cooking is complete, let the pressure release naturally. Unlock the lid. Carefully remove the chicken and set aside. 3. Using an immersion blender in the pot, blend together all the ingredients into a smooth sauce. (Or use a stand blender, but be careful with the hot sauce and be sure to leave the inside lid open to vent.) After blending, let the sauce cool before adding the remaining ingredients or it will be thinner than is ideal. 4. Add the butter cubes, cream, remaining 1 teaspoon of garam masala, and cilantro. Stir until well incorporated. The sauce should be thick enough to coat the back of a spoon when you're done. 5. Remove half the sauce and freeze it for later or refrigerate for up to 2 to 3 days. 6. Cut the chicken into bite-size pieces. Add it back to the sauce. 7. Preheat the Instant Pot by selecting Sauté and adjust to Less for low heat. Let the chicken heat through. Break it up into smaller pieces if you like, but don't shred it. 8. Serve over cauliflower rice or raw cucumber noodles.

Chicken Fajitas with Bell Peppers

Prep time: 10 minutes | Cook time: 5 minutes | Serves 4

- 1½ pounds (680 g) boneless, skinless chicken breasts
- ¼ cup avocado oil
- 2 tablespoons water
- 1 tablespoon Mexican hot sauce
- 2 cloves garlic, minced
- 1 teaspoon lime juice
- 1 teaspoon ground cumin
- 1 teaspoon salt
- 1 teaspoon erythritol
- ¼ teaspoon chili powder
- ¼ teaspoon smoked paprika
- 5 ounces (142 g) sliced yellow bell pepper strips
- 5 ounces (142 g) sliced red bell pepper strips
- 5 ounces (142 g) sliced green bell pepper strips

1. Begin by slicing the chicken into very thin strips lengthwise, then cut each strip in half again, aiming for a thickness similar to restaurant-style fajitas. 2. In a measuring cup, combine the avocado oil, water, hot sauce, minced garlic, lime juice, cumin, salt, erythritol, chili powder, and paprika to create a flavorful marinade. Pour this marinade into the Instant Pot, along with the chicken and sliced peppers. 3. Secure the lid of the Instant Pot and seal the vent. Set the cooker to High Pressure and cook for 5 minutes. Once cooking is complete, perform a quick release of the steam.

Mexican-Spiced Turkey Tenderloin

Prep time: 5 minutes | Cook time: 8 minutes | Serves 6

- 1 cup Low-Sodium Salsa or bottled salsa
- 1 teaspoon chili powder
- ½ teaspoon ground cumin
- ¼ teaspoon dried oregano
- 1½ pounds unseasoned turkey tenderloin or
- boneless turkey breast, cut into 6 pieces
- Freshly ground black pepper
- ½ cup shredded Monterey Jack cheese or Mexican cheese blend

1. In a small bowl or measuring cup, combine the salsa, chili powder, cumin, and oregano. Pour half of the mixture into the electric pressure cooker. 2. Nestle the turkey into the sauce. Grind some pepper onto each piece of turkey. Pour the remaining salsa mixture on top. 3. Close and lock the lid of the pressure cooker. Set the valve to sealing. 4. Cook on high pressure for 8 minutes. 5. When the cooking is complete, hit Cancel. Allow the pressure to release naturally for 10 minutes, then quick release any remaining pressure. 6. Once the pin drops, unlock and remove the lid. 7. Sprinkle the cheese on top, and put the lid back on for a few minutes to let the cheese melt. 8. Serve immediately.

Sesame-Ginger Chicken

Prep time: 20 minutes | Cook time: 8 minutes | Serves 5

- 2 tablespoons tahini (sesame sauce)
- ¼ cup water
- 1 tablespoon low-sodium soy sauce
- ¼ cup chopped onion
- 1 teaspoon red wine
- vinegar
- 2 teaspoons minced garlic
- 1 teaspoon shredded ginger root (Microplane works best)
- 2 pounds chicken breast, chopped into 8 portions

1. Place first seven ingredients in bottom of the inner pot of the Instant Pot. 2. Add coarsely chopped chicken on top. 3. Secure the lid and make sure vent is at sealing. Set for 8 minutes using Manual setting. When cook time is up, let the pressure release naturally for 10 minutes, then perform a quick release. 4. Remove ingredients and shred chicken with fork. Combine with other ingredients in pot for a tasty sandwich filling or sauce.

Creamy Nutmeg Chicken

Prep time: 20 minutes | Cook time: 10 minutes | Serves 6

- 1 tablespoon canola oil
- 6 boneless chicken breast halves, skin and visible fat removed
- ¼ cup chopped onion
- ¼ cup minced parsley
- 2 (10¾-ounce) cans 98% fat-free, reduced-sodium cream of mushroom soup
- ½ cup fat-free sour cream
- ½ cup fat-free milk
- 1 tablespoon ground nutmeg
- ¼ teaspoon sage
- ¼ teaspoon dried thyme
- ¼ teaspoon crushed rosemary

1. Start by pressing the Sauté button on the Instant Pot, then add the canola oil. Place the chicken in the hot oil and brown it on both sides. Once browned, remove the chicken to a plate. 2. In the remaining oil, sauté the onion and parsley in the Instant Pot until the onions become tender. After that, press Cancel on the Instant Pot and return the chicken to the pot. 3. In a separate bowl, mix together the remaining ingredients, then pour the mixture over the chicken in the pot. 4. Secure the lid on the Instant Pot and set the vent to sealing. Choose Manual mode and set the cooking time for 10 minutes. 5. Once the cooking time is complete, allow the pressure to release naturally for optimal flavor and tenderness.

Chicken Tagine

Prep time: 15 minutes | Cook time: 11 minutes | Serves 4

- 2 (15-ounce / 425-g) cans chickpeas, rinsed, divided
- 1 tablespoon extra-virgin olive oil
- 5 garlic cloves, minced
- 1½ teaspoons paprika
- ½ teaspoon ground turmeric
- ½ teaspoon ground cumin
- ¼ teaspoon ground ginger
- ¼ teaspoon cayenne pepper
- 1 fennel bulb, 1 tablespoon fronds minced, stalks discarded, bulb halved and cut lengthwise
- into ½-inch-thick wedges
- 1 cup chicken broth
- 3 (2-inch) strips lemon zest, plus lemon wedges for serving
- 4 (5- to 7-ounce / 142- to 198-g) bone-in chicken thighs, skin removed, trimmed
- ½ teaspoon table salt
- ½ cup pitted large brine-cured green or black olives, halved
- ⅓ cup raisins
- 2 tablespoons chopped fresh parsley

1. Using a potato masher, mash ½ cup of chickpeas in a bowl until they form a paste. Set the Instant Pot to the highest sauté function and heat the oil. Add garlic, paprika, turmeric, cumin, ginger, and cayenne, cooking until fragrant, about 1 minute. Turn off the Instant Pot, then stir in the remaining whole chickpeas, the mashed chickpeas, fennel wedges, broth, and lemon zest.2. Season the chicken with salt. Nestle the chicken, skin side up, into the pot, and spoon some of the cooking liquid over the top. Lock the lid in place and close the pressure release valve. Select the high-pressure cooking function and set the timer for 10 minutes.3. Once the cooking time is complete, turn off the Instant Pot and perform a quick release of the pressure. Carefully remove the lid, allowing the steam to escape away from you. Discard the lemon zest, then stir in the olives, raisins, parsley, and fennel fronds. Adjust seasoning with salt and pepper to taste. Serve with lemon wedges for added flavor.

BBQ Pulled Chicken

Prep time: 5 minutes | Cook time: 25 minutes | Serves 4

- 1 (5-pound / 2.2-kg) whole chicken
- 3 teaspoons salt
- 1 teaspoon pepper
- 1 teaspoon dried parsley
- 1 teaspoon garlic powder
- ½ medium onion, cut into 3 to 4 large pieces
- 1 cup water
- ½ cup sugar-free barbecue sauce, divided

1. Scatter the chicken with salt, pepper, parsley, and garlic powder. Put the onion pieces inside the chicken cavity. 2. Pour the water into the Instant Pot and insert the trivet. Place seasoned chicken on the trivet. Brush with half of the barbecue sauce. 3. Lock the lid. Select the Manual mode and set the cooking time for 25 minutes at High Pressure. 4. When the timer beeps, perform a natural pressure release for 10 minutes, then release any remaining pressure. Carefully remove the lid. 5. Using a clean brush, add the remaining half of the sauce to chicken. For crispy skin or thicker sauce, you can broil in the oven for 5 minutes until lightly browned. 6. Slice or shred the chicken and serve warm.

Lemon Chicken Kale Sandwiches

Prep time: 10 minutes | Cook time: 10 minutes | Serves 2

- 4 ounces (113 g) kale leaves
- 8 ounces (227 g) chicken fillet
- 1 tablespoon butter
- 1 ounce (28 g) lemon
- ¼ cup water

1. Dice the chicken fillet. 2. Squeeze the lemon juice over the poultry. 3. Transfer the poultry into the instant pot; add water and butter. 4. Close the lid and cook the chicken on the Poultry mode for 10 minutes. 5. When the chicken is cooked, place it on the kale leaves to make the medium sandwiches.

Pecorino Chicken

Prep time: 10 minutes | Cook time: 15 minutes | Serves 3

- 2 ounces (57 g) Pecorino cheese, grated
- 10 ounces (283 g) chicken breast, skinless, boneless
- 1 tablespoon butter
- ¾ cup heavy cream
- ½ teaspoon salt
- ½ teaspoon red hot pepper

1. Begin by chopping the chicken breast into bite-sized cubes.2. Add butter to the Instant Pot and preheat it using the Sauté mode.3. Once the butter is melted, add the chicken cubes to the pot.4. Season the chicken with salt and red hot pepper to taste.5. Pour in the cream and stir to combine all the ingredients thoroughly.6. Close the lid of the Instant Pot and ensure it is sealed properly.7. Select Poultry mode and set the timer for 15 minutes.8. When the cooking time is complete, allow the chicken to rest for an additional 5 minutes.9. Carefully transfer the chicken to plates and sprinkle with grated cheese, allowing it to sit for a moment so it doesn't melt immediately.

Chicken Piccata

Prep time: 5 minutes | Cook time: 25 minutes | Serves 4

- 4 (6-ounce / 170-g) boneless, skinless chicken breasts
- ½ teaspoon salt
- ½ teaspoon garlic powder
- ¼ teaspoon pepper
- 2 tablespoons coconut oil
- 1 cup water
- 2 cloves garlic, minced
- 4 tablespoons butter
- Juice of 1 lemon
- ¼ teaspoon xanthan gum

1. Begin by seasoning the chicken with salt, garlic powder, and pepper.2. Set your Instant Pot to Sauté mode and melt the coconut oil.3. Add the seasoned chicken to the pot and sear each side for about 5 to 7 minutes until golden brown.4. Once browned, remove the chicken from the pot and place it on a plate.5. Pour water into the Instant Pot, using a wooden spoon to scrape the bottom if needed to remove any stuck seasoning or bits of chicken. Insert the trivet and place the seared chicken on top of it.6. Secure the lid of the Instant Pot. Select Manual mode and set the cooking time for 10 minutes at High Pressure.7. After the cooking time is complete, allow for a natural pressure release for 10 minutes, then release any remaining pressure. Carefully open the lid.8. Remove the chicken and set it aside. Strain the broth from the Instant Pot into a large bowl, then return the strained broth to the pot.9. Switch the Instant Pot back to Sauté mode and add the remaining ingredients. Cook for at least 5 minutes, stirring frequently, until the sauce reaches your desired thickness.10. Pour the sauce over the chicken and serve warm for a delicious meal.

Stuffed Chicken with Spinach and Feta

Prep time: 10 minutes | Cook time: 25 minutes | Serves 4

- ½ cup frozen spinach
- ⅓ cup crumbled feta cheese
- 1¼ teaspoons salt, divided
- 4 (6-ounce / 170-g) boneless, skinless chicken
- breasts, butterflied
- ¼ teaspoon pepper
- ¼ teaspoon dried oregano
- ¼ teaspoon dried parsley
- ¼ teaspoon garlic powder
- 2 tablespoons coconut oil
- 1 cup water

1. In a medium bowl, mix together the spinach, feta cheese, and ¼ teaspoon of salt. Divide this mixture evenly and spoon it onto the chicken breasts.2. Fold the chicken breasts closed and secure them with toothpicks or butcher's string. Season the outside of the chicken with the remaining 1 teaspoon of salt, pepper, oregano, parsley, and garlic powder.3. Set your Instant Pot to Sauté mode and heat the coconut oil.4. Sear each chicken breast in the hot oil until golden brown, about 4 to 5 minutes per side.5. Once browned, remove the chicken breasts from the pot and set them aside.6. Pour water into the Instant Pot, scraping the bottom to release any browned bits or seasoning stuck to the bottom. Add the trivet to the pot and place the chicken on top of it.7. Secure the lid on the Instant Pot. Select the Manual mode and set the cooking time to 15 minutes at High Pressure.8. After cooking is complete, allow for a natural pressure release for 15 minutes before releasing any remaining pressure. Carefully open the lid and serve the chicken warm.

Rustic Tomato and Mushroom Braised Chicken

Prep time: 20 minutes | Cook time: 25 minutes | Serves 4

- 1 tablespoon extra-virgin olive oil
- 1 pound (454 g) portobello mushroom caps, gills removed, caps halved and sliced ½ inch thick
- 1 onion, chopped fine
- ¾ teaspoon salt, divided
- 4 garlic cloves, minced
- 1 tablespoon tomato paste
- 1 tablespoon all-purpose flour
- 2 teaspoons minced fresh
- sage
- ½ cup dry red wine
- 1 (14½ ounces / 411 g) can diced tomatoes, drained
- 4 (5 to 7 ounces / 142 to 198 g) bone-in chicken thighs, skin removed, trimmed
- ¼ teaspoon pepper
- 2 tablespoons chopped fresh parsley
- Shaved Parmesan cheese

1. Using highest sauté function, heat oil in Instant Pot until shimmering. Add mushrooms, onion, and ¼ teaspoon salt. Partially cover and cook until mushrooms are softened and have released their liquid, about 5 minutes. Stir in garlic, tomato paste, flour, and sage and cook until fragrant, about 1 minute. Stir in wine, scraping up any browned bits, then stir in tomatoes. 2. Sprinkle chicken with remaining ½ teaspoon salt and pepper. Nestle chicken skinned side up into pot and spoon some of sauce on top. Lock lid in place and close pressure release valve. Select high pressure cook function and cook for 15 minutes. 3. Turn off Instant Pot and quick-release pressure. Carefully remove lid, allowing steam to escape away from you. Transfer chicken to serving dish, tent with aluminum foil, and let rest while finishing sauce. 4. Using highest sauté function, bring sauce to simmer and cook until thickened slightly, about 5 minutes. Season sauce with salt and pepper to taste. Spoon sauce over chicken and sprinkle with parsley and Parmesan. Serve.

Cheesy Chicken Alfredo Casserole

Prep time: 15 minutes | Cook time: 15 minutes | Serves 4

- 1 cup broccoli florets
- 1½ cups Alfredo sauce
- ½ cup chopped fresh spinach
- ¼ cup whole-milk ricotta cheese
- ½ teaspoon salt
- ¼ teaspoon pepper
- 1 pound (454 g) thin-sliced deli chicken
- 1 cup shredded whole-milk Mozzarella cheese
- 1 cup water

1. Put the broccoli florets in a large bowl. Add the Alfredo sauce, spinach, ricotta, salt, and pepper to the bowl and stir to mix well. Using a spoon, separate the veggie mix into three sections. 2. Layer the chicken into the bottom of a 7-cup glass bowl. Place one section of the veggie mix on top in an even layer and top with a layer of shredded Mozzarella cheese. Repeat until all veggie mix has been used and finish with a layer of Mozzarella cheese. Cover the dish with aluminum foil. 3. Pour the water into the Instant Pot and insert the trivet. Place the dish on the trivet. 4. Secure the lid. Select the Manual mode and set the cooking time for 15 minutes at High Pressure. 5. Once cooking is complete, do a quick pressure release. Carefully open the lid. 6. If desired, broil in oven for 3 to 5 minutes until golden. Serve warm.

Chicken and Scallions Stuffed Peppers

Prep time: 5 minutes | Cook time: 20 minutes | Serves 5

- 1 tablespoon butter, at room temperature
- ½ cup scallions, chopped
- 1 pound (454 g) ground chicken
- ½ teaspoon sea salt
- ½ teaspoon chili powder
- ⅓ teaspoon paprika
- ⅓ teaspoon ground cumin
- ¼ teaspoon shallot powder
- 6 ounces (170 g) goat cheese, crumbled
- 1½ cups water
- 5 bell peppers, tops, membrane, and seeds removed
- ½ cup sour cream

1. Begin by setting your Instant Pot to Sauté mode and melting the butter. 2. Add the scallions and chicken to the pot, sautéing for 2 to 3 minutes until the chicken is lightly browned. 3. Stir in the sea salt, chili powder, paprika, cumin, and shallot powder. Add the crumbled goat cheese, mixing well, then transfer the mixture to a bowl and set aside. 4. Clean the Instant Pot to prepare for steaming. Pour the water into the pot and insert the trivet. 5. Stuff the bell peppers with the chicken mixture, being careful not to pack them too tightly. Place the stuffed peppers on the trivet. 6. Secure the lid on the Instant Pot. Select the Poultry mode and set the cooking time for 15 minutes at High Pressure. 7. When the cooking timer goes off, allow for a natural pressure release for 10 minutes, then release any remaining pressure. Carefully remove the lid. 8. Take the stuffed peppers out of the Instant Pot and serve them with sour cream for a delicious finishing touch.

Tomato Chicken Legs

Prep time: 10 minutes | Cook time: 35 minutes | Serves 2

- 2 chicken legs
- 2 tomatoes, chopped
- 1 cup chicken stock
- 1 teaspoon peppercorns

1. Place all the ingredients into the Instant Pot. 2. Secure the lid and seal it properly. Select Manual mode and set it to High Pressure. 3. Cook the chicken legs for 35 minutes. 4. Once cooking is complete, perform a quick release of the pressure. 5. Carefully transfer the cooked chicken legs to serving bowls and ladle in 1 scoop of the chicken stock over them for added flavor.

Herb-Seasoned Shredded Chicken

Prep time: 5 minutes | Cook time: 14 minutes | Serves 4

- ½ teaspoon salt
- ½ teaspoon pepper
- ½ teaspoon dried oregano
- ½ teaspoon dried basil
- ½ teaspoon garlic powder
- 2 (6-ounce / 170-g) boneless, skinless chicken breasts
- 1 tablespoon coconut oil
- 1 cup water

1. In a small bowl, combine the salt, pepper, oregano, basil, and garlic powder. Rub this mix over both sides of the chicken. 2. Set your Instant Pot to Sauté and heat the coconut oil until sizzling. 3. Add the chicken and sear for 3 to 4 minutes until golden on both sides. 4. Remove the chicken and set aside. 5. Pour the water into the Instant Pot and use a wooden spoon or rubber spatula to make sure no seasoning is stuck to bottom of pot. 6. Add the trivet to the Instant Pot and place the chicken on top. 7. Secure the lid. Select the Manual mode and set the cooking time for 10 minutes at High Pressure. 8. Once cooking is complete, do a natural pressure release for 5 minutes, then release any remaining pressure. Carefully open the lid. 9. Remove the chicken and shred, then serve.

Pizza in a Pot

Prep time: 25 minutes | Cook time: 15 minutes | Serves 8

- 1 pound bulk lean sweet Italian turkey sausage, browned and drained
- 28 ounces can crushed tomatoes
- 15½ ounces can chili beans
- 2¼ ounces can sliced black olives, drained
- 1 medium onion, chopped
- 1 small green bell pepper, chopped
- 2 garlic cloves, minced
- ¼ cup grated Parmesan cheese
- 1 tablespoon quick-cooking tapioca
- 1 tablespoon dried basil
- 1 bay leaf

1. Start by setting the Instant Pot to Sauté mode, then add the turkey sausage. Sauté the sausage until it is nicely browned. 2. Add the remaining ingredients into the Instant Pot and stir well to combine everything. 3. Secure the lid on the Instant Pot, ensuring the vent is set to sealing. Cook on Manual mode for 15 minutes. 4. Once the cooking time is complete, allow the pressure to release naturally for 5 minutes, then perform a quick release for any remaining pressure. Don't forget to discard the bay leaf before serving.

Barbecue Glazed Turkey Meatloaf

Prep time: 5 minutes | Cook time: 40 minutes | Serves 6

- 1 pound 93 percent lean ground turkey
- ⅓ cup low-sugar or unsweetened barbecue sauce, plus 2 tablespoons
- ⅓ cup gluten-free panko (Japanese bread crumbs)
- 1 large egg
- ½ small yellow onion,
- finely diced
- 1 garlic clove, minced
- ½ teaspoon fine sea salt
- ½ teaspoon freshly ground black pepper
- Cooked cauliflower "rice" or brown rice for serving

1. Pour 1 cup water into the Instant Pot. Lightly grease a 7 by 3-inch round cake pan or a 5½ by 3-inch loaf pan with olive oil or coat with nonstick cooking spray. 2. In a medium bowl, combine the turkey, ⅓ cup barbecue sauce, panko, egg, onion, garlic, salt, and pepper and mix well with your hands until all of the ingredients are evenly distributed. Transfer the mixture to the prepared pan, pressing it into an even layer. Cover the pan tightly with aluminum foil. Place the pan on a long-handled silicone steam rack, then, holding the handles of the steam rack, lower it into the pot.

(If you don't have the long-handled rack, use the wire metal steam rack and a homemade sling) 3. Secure the lid and set the Pressure Release to Sealing. Select the Pressure Cook or Manual setting and set the cooking time for 25 minutes at high pressure if using a 7-inch round cake pan, or for 35 minutes at high pressure if using a 5½ by 3-inch loaf pan. (The pot will take about 10 minutes to come up to pressure before the cooking program begins.) 4. Preheat a toaster oven or position an oven rack 4 to 6 inches below the heat source and preheat the broiler. 5. When the cooking program ends, perform a quick pressure release by moving the Pressure Release to Venting. Open the pot and, wearing heat-resistant mitts, grasp the handles of the steam rack and lift it out of the pot. Uncover the pan, taking care not to get burned by the steam or to drip condensation onto the meat loaf. Brush the remaining 2 tablespoons barbecue sauce on top of the meat loaf. 6. Broil the meat loaf for a few minutes, just until the glaze becomes bubbly and browned. Cut the meat loaf into slices and serve hot, with the cauliflower "rice" alongside.

Herbed Whole Turkey Breast

Prep time: 10 minutes | Cook time:30 minutes | Serves 12

- 3 tablespoons extra-virgin olive oil
- 1½ tablespoons herbes de Provence or poultry seasoning
- 2 teaspoons minced garlic
- 1 teaspoon lemon zest (from 1 small lemon)
- 1 tablespoon kosher salt
- 1½ teaspoons freshly ground black pepper
- 1 (6 pounds) bone-in, skin-on whole turkey breast, rinsed and patted dry

1. In a small bowl, whisk together the olive oil, herbes de Provence, minced garlic, lemon zest, salt, and pepper until well combined. 2. Rub the olive oil mixture all over the outside of the turkey and under the skin for added flavor. 3. Pour 1 cup of water into the electric pressure cooker and insert a wire rack or trivet to elevate the turkey. 4. Place the turkey on the rack, ensuring the skin side is facing up. 5. Close and lock the lid of the pressure cooker, making sure the valve is set to sealing. 6. Cook the turkey on high pressure for 30 minutes. 7. When cooking is complete, press Cancel. Allow the pressure to release naturally for 20 minutes, then perform a quick release for any remaining pressure. 8. Once the pressure pin drops, carefully unlock and remove the lid. 9. Gently transfer the turkey to a cutting board. Remove the skin, slice the turkey, and serve for a delicious meal.

Creamy Tuscan Drumsticks

Prep time: 15 minutes | Cook time: 12 minutes | Serves 4

- 4 chicken drumsticks
- 1 cup chopped spinach
- 1 teaspoon minced garlic
- 1 teaspoon ground paprika
- 1 cup heavy cream
- 1 teaspoon cayenne pepper
- 1 ounce (28 g) sun-dried tomatoes, chopped

1. Put all ingredients in the instant pot. 2. Close and seal the lid. 3. Cook the meal on Manual mode (High Pressure) for 12 minutes. 4. Then allow the natural pressure release for 10 minutes. 5. Serve the chicken with hot sauce from the instant pot.

Creamy Turkey Tetrazzini

Prep time: 5 minutes | Cook time: 20 minutes | Serves 6

- 1 tablespoon extra-virgin olive oil
- 2 garlic cloves, minced
- 1 yellow onion, diced
- 8 ounces cremini or button mushrooms, sliced
- ½ teaspoon fine sea salt
- ¼ teaspoon freshly ground black pepper
- 1 pound 93 percent lean ground turkey
- 1 teaspoon poultry seasoning
- 6 ounces whole-grain extra-broad egg-white pasta (such as No Yolks brand) or whole-wheat
- elbow pasta
- 2 cups low-sodium chicken broth
- 1½ cups frozen green peas, thawed
- 3 cups baby spinach
- Three ¾-ounce wedges Laughing Cow creamy light Swiss cheese, or 2 tablespoons Neufchâtel cheese, at room temperature
- ⅓ cup grated Parmesan cheese
- 1 tablespoon chopped fresh flat-leaf parsley

1. Select the Sauté setting on the Instant Pot and heat the oil and garlic for 2 minutes, until the garlic is bubbling but not browned. Add the onion, mushrooms, salt, and pepper and sauté for about 5 minutes, until the mushrooms have wilted and begun to give up their liquid. Add the turkey and poultry seasoning and sauté, using a wooden spoon or spatula to break up the meat as it cooks, for about 4 minutes more, until cooked through and no streaks of pink remain. 2. Stir in the pasta. Pour in the broth and use the spoon or spatula to nudge the pasta into the liquid as much as possible. It's fine if some pieces are not completely submerged. 3. Secure the lid and set the Pressure Release to Sealing. Press the Cancel button to reset the cooking program, then select the Pressure Cook or Manual setting and set the cooking time for 5 minutes at high pressure. (The pot will take about 5 minutes to come up to pressure before the cooking program begins.) 4. When the cooking program ends, let the pressure release naturally for 5 minutes, then move the Pressure Release to Venting to release any remaining steam. Open the pot and stir in the peas, spinach, Laughing Cow cheese, and Parmesan. Let stand for 2 minutes, then stir the mixture once more. 5. Ladle into bowls or onto plates and sprinkle with the parsley. Serve right away.

Stuffed Provolone Chicken Rolls

Prep time: 15 minutes | Cook time: 20 minutes | Serves 4

- 12 ounces (340 g) chicken fillet
- 4 ounces (113 g) provolone cheese, sliced
- 1 tablespoon cream
- cheese
- ½ teaspoon dried cilantro
- ½ teaspoon smoked paprika
- 1 cup water, for cooking

1. Beat the chicken fillet well and rub it with dried cilantro and smoked paprika. 2. Then spread it with cream cheese and top with Provolone cheese. 3. Roll the chicken fillet into the roll and wrap in the foil. 4. Pour water and insert the rack in the instant pot. 5. Place the chicken roll on the rack. Close and seal the lid. 6. Cook it on Manual mode (High Pressure) for 20 minutes. 7. Make a quick pressure release and slice the chicken roll into the servings.

Ann's Classic Chicken Cacciatore

Prep time: 25 minutes | Cook time: 3 to 9 minutes | Serves 8

- 1 large onion, thinly sliced
- 3 pound chicken, cut up, skin removed, trimmed of fat
- 2 6-ounce cans tomato paste
- 4-ounce can sliced mushrooms, drained
- 1 teaspoon salt
- ¼ cup dry white wine
- ¼ teaspoons pepper
- 1 to 2 garlic cloves, minced
- 1 to 2 teaspoons dried oregano
- ½ teaspoon dried basil
- ½ teaspoon celery seed, optional
- 1 bay leaf

1. In the inner pot of the Instant Pot, place the onion and chicken. 2. Combine remaining ingredients and pour over the chicken. 3. Secure the lid and make sure vent is at sealing. Cook on Slow Cook mode, low 7 to 9 hours, or high 3 to 4 hours.

Creamy Pesto Chicken Bake

Prep time: 5 minutes | Cook time: 25 minutes | Serves 2

- 2 (6-ounce / 170-g) boneless, skinless chicken breasts, butterflied
- ½ teaspoon salt
- ¼ teaspoon pepper
- ¼ teaspoon dried parsley
- ¼ teaspoon garlic powder
- 2 tablespoons coconut oil
- 1 cup water
- ¼ cup whole-milk ricotta cheese
- ¼ cup pesto
- ¼ cup shredded whole-milk Mozzarella cheese
- Chopped parsley, for garnish (optional)

1. Sprinkle the chicken breasts with salt, pepper, parsley, and garlic powder. 2. Set your Instant Pot to Sauté and melt the coconut oil. 3. Add the chicken and brown for 3 to 5 minutes. Remove the chicken from the pot to a 7-cup glass bowl. 4. Pour the water into the Instant Pot and use a wooden spoon or rubber spatula to make sure no seasoning is stuck to bottom of pot. 5. Scatter the ricotta cheese on top of the chicken. Pour the pesto over chicken, and sprinkle the Mozzarella cheese over chicken. Cover with aluminum foil. Add the trivet to the Instant Pot and place the bowl on the trivet. 6. Secure the lid. Select the Manual mode and set the cooking time for 20 minutes at High Pressure. 7. Once cooking is complete, do a natural pressure release for 10 minutes, then release any remaining pressure. Carefully open the lid. 8. Serve the chicken garnished with the chopped parsley, if desired.

Moroccan Chicken Casablanca

Prep time: 20 minutes | Cook time: 12 minutes | Serves 8

- 2 large onions, sliced
- 1 teaspoon ground ginger
- 3 garlic cloves, minced
- 2 tablespoons canola oil, divided
- 3 pounds skinless chicken pieces
- 3 large carrots, diced
- 2 large potatoes, unpeeled, diced
- ½ teaspoon ground cumin
- ½ teaspoon salt
- ½ teaspoon pepper
- ¼ teaspoon cinnamon
- 2 tablespoons raisins
- 14½-ounce can chopped tomatoes
- 3 small zucchini, sliced
- 15-ounce can garbanzo beans, drained
- 2 tablespoons chopped parsley

1. Using the Sauté function of the Instant Pot, cook the onions, ginger, and garlic in 1 tablespoon of the oil for 5 minutes, stirring constantly. Remove onions, ginger, and garlic from pot and set aside. 2. Brown the chicken pieces with the remaining oil, then add the cooked onions, ginger and garlic back in as well as all of the remaining ingredients, except the parsley. 3. Secure the lid and make sure vent is in the sealing position. Cook on Manual mode for 12 minutes. 4. When cook time is up, let the pressure release naturally for 5 minutes and then release the rest of the pressure manually.

BBQ Pulled Chicken with Texas Slaw

Prep time: 5 minutes | Cook time: 20 minutes | Serves 6

- Chicken
- 1 cup water
- ¼ teaspoon fine sea salt
- 3 garlic cloves, peeled
- 2 bay leaves
- 2 pounds boneless, skinless chicken thighs (see Note)
- Cabbage Slaw
- ½ head red or green cabbage, thinly sliced
- 1 red bell pepper, seeded and thinly sliced
- 2 jalapeño chiles, seeded and cut into narrow strips
- 2 carrots, julienned
- 1 large Fuji or Gala apple, julienned
- ½ cup chopped fresh cilantro
- 3 tablespoons fresh lime juice
- 3 tablespoons extra-virgin olive oil
- ½ teaspoon ground cumin
- ¼ teaspoon fine sea salt
- ¾ cup low-sugar or unsweetened barbecue sauce
- Cornbread, for serving

1. To make the chicken: Combine the water, salt, garlic, bay leaves, and chicken thighs in the Instant Pot, arranging the chicken in a single layer. 2. Secure the lid and set the Pressure Release to Sealing. Select the Poultry, Pressure Cook, or Manual setting and set the cooking time for 10 minutes at high pressure. (The pot will take about 10 minutes to come up to pressure before the cooking program begins.) 3. To make the slaw: While the chicken is cooking, in a large bowl, combine the cabbage, bell pepper, jalapeños, carrots, apple, cilantro, lime juice, oil, cumin, and salt and toss together until the vegetables and apples are evenly coated. 4. When the cooking program ends, perform a quick pressure release by moving the Pressure Release to Venting, or let the pressure release naturally. Open the pot and, using tongs, transfer the chicken to a cutting board. Using two forks, shred the chicken into bite-size pieces. Wearing heat-resistant mitts, lift out the inner pot and discard the cooking liquid. Return the inner pot to the housing. 5. Return the chicken to the pot and stir in the barbecue sauce. You can serve it right away or heat it for a minute or two on the Sauté setting, then return the pot to its Keep Warm setting until ready to serve. 6. Divide the chicken and slaw evenly among six plates. Serve with wedges of cornbread on the side.

Parmesan-Crusted Chicken

Prep time: 15 minutes | Cook time: 13 minutes | Serves 2

- 1 tomato, sliced
- 8 ounces (227 g) chicken fillets
- 2 ounces (57 g) Parmesan, sliced
- 1 teaspoon butter
- 4 tablespoons water, for sprinkling
- 1 cup water, for cooking

1. Begin by pouring water into the Instant Pot and inserting the steamer rack.2. Next, grease the baking mold with butter to prevent sticking.3. Slice the chicken fillets in half and arrange them in the greased mold.4. Sprinkle a little water over the chicken and then top with slices of tomato and grated Parmesan cheese.5. Cover the baking mold with aluminum foil and place it on the steamer rack in the Instant Pot.6. Secure the lid tightly and seal it.7. Set the Instant Pot to Manual mode and cook for 13 minutes. After cooking, allow for a natural pressure release for 10 minutes before opening the lid.

African Chicken Peanut Stew

Prep time: 10 minutes | Cook time: 10 minutes | Serves 6

- 1 cup chopped onion
- 2 tablespoons minced garlic
- 1 tablespoon minced fresh ginger
- 1 teaspoon salt
- ½ teaspoon ground cumin
- ½ teaspoon ground coriander
- ½ teaspoon freshly ground black pepper
- ½ teaspoon ground cinnamon
- ⅛ teaspoon ground cloves
- 1 tablespoon sugar-free tomato paste
- 1 pound (454 g) boneless, skinless chicken breasts or thighs, cut into large chunks
- 3 to 4 cups chopped Swiss chard
- 1 cup cubed raw pumpkin
- ½ cup water
- 1 cup chunky peanut butter

1. In the inner cooking pot of the Instant Pot, combine the onion, garlic, ginger, salt, cumin, coriander, pepper, cinnamon, cloves, and tomato paste. Then, add the chicken, chard, pumpkin, and water, stirring to mix everything together.2. Lock the lid securely into place. Select the Manual setting and adjust the pressure to High. Set the cooking time for 10 minutes. Once cooking is complete, allow the pressure to release naturally before unlocking the lid.3. Gradually mix in the peanut butter, adding it a little at a time. Taste the sauce with each addition to ensure it's to

your liking. The final sauce should be thick enough to coat the back of a spoon in a thin layer.4. Serve the dish over mashed cauliflower, cooked zucchini noodles, steamed vegetables, or alongside a fresh side salad for a delicious and nutritious meal.

Unstuffed Turkey and Quinoa Pepper Bowls

Prep time: 0 minutes | Cook time: 35 minutes | Serves 8

- 2 tablespoons extra-virgin olive oil
- 1 yellow onion, diced
- 2 celery stalks, diced
- 2 garlic cloves, chopped
- 2 pounds 93 percent lean ground turkey
- 2 teaspoons Cajun seasoning blend (plus 1 teaspoon fine sea salt if using a salt-free blend)
- ½ teaspoon freshly ground black pepper
- ¼ teaspoon cayenne pepper
- 1 cup quinoa, rinsed
- 1 cup low-sodium chicken broth
- One 14½-ounce can fire-roasted diced tomatoes and their liquid
- 3 red, orange, and/or yellow bell peppers, seeded and cut into 1-inch squares
- 1 green onion, white and green parts, thinly sliced
- 1½ tablespoons chopped fresh flat-leaf parsley
- Hot sauce (such as Crystal or Frank's RedHot) for serving

1. Select the Sauté setting on the Instant Pot and heat the oil for 2 minutes. Add the onion, celery, and garlic and sauté for about 4 minutes, until the onion begins to soften. Add the turkey, Cajun seasoning, black pepper, and cayenne and sauté, using a wooden spoon or spatula to break up the meat as it cooks, for about 6 minutes, until cooked through and no streaks of pink remain. 2. Sprinkle the quinoa over the turkey in an even layer. Pour the broth and the diced tomatoes and their liquid over the quinoa, spreading the tomatoes on top. Sprinkle the bell peppers over the top in an even layer. 3. Secure the lid and set the Pressure Release to Sealing. Press the Cancel button to reset the cooking program, then select the Pressure Cook or Manual setting and set the cooking time for 8 minutes at high pressure. (The pot will take about 15 minutes to come up to pressure before the cooking program begins.) 4. When the cooking program ends, let the pressure release naturally for at least 15 minutes, then move the Pressure Release to Venting to release any remaining steam. Open the pot and sprinkle the green onion and parsley over the top in an even layer. 5. Spoon the unstuffed peppers into bowls, making sure to dig down to the bottom of the pot so each person gets an equal amount of peppers, quinoa, and meat. Serve hot, with hot sauce on the side.

Garlic Paprika Chicken Wings

Prep time: 10 minutes | Cook time: 13 minutes | Serves 4

- 1 pound (454 g) boneless chicken wings
- 1 teaspoon ground paprika
- 1 teaspoon avocado oil
- ¼ teaspoon minced garlic
- ¾ cup beef broth

1. Pour the avocado oil in the instant pot. 2. Rub the chicken wings with ground paprika and minced garlic and put them in the instant pot. 3. Cook the chicken on Sauté mode for 4 minutes from each side. 4. Then add beef broth and close the lid. 5. Sauté the meal for 5 minutes more.

Cheesy Stuffed Cabbage

Prep time: 30 minutes | Cook time: 18 minutes | Serves 6 to 8

- 1 to 2 heads savoy cabbage
- 1 pound ground turkey
- 1 egg
- 1 cup reduced-fat shredded cheddar cheese
- 2 tablespoons evaporated skim milk
- ¼ cup reduced-fat shredded Parmesan cheese
- ¼ cup reduced-fat shredded mozzarella cheese
- ¼ cup finely diced onion
- ¼ cup finely diced bell pepper
- ¼ cup finely diced mushrooms
- 1 teaspoon salt
- ½ teaspoon black pepper
- 1 teaspoon garlic powder
- 6 basil leaves, fresh and cut chiffonade
- 1 tablespoon fresh parsley, chopped
- 1 quart of your favorite pasta sauce

1. Start by removing the core from the cabbages to prepare them for cooking.2. Bring a large pot of water to a boil and place one head of cabbage at a time into the water. Boil for approximately 10 minutes until the leaves soften.3. Once boiled, allow the cabbage to cool slightly. Carefully remove the leaves and set them aside; you will need about 15 or 16 leaves.4. In a separate bowl, mix together the ground meat and all remaining ingredients, reserving the pasta sauce for later.5. Take one cabbage leaf at a time and place a heaping tablespoon of the meat mixture in the center of the leaf.6. Tuck in the sides of the leaf and roll it tightly to secure the filling.7. Pour ½ cup of sauce into the bottom of the inner pot of the Instant Pot.8. Place the rolled cabbage leaves, fold-side down, into the pot, layering them as you go. Add a bit of sauce between each layer and pour any remaining sauce on top. (You may want to cook the rolls in two batches if needed.)9. Lock the lid in place and ensure the vent is set to sealing. Set the timer for 18 minutes on Manual mode at high pressure. Once the cooking time is complete, manually release the pressure to open the pot.

Spiced Chicken with Lentils and Butternut Squash

Prep time: 15 minutes | Cook time: 28 minutes | Serves 4

- 2 large shallots, halved and sliced thin, divided
- 5 teaspoons extra-virgin olive oil, divided
- ½ teaspoon grated lemon zest plus 2 teaspoons juice
- 1 teaspoon table salt, divided
- 4 (5 to 7 ounces / 142 to 198 g) bone-in chicken thighs, trimmed
- ¼ teaspoon pepper
- 2 garlic cloves, minced
- 1½ teaspoons caraway seeds
- 1 teaspoon ground coriander
- 1 teaspoon ground cumin
- ½ teaspoon paprika
- ⅛ teaspoon cayenne pepper
- 2 cups chicken broth
- 1 cup French green lentils, picked over and rinsed
- 2 pounds (907 g) butternut squash, peeled, seeded, and cut into 1½-inch pieces
- 1 cup fresh parsley or cilantro leaves

1. Combine half of shallots, 1 tablespoon oil, lemon zest and juice, and ¼ teaspoon salt in bowl; set aside. Pat chicken dry with paper towels and sprinkle with ½ teaspoon salt and pepper. Using highest sauté function, heat remaining 2 teaspoons oil in Instant Pot for 5 minutes (or until just smoking). Place chicken skin side down in pot and cook until well browned on first side, about 5 minutes; transfer to plate. 2. Add remaining shallot and remaining ¼ teaspoon salt to fat left in pot and cook, using highest sauté function, until shallot is softened, about 2 minutes. Stir in garlic, caraway, coriander, cumin, paprika, and cayenne and cook until fragrant, about 30 seconds. Stir in broth, scraping up any browned bits, then stir in lentils. 3. Nestle chicken skin side up into lentils and add any accumulated juices. Arrange squash on top. Lock lid in place and close pressure release valve. Select high pressure cook function and cook for 15 minutes. 4. Turn off Instant Pot and quick-release pressure. Carefully remove lid, allowing steam to escape away from you. Transfer chicken to plate and discard skin, if desired. Season lentil mixture with salt and pepper to taste. Add parsley to shallot mixture and toss to combine. Serve chicken with lentil mixture, topping individual portions with shallot-parsley salad.

Mushroom Chicken Alfredo

Prep time: 15 minutes | Cook time: 10 minutes | Serves 4

- ½ cup sliced cremini mushrooms
- ¼ cup chopped leek
- 1 tablespoon sesame oil
- 1 teaspoon chili flakes
- 1 cup heavy cream
- 1 pound (454 g) chicken fillet, chopped
- 1 teaspoon Italian seasoning
- 1 tablespoon cream cheese

1. Start by brushing the inside of the Instant Pot bowl with sesame oil to coat it evenly.2. Place the chicken in the Instant Pot in a single layer to ensure even cooking.3. Top the chicken with the sliced mushrooms and leeks for added flavor and texture.4. Sprinkle the ingredients with chili flakes, then add the heavy cream, Italian seasoning, and cream cheese on top.5. Securely close and seal the lid of the Instant Pot.6. Cook the meal on Manual mode at High Pressure for 10 minutes.7. Once the cooking time is complete, allow for a natural pressure release for 10 minutes before opening the lid.

Thai Yellow Curry Chicken Meatballs

Prep time: 5 minutes | Cook time: 30 minutes | Serves 4

- 1 pound 95 percent lean ground chicken
- ⅓ cup gluten-free panko (Japanese bread crumbs)
- 1 egg white
- 1 tablespoon coconut oil
- 1 yellow onion, cut into 1-inch pieces
- One 14-ounce can light coconut milk
- 3 tablespoons yellow curry paste
- ¾ cup water
- 8 ounces carrots, halved lengthwise, then cut crosswise into 1-inch lengths (or quartered if
- very large)
- 8 ounces zucchini, quartered lengthwise, then cut crosswise into 1-inch lengths (or cut into halves, then thirds if large)
- 8 ounces cremini mushrooms, quartered
- Fresh Thai basil leaves for serving (optional)
- Fresno or jalapeño chile, thinly sliced, for serving (optional)
- 1 lime, cut into wedges
- Cooked cauliflower "rice" for serving

1. In a medium bowl, combine the chicken, panko, and egg white and mix until evenly combined. Set aside. 2. Select the Sauté setting on the Instant Pot and heat the oil for 2 minutes. Add the onion and sauté for 5 minutes, until it begins to soften and brown. Add ½ cup of the coconut milk and the curry paste and sauté for 1 minute more, until bubbling and fragrant. Press the Cancel button to turn off the pot, then stir in the water. 3. Using a 1½-tablespoon cookie scoop, shape and drop meatballs into the pot in a single layer. 4. Secure the lid and set the Pressure Release to Sealing. Select the Pressure Cook or Manual setting and set the cooking time for 5 minutes at high pressure. (The pot will take about 5 minutes to come up to pressure before the cooking program begins.) 5. When the cooking program ends, perform a quick pressure release by moving the Pressure Release to Venting, or let the pressure release naturally. Open the pot and stir in the carrots, zucchini, mushrooms, and remaining 1¼ cups coconut milk. 6. Press the Cancel button to reset the cooking program, then select the Sauté setting. Bring the curry to a simmer (this will take about 2 minutes), then let cook, uncovered, for about 8 minutes, until the carrots are fork-tender. Press the Cancel button to turn off the pot. 7. Ladle the curry into bowls. Serve piping hot, topped with basil leaves and chile slices, if desired, and the lime wedges and cauliflower "rice" on the side.

Herb and Lemon Whole Chicken

Prep time: 5 minutes | Cook time: 30 to 32 minutes | Serves 4

- 3 teaspoons garlic powder
- 3 teaspoons salt
- 2 teaspoons dried parsley
- 2 teaspoons dried rosemary
- 1 teaspoon pepper
- 1 (4-pound / 1.8-kg) whole chicken
- 2 tablespoons coconut oil
- 1 cup chicken broth
- 1 lemon, zested and quartered

1. In a small bowl, mix together the garlic powder, salt, parsley, rosemary, and pepper. Rub this herb mixture all over the whole chicken.2. Set your Instant Pot to Sauté mode and heat the coconut oil.3. Add the seasoned chicken to the pot and brown it for 5 to 7 minutes. Using tongs, transfer the chicken to a plate.4. Pour the broth into the Instant Pot, using a rubber spatula or wooden spoon to scrape the bottom until all seasoning is removed. Then, insert the trivet.5. Scatter the lemon zest over the chicken and place the lemon quarters inside the cavity. Position the chicken on the trivet.6. Secure the lid on the Instant Pot. Select the Meat/Stew mode and set the cooking time to 25 minutes at High Pressure.7. Once cooking is complete, allow for a natural pressure release for 10 minutes before releasing any remaining pressure. Carefully open the lid.8. Shred the chicken and serve it warm for a delightful meal.

Chicken Reuben Bake

Prep time: 10 minutes | Cook time: 6 to 8 hours | Serves 6

- 4 boneless, skinless chicken-breast halves
- ¼ cup water
- 1-pound bag sauerkraut, drained and rinsed
- 4 to 5 (1 ounce each)
- slices Swiss cheese
- ¾ cup fat-free Thousand Island salad dressing
- 2 tablespoons chopped fresh parsley

1. Begin by placing the chicken and ¼ cup of water in the inner pot of the Instant Pot. Layer the sauerkraut over the chicken, then add the cheese on top. Drizzle the salad dressing over the cheese and finish by sprinkling parsley on top.2. Secure the lid of the Instant Pot and set it to the Slow Cook function, adjusting the temperature to low. Cook for 6 to 8 hours until the chicken is tender and fully cooked.

Speedy Chicken Cacciatore

Prep time: 5 minutes | Cook time: 30 minutes | Serves 6

- 2 pounds boneless, skinless chicken thighs
- 1½ teaspoons fine sea salt
- ½ teaspoon freshly ground black pepper
- 2 tablespoons extra-virgin olive oil
- 3 garlic cloves, chopped
- 2 large red bell peppers, seeded and cut into ¼ by 2-inch strips
- 2 large yellow onions, sliced
- ½ cup dry red wine
- 1½ teaspoons Italian seasoning
- ½ teaspoon red pepper flakes (optional)
- One 14½ ounces can diced tomatoes and their liquid
- 2 tablespoons tomato paste
- Cooked brown rice or whole-grain pasta for serving

1. Season the chicken thighs on both sides with 1 teaspoon of salt and black pepper to enhance their flavor.2. Select the Sauté setting on the Instant Pot and heat the oil along with minced garlic for about 2 minutes, allowing the garlic to become fragrant but not browned. Add the bell peppers, onions, and the remaining ½ teaspoon of salt, sautéing for 3 minutes until the onions start to soften. Stir in the wine, Italian seasoning, and red pepper flakes (if using). Using tongs, carefully add the chicken to the pot, turning each piece to coat it with the wine and spices, and nestle them into a single layer in the liquid. Pour the tomatoes, along with their juices, over the chicken and place dollops of tomato paste on top without stirring.3. Secure the lid on the Instant Pot and set the Pressure Release valve to Sealing. Press Cancel to reset the cooking program, then select the Poultry, Pressure Cook, or Manual setting and set the cooking time for 12 minutes at high pressure. (Keep in mind that the pot will take about 15 minutes to build pressure before the cooking program starts.)4. Once the cooking program ends, you can perform a quick pressure release by moving the Pressure Release valve to Venting, or let the pressure release naturally. Carefully open the pot, and using tongs, transfer the chicken and vegetables to a serving dish.5. Spoon some of the delicious sauce over the chicken and serve hot, alongside rice for a complete meal.

Chicken and Bacon Ranch Casserole

Prep time: 5 minutes | Cook time: 30 minutes | Serves 4

- 4 slices bacon
- 4 (6-ounce / 170-g) boneless, skinless chicken breasts, cut into 1-inch cubes
- ½ teaspoon salt
- ¼ teaspoon pepper
- 1 tablespoon coconut oil
- ½ cup chicken broth
- ½ cup ranch dressing
- ½ cup shredded Cheddar cheese
- 2 ounces (57 g) cream cheese

1. Begin by pressing the Sauté button to heat your Instant Pot.2. Add the bacon slices to the pot and cook for about 7 minutes, flipping occasionally, until they are crisp.3. Once cooked, remove the bacon from the pot and place it on a paper towel to drain excess grease. Set it aside.4. Season the chicken cubes with salt and pepper to enhance their flavor.5. Set your Instant Pot back to Sauté mode and melt the coconut oil in the pot.6. Add the seasoned chicken cubes to the pot and brown them for 3 to 4 minutes until they achieve a golden color.7. Stir in the broth and ranch dressing, mixing well.8. Secure the lid on the Instant Pot, select Manual mode, and set the cooking time for 20 minutes at High Pressure.9. Once cooking is complete, perform a quick release of the pressure. Carefully open the lid once the pressure is released.10. Stir in the Cheddar cheese and cream cheese until well combined. Crumble the cooked bacon and sprinkle it on top. Serve immediately for a delicious mea

Chapter 3

Beef, Pork, and Lamb

Hearty Beef and Red Cabbage Stew

Prep time: 10 minutes | Cook time: 20 minutes | Serves 4

- 2 tablespoons butter, at room temperature
- 1 onion, chopped
- 2 garlic cloves, minced
- 1½ pounds (680 g) beef stew meat, cubed
- 2½ cups beef stock
- 8 ounces (227 g) sugar-free tomato sauce
- 2 cups shredded red cabbage
- 1 tablespoon coconut aminos
- 2 bay leaves
- 1 teaspoon dried parsley flakes
- ½ teaspoon crushed red pepper flakes
- Sea salt and ground black pepper, to taste

1. Press the Sauté button to heat up the Instant Pot. Then, melt the butter. Cook the onion and garlic until softened. 2. Add beef stew meat and cook an additional 3 minutes or until browned. Stir the remaining ingredients into the Instant Pot. 3. Secure the lid. Choose Manual mode and High Pressure; cook for 15 minutes. Once cooking is complete, use a quick pressure release; carefully remove the lid. 4. Discard bay leaves and ladle into individual bowls. Enjoy!

Osso Buco with Gremolata

Prep time: 35 minutes | Cook time: 1 hour 2 minutes | Serves 6

- 4 bone-in beef shanks
- Sea salt, to taste
- 2 tablespoons avocado oil
- 1 small turnip, diced
- 1 medium onion, diced
- 1 medium stalk celery, diced
- 4 cloves garlic, smashed
- 1 tablespoon unsweetened tomato purée
- ½ cup dry white wine
- 1 cup chicken broth
- 1 sprig fresh rosemary
- 2 sprigs fresh thyme
- 3 Roma tomatoes, diced
- For the Gremolata:
- ½ cup loosely packed parsley leaves
- 1 clove garlic, crushed
- Grated zest of 2 lemons

1. Begin by seasoning the shanks generously with salt on a clean work surface.2. Set the Instant Pot to Sauté mode and add the oil. Once the oil shimmers, add 2 shanks and sear them for 4 minutes on each side. Remove the shanks to a bowl and repeat the process with the remaining shanks, setting them aside afterward.3. Add the turnip, onion, and celery to the pot, cooking for 5 minutes or until the vegetables are softened.4. Stir in the garlic and unsweetened tomato purée, cooking for an additional minute while stirring frequently.5. Deglaze the pot with the wine, using a wooden spoon to scrape the bottom and loosen any browned bits. Bring the mixture to a boil.6. Add the broth, rosemary, thyme, and the seared shanks back into the pot. Top the shanks with the tomatoes.7. Secure the lid of the Instant Pot. Press the Manual button and set the cooking time for 40 minutes at High Pressure.8. While the shanks are cooking, prepare the gremolata: In a small food processor, combine the parsley, garlic, and lemon zest, pulsing until the parsley is finely chopped. Refrigerate the gremolata until ready to use.9. When the timer beeps, allow the pressure to release naturally for 20 minutes, then release any remaining pressure before carefully opening the lid.10. To serve, transfer the shanks to a large, shallow serving bowl. Ladle the braising sauce over the top and finish by sprinkling with the prepared gremolata for added flavor.

Golden Bacon Sticks

Prep time: 5 minutes | Cook time: 6 minutes | Serves 4

- 6 ounces (170 g) bacon, sliced
- 2 tablespoons almond
- flour
- 1 tablespoon water
- ¾ teaspoon chili pepper

1. Begin by coating the sliced bacon with almond flour, then drizzle it with a bit of water and mix in the chili pepper to enhance the flavor. 2. Transfer the seasoned bacon into the Instant Pot, ensuring it's spread out evenly. 3. Set the Instant Pot to Sauté mode and cook the bacon for 3 minutes on each side until it reaches your desired level of crispiness. Enjoy your delicious bacon immediately after cooking!

Filipino Pork Loin

Prep time: 10 minutes | Cook time: 40 minutes | Serves 4

- 1 pound (454 g) pork loin, chopped
- ½ cup apple cider vinegar
- 1 cup chicken broth
- 1 chili pepper, chopped
- 1 tablespoon coconut oil
- 1 teaspoon salt

1. Start by melting the coconut oil in the Instant Pot using Sauté mode.2. Once the oil is hot, add the chili pepper and cook for 2 minutes, stirring occasionally.3. Next, add the chopped pork loin and salt to the pot. Cook the mixture for 5 minutes, allowing the pork to brown slightly.4. After the pork is cooked, pour in the apple cider vinegar and chicken broth, stirring to combine.5. Secure the lid on the Instant Pot, ensuring it is sealed. Set it to cook the Filipino pork for 30 minutes on High Pressure (Manual mode). Once the cooking time is complete, perform a quick pressure release to open the pot.

Tender Pork Butt Roast

Prep time: 10 minutes | Cook time: 9 minutes | Serves 6 to 8

- 3 to 4 pounds pork butt roast
- 2 to 3 tablespoons of your

- favorite rub
- 2 cups water

1. Place pork in the inner pot of the Instant Pot. 2. Sprinkle in the rub all over the roast and add the water, being careful not to wash off the rub. 3. Secure the lid and set the vent to sealing. Cook for 9 minutes on the Manual setting. 4. Let the pressure release naturally.

Beef, Bacon and Cauliflower Rice Casserole

Prep time: 15 minutes | Cook time: 26 minutes | Serves 5

- 2 cups fresh cauliflower florets
- 1 pound (454 g) ground beef
- 5 slices uncooked bacon, chopped
- 8 ounces (227 g) unsweetened tomato purée
- 1 cup shredded Cheddar

- cheese, divided
- 1 teaspoon garlic powder
- ½ teaspoon paprika
- ½ teaspoon sea salt
- ¼ teaspoon ground black pepper
- ¼ teaspoon celery seed
- 1 cup water
- 1 medium Roma tomato, sliced

1. Start by spraying a round soufflé dish with coconut oil cooking spray and set it aside.2. Add the cauliflower florets to a food processor and pulse until they resemble rice. Set the riced cauliflower aside.3. Select Sauté mode on the Instant Pot. Once the pot is hot, crumble the ground beef into the pot and add the bacon. Sauté for 6 minutes, or until the ground beef is browned and the bacon is cooked through.4. Transfer the cooked beef, bacon, and rendered fat to a large bowl.5. To the bowl with the beef and bacon, add the riced cauliflower, tomato purée, ½ cup of Cheddar cheese, garlic powder, paprika, sea salt, black pepper, and celery seed. Mix well to combine all the ingredients.6. Pour the mixture into the prepared soufflé dish, using a spoon to press and smooth it into an even layer.7. Place the trivet in the Instant Pot and add water to the bottom of the pot. Carefully set the dish on top of the trivet.8. Secure the lid on the Instant Pot. Select Manual mode and set the cooking time for 20 minutes at High Pressure.9. Once cooking is complete, perform a quick release of the pressure.10. Carefully open the lid. Arrange tomato slices in a single layer on top of the casserole and sprinkle the remaining cheese over them.11.

Secure the lid again and let the residual heat melt the cheese for about 5 minutes.12. Open the lid and carefully remove the dish from the pot.13. Transfer the casserole to a serving plate and slice it into 5 equal-sized wedges. Serve warm for a delicious meal!

Romano-Crusted Pork Chops

Prep time: 10 minutes | Cook time: 18 minutes | Serves 3

- 3 pork chops
- 4 ounces (113 g) Romano cheese, grated
- ½ teaspoon Cajun seasoning

- 1 egg, beaten
- 1 tablespoon cream cheese
- ⅓ cup almond flour
- 3 tablespoons avocado oil

1. Generously coat the pork chops with Cajun seasoning, ensuring they are well covered. 2. In a separate mixing bowl, combine grated Romano cheese with almond flour until blended. 3. In another bowl, whisk together the eggs and cream cheese until smooth and creamy. 4. Dip each seasoned pork chop into the egg mixture, allowing any excess to drip off, and then coat them in the cheese mixture thoroughly. 5. Repeat the dipping and coating process for an extra layer of flavor and crunch. 6. Pour avocado oil into the Instant Pot and preheat it on Sauté mode for 2 minutes until the oil is hot. 7. Place the coated pork chops into the pot and cook for 8 minutes on each side until golden brown and cooked through.

Beef Shami Kabob

Prep time: 15 minutes | Cook time: 35 minutes | Serves 4

- 1 pound (454 g) beef chunks, chopped
- 1 teaspoon ginger paste
- ½ teaspoon ground cumin

- 2 cups water
- ¼ cup almond flour
- 1 egg, beaten
- 1 tablespoon coconut oil

1. Start by placing the beef chunks, ginger paste, ground cumin, and water into the Instant Pot.2. Select Manual mode and set the cooking time for 30 minutes on High Pressure.3. When the timer beeps, perform a quick pressure release and carefully open the lid.4. Drain the water from the meat and transfer the beef to a blender. Add the almond flour and beaten egg, then blend until smooth. Shape the mixture into small meatballs.5. On Sauté mode, heat the coconut oil in the Instant Pot and add the meatballs to the pot.6. Cook the meatballs for 2 minutes on each side, or until they are golden brown.7. Serve the meatballs immediately for a delicious dish!

Garlic-Infused Buttered Italian Sausages

Prep time: 15 minutes | Cook time: 20 minutes | Serves 4

- 1 teaspoon garlic powder
- 1 cup water
- 1 teaspoon butter
- 12 ounces (340 g) Italian sausages, chopped
- ½ teaspoon Italian seasoning

1. Sprinkle the chopped Italian sausages with Italian seasoning and garlic powder and place in the instant pot. 2. Add butter and cook the sausages on Sauté mode for 10 minutes. Stir them from time to time with the help of the spatula. 3. Then add water and close the lid. 4. Cook the sausages on Manual mode (High Pressure) for 10 minutes. 5. Allow the natural pressure release for 10 minutes more.

Mustard Leek Smothered Pork Chops

Prep time: 15 minutes | Cook time: 35 minutes | Serves 4

- 4 (8- to 10-ounce/ 227- to 283-g) bone-in blade-cut pork chops, about ¾ inch thick, trimmed
- ½ teaspoon table salt
- ½ teaspoon pepper
- 4 teaspoons extra-virgin olive oil, divided
- 2 ounces (57 g) pancetta, chopped fine
- 1 tablespoon all-purpose flour
- ¾ cup dry white wine
- 1½ pounds (680 g) leeks, ends trimmed, halved lengthwise, sliced into 3-inch lengths, and washed thoroughly
- 1 tablespoon Dijon mustard
- 2 tablespoons chopped fresh parsley

1. Pat pork chops dry with paper towels. Using sharp knife, cut 2 slits, about 2 inches apart, through fat on edge of each chop. Sprinkle with salt and pepper. Using highest sauté function, heat 2 teaspoons oil in Instant Pot for 5 minutes (or until just smoking). Brown 2 chops on both sides, 6 to 8 minutes; transfer to plate. Repeat with remaining 2 teaspoons oil and remaining chops; transfer to plate. 2. Add pancetta to fat left in pot and cook, using highest sauté function, until softened and lightly browned, about 2 minutes. Stir in flour and cook for 30 seconds. Stir in wine, scraping up any browned bits and smoothing any lumps. Stir in leeks and cook until softened, about 3 minutes. Nestle chops into pot (chops will overlap) and add any accumulated juices. Lock lid in place and close pressure release valve. Select high pressure cook function and cook for 10 minutes. 3. Turn off Instant Pot and let pressure release naturally for

15 minutes. Quick-release any remaining pressure, then carefully remove lid, allowing steam to escape away from you. Transfer chops to serving platter, tent with aluminum foil, and let rest while finishing leeks. 4. Using highest sauté function, bring leek mixture to simmer. Stir in mustard and cook until slightly thickened, about 5 minutes. Season with salt and pepper to taste. Spoon leek mixture over chops and sprinkle with parsley. Serve.

Stuffed Meatballs with Mozzarella

Prep time: 10 minutes | Cook time: 20 minutes | Serves 6

- 1 pound (454 g) ground pork
- 1 teaspoon chili flakes
- ½ teaspoon salt
- ⅓ cup shredded
- Mozzarella cheese
- 1 tablespoon butter
- ¼ cup chicken broth
- ½ teaspoon garlic powder

1. In a bowl, mix together the ground pork, chili flakes, salt, and garlic powder until well combined. 2. Using your fingertips, shape the mixture into meatballs. 3. Roll the cheese into small balls to create mini cheese portions. 4. Stuff each meatball with a mini cheese ball, ensuring they are well sealed. 5. Add butter to the Instant Pot and set it to Sauté mode. 6. Once the butter has melted and is hot, add the prepared meatballs to the pot. 7. Sauté the meatballs for 3 minutes on each side until they are browned. 8. After browning, pour in the chicken broth and close the lid securely. 9. Set the Instant Pot to Meat/Stew mode and cook for 10 minutes for a delicious finish.

Garlic Beef Roast

Prep time: 2 minutes | Cook time: 70 minutes | Serves 6

- 2 pounds (907 g) top round roast
- ½ cup beef broth
- 2 teaspoons salt
- 1 teaspoon black pepper
- 3 whole cloves garlic
- 1 bay leaf

1. Begin by adding the roast, broth, salt, pepper, minced garlic, and bay leaf to the pot. 2. Secure the lid and seal the vent. Set the Instant Pot to cook on High Pressure for 15 minutes. After the cooking time is complete, allow the steam to naturally release for 15 minutes before performing a manual release for any remaining pressure. 3. Carefully remove the beef from the pot, then slice or shred it as desired. Store the prepared beef in an airtight container in the refrigerator or freezer for later use.

Creamy Pork and Mushroom Stroganoff

Prep time: 10 minutes | Cook time: 25 minutes | Serves 4

- ½ cup chopped cremini mushrooms
- 1 teaspoon dried oregano
- ½ teaspoon ground nutmeg
- ½ cup coconut milk
- 1 cup ground pork
- ½ teaspoon salt
- 2 tablespoons butter

1. Heat up butter on Sauté mode for 3 minutes. 2. Add mushrooms. Sauté the vegetables for 5 minutes. 3. Then stir them and add salt, ground pork, ground nutmeg, and dried oregano. 4. Stir the ingredients and cook for 5 minutes more. 5. Add coconut milk and close the lid. 6. Sauté the stroganoff for 15 minutes. Stir it from time to time to avoid burning.

Braised Pork with Broccoli Rabe and Sage

Prep time: 15 minutes | Cook time: 50 minutes | Serves 4

- 1½ pounds (680 g) boneless pork butt roast, trimmed and cut into 2-inch pieces
- ½ teaspoon table salt
- ½ teaspoon pepper
- 1 tablespoon extra-virgin olive oil
- 2 tablespoons minced fresh sage, divided
- 5 garlic cloves, peeled
- and smashed
- 1 tablespoon all-purpose flour
- ¼ cup chicken broth
- ¼ cup dry white wine
- 1 pound (454 g) broccoli rabe, trimmed and cut into 1-inch pieces
- ½ teaspoon grated orange zest

1. Pat the pork dry with paper towels and season it generously with salt and pepper. Using the highest sauté function, heat oil in the Instant Pot for about 5 minutes, or until it begins to smoke slightly. Brown the pork on all sides for 6 to 8 minutes, then transfer it to a plate.2. In the remaining fat in the pot, add 1 tablespoon of sage, minced garlic, and flour. Cook on the highest sauté setting until fragrant, about 1 minute. Stir in the broth and wine, scraping up any browned bits from the bottom of the pot. Return the browned pork to the pot along with any accumulated juices. Secure the lid in place and close the pressure release valve. Select the high-pressure cook function and set the timer for 30 minutes.3. After the cooking time is complete, turn off the Instant Pot and allow the pressure to release naturally for 15 minutes. Then, perform a quick release for any remaining pressure. Carefully remove the lid, allowing steam to escape away from you. Transfer the pork to a serving dish and cover it loosely with aluminum foil to rest while you prepare the broccoli rabe.4. Whisk the sauce until smooth and bring it to a simmer using the highest sauté function. Add the broccoli rabe and cook, partially covered, until it becomes tender and bright green, about 3 minutes. Stir in the orange zest and the remaining 1 tablespoon of sage. Serve the pork alongside the broccoli rabe mixture for a delicious meal.

Chipotle-Glazed Pork Chops with Fire-Roasted Tomatoes

Prep time: 7 minutes | Cook time: 15 minutes | Serves 4

- 2 tablespoons coconut oil
- 3 chipotle chilies
- 2 tablespoons adobo sauce
- 2 teaspoons cumin
- 1 teaspoon dried thyme
- 1 teaspoon salt
- 4 (5-ounce / 142-g) boneless pork chops
- ½ medium onion, chopped
- 2 bay leaves
- 1 cup chicken broth
- ½ (7-ounce / 198-g) can fire-roasted diced tomatoes
- ⅓ cup chopped cilantro

1. Press the Sauté button and add coconut oil to Instant Pot. While it heats, add chilies, adobo sauce, cumin, thyme, and salt to food processor. Pulse to make paste. Rub paste into pork chops. Place in Instant Pot and sear each side 5 minutes or until browned. 2. Press the Cancel button and add onion, bay leaves, broth, tomatoes, and cilantro to Instant Pot. Click lid closed. Press the Manual button and adjust time for 15 minutes. When timer beeps, allow a 10-minute natural release, then quick-release the remaining pressure. Serve warm with additional cilantro as garnish if desired.

Fajita Pork Shoulder

Prep time: 5 minutes | Cook time: 45 minutes | Serves 2

- 11 ounces (312 g) pork shoulder, boneless, sliced
- 1 teaspoon fajita
- seasoning
- 2 tablespoons butter
- ½ cup water

1. Begin by sprinkling the meat with fajita seasoning, then place it in the Instant Pot.2. Add the butter and set the Instant Pot to Sauté mode, cooking for 5 minutes.3. After 5 minutes, stir the pork strips and add water to the pot.4. Secure the lid on the Instant Pot and set it to Manual mode (High Pressure).5. Adjust the timer to 40 minutes for cooking.6. When the cooking time is nearing completion, allow for a natural pressure release for 10 minutes before carefully opening the lid.

Spiced Pork and Cauliflower Keema

Prep time: 15 minutes | Cook time: 8 minutes | Serves 6

- 1 tablespoon sesame oil
- ½ cup yellow onion, chopped
- 1 garlic cloves, minced
- 1 (1-inch) piece fresh ginger, minced
- 1½ pounds (680 g) ground pork
- 1 cup cauliflower, chopped into small florets
- 1 ripe tomatoes, puréed
- 1 jalapeño pepper, seeded and minced
- 4 cloves, whole
- 1 teaspoon garam masala
- ½ teaspoon ground cumin
- ¼ teaspoon turmeric powder
- 1 teaspoon brown mustard seeds
- ½ teaspoon hot paprika
- Sea salt and ground black pepper, to taste
- 1 cup wate

1. Press the Sauté button to heat up the Instant Pot. Heat the sesame oil. Once hot, sauté yellow onion for 3 minutes or until softened. 2. Stir in garlic and ginger; cook for an additional minute. Add the remaining ingredients. 3. Secure the lid. Choose the Manual mode and set cooking time for 5 minutes on High pressure. 4. Once cooking is complete, use a quick pressure release. Carefully remove the lid. 5. Serve immediately.

Mary's Classic Sunday Pot Roast

Prep time: 10 minutes | Cook time:1 hour 30 minutes | Serves 10

- 1 (3 to 4 pounds) beef rump roast
- 2 teaspoons kosher salt, divided
- 2 tablespoons avocado oil
- 1 large onion, coarsely chopped (about 1½ cups)
- 4 large carrots, each cut into 4 pieces
- 1 tablespoon minced garlic
- 3 cups low-sodium beef broth
- 1 teaspoon freshly ground black pepper
- 1 tablespoon dried parsley
- 2 tablespoons all-purpose flour

1. Rub the roast all over with 1 teaspoon of the salt. 2. Set the electric pressure cooker to the Sauté setting. When the pot is hot, pour in the avocado oil. 3. Carefully place the roast in the pot and sear it for 6 to 9 minutes on each side. (You want a dark caramelized crust.) Hit Cancel. 4. Transfer the roast from the pot to a plate. 5. In order, put the onion, carrots, and garlic in the pot. Place the roast on top of the vegetables along with any juices that accumulated on the plate. 6. In a medium bowl, whisk together the broth, remaining 1 teaspoon of salt, pepper, and parsley. Pour the broth mixture over the roast. 7. Close and lock the lid of the pressure cooker. Set the valve to sealing. 8. Cook on high pressure for 1 hour and 30 minutes. 9. When the cooking is complete, hit Cancel and allow the pressure to release naturally. 10. Once the pin drops, unlock and remove the lid. 11. Using large slotted spoons, transfer the roast and vegetables to a serving platter while you make the gravy. 12. Using a large spoon or fat separator, remove the fat from the juices in the pot. Set the electric pressure cooker to the Sauté setting and bring the liquid to a boil. 13. In a small bowl, whisk together the flour and 4 tablespoons of water to make a slurry. Pour the slurry into the pot, whisking occasionally, until the gravy is the thickness you like. Season with salt and pepper, if necessary. 14. Serve the meat and carrots with the gravy.

Garlic Beef Stroganoff

Prep time: 20 minutes | Cook time: 25 minutes | Serves 6

- 2 tablespoons canola oil
- 1½ pounds boneless round steak, cut into thin strips, trimmed of fat
- 2 teaspoons sodium-free beef bouillon powder
- 1 cup mushroom juice, with water added to make a full cup
- 2 (4½ ounces) jars sliced mushrooms, drained with juice reserved
- 10¾ ounces can 98% fat-free, lower-sodium cream of mushroom soup
- 1 large onion, chopped
- 3 garlic cloves, minced
- 1 tablespoon Worcestershire sauce
- 6 ounces fat-free cream cheese, cubed and softened

1. Begin by pressing the Sauté button on your Instant Pot and pouring the oil into the inner pot. 2. When the oil is hot, add the beef and sauté it until it's lightly browned, about 2 minutes on each side. Set the browned beef aside for now. Press Cancel and clean the inner pot with a paper towel. 3. Press Sauté again and combine the bouillon with the mushroom juice and water in the inner pot. Stir until completely dissolved, then press Cancel. 4. Add the sliced mushrooms, soup, diced onion, minced garlic, and Worcestershire sauce to the pot, stirring everything together. Return the beef to the pot. 5. Close the lid securely and ensure the vent is set to sealing. Select Manual mode and set the timer for 15 minutes. 6. After the cooking time ends, allow the pressure to release naturally for 15 minutes before doing a quick release. 7. Once the lid is removed, press Cancel and then select Sauté. Stir in the cream cheese, mixing until smooth and creamy. 8. Serve the flavorful mixture over your choice of noodles for a delicious meal.

Cider-Herb Pork Tenderloin

Prep time: 15 minutes | Cook time: 18 minutes | Serves 4

- ¼ teaspoon ground cumin
- ½ teaspoon ground nutmeg
- ½ teaspoon dried thyme
- ½ teaspoon ground coriander
- 1 tablespoon sesame oil
- 1 pound (454 g) pork tenderloin
- 2 tablespoons apple cider vinegar
- 1 cup water

1. In a mixing bowl, combine ground cumin, ground nutmeg, dried thyme, ground coriander, and apple cider vinegar to create a flavorful spice mixture. 2. Rub the spice blend all over the pork, ensuring it is evenly coated. 3. Heat sesame oil in the Instant Pot on Sauté mode for 2 minutes until hot. 4. Carefully place the pork tenderloin into the hot oil and sear it for 5 minutes on each side, or until it develops a light brown crust. 5. Pour in water to add moisture to the pot. 6. Secure the lid and seal the vent. Set the pot to Manual mode and cook on High Pressure for 5 minutes. 7. Once the cooking time is complete, let the pressure release naturally for 15 minutes before opening the lid.

Basic Nutritional Values

Prep time: 20 minutes | Cook time: 2 hours | Serves 4 to 6

- 2 pounds beef roast, boneless
- ¼ teaspoon salt
- ¼ teaspoon pepper
- 1 tablespoon olive oil
- 2 stalks celery, chopped
- 4 tablespoons margarine
- 2 cups low-sodium tomato juice
- 2 cloves garlic, finely chopped, or 1 teaspoon garlic powder
- 1 teaspoon thyme
- 1 bay leaf
- 4 carrots, chopped
- 1 medium onion, chopped
- 4 medium potatoes, chopped

1. Pat the beef dry with paper towels and season all sides generously with salt and pepper. 2. Select the Sauté function on the Instant Pot and adjust the heat to More. Add the oil to the inner pot and cook the beef for 6 minutes, turning it once, until browned. Transfer the beef to a plate. 3. Add the chopped celery and margarine to the inner pot and cook for 2 minutes. Stir in the tomato juice, minced garlic, thyme, and bay leaf, then hit Cancel to turn off the Sauté function. 4. Place the browned beef on top of the mixture in the inner pot, pressing it into the sauce. Cover and lock the lid, ensuring the vent is set to sealing. Select Manual and cook at high pressure for 1 hour and 15 minutes. 5. Once cooking is complete, release the pressure using the natural release function. Carefully transfer the beef to a cutting board and

discard the bay leaf. 6. Skim off any excess fat from the surface of the sauce. Then, select the Sauté function again and adjust the heat to More. Cook for 18 minutes, or until the sauce is reduced by about half (approximately 2½ cups). Hit Cancel to turn off the Sauté function. 7. Add the chopped carrots, onion, and potatoes to the pot. Cover and lock the lid, ensuring the vent is set to sealing. Select Manual and cook at high pressure for 10 minutes. 8. Once cooking is complete, use a quick release to release the pressure. With the Sauté function still on, bring the mixture to a simmer. 9. Season the stew with additional salt and pepper to taste before serving. Enjoy your hearty beef stew!

Chile Verde Pulled Pork with Tomatillos

Prep time: 15 minutes | Cook time: 1 hour 3 minutes | Serves 6

- 2 pounds (907 g) pork shoulder, cut into 6 equal-sized pieces
- 1 teaspoon sea salt
- ½ teaspoon ground black pepper
- 2 jalapeño peppers, deseeded and stemmed
- 1 pound (454 g) tomatillos, husks removed and quartered
- 3 garlic cloves
- 1 tablespoon lime juice
- 3 tablespoons fresh cilantro, chopped
- 1 medium white onion, chopped
- 1 teaspoon ground cumin
- ½ teaspoon dried oregano
- 1⅔ cups chicken broth
- 1½ tablespoons olive oil

1. Begin by seasoning the pork pieces generously with salt and freshly ground black pepper. Massage the seasonings into the meat thoroughly and set them aside. 2. In a blender, combine chopped jalapeños, tomatillos, garlic cloves, lime juice, fresh cilantro, diced onions, ground cumin, dried oregano, and chicken broth. Blend the mixture until it achieves a smooth consistency, then set it aside. 3. Activate the Sauté function on your pot and pour in the olive oil. Once heated, add the seasoned pork cuts and sear them for approximately 4 minutes on each side until they develop a nice golden-brown color. 4. Carefully pour the blended jalapeño sauce over the browned pork, stirring gently to ensure the pieces are evenly coated. 5. Secure the lid tightly. Switch to Manual mode and adjust the cooking time to 55 minutes at High Pressure. 6. After cooking, let the pressure release naturally for 10 minutes before carefully releasing any remaining pressure. 7. Once the lid is removed, transfer the pork onto a cutting board and shred it using two forks until it is fully pulled apart. 8. Return the shredded pork to the pot, mixing it thoroughly with the sauce. Serve the dish warm on a platter for an inviting presentation.

Herb-Infused Rosemary Pork Belly

Prep time: 10 minutes | Cook time: 75 minutes | Serves 4

- 10 ounces (283 g) pork belly
- 1 teaspoon dried rosemary
- ½ teaspoon dried thyme
- ¼ teaspoon ground cinnamon
- 1 teaspoon salt
- 1 cup water

1. Rub the pork belly with dried rosemary, thyme, ground cinnamon, and salt and transfer in the instant pot bowl. 2. Add water, close and seal the lid. 3. Cook the pork belly on Manual mode (High Pressure) for 75 minutes. 4. Remove the cooked pork belly from the instant pot and slice it into servings.

Spicy Butternut Squash Beef Stew

Prep time: 15 minutes | Cook time: 30 minutes | Serves 8

- 1½ tablespoons smoked paprika
- 2 teaspoons ground cinnamon
- 1½ teaspoons kosher salt
- 1 teaspoon ground ginger
- 1 teaspoon red pepper flakes
- ½ teaspoon freshly ground black pepper
- 2 pounds beef shoulder roast, cut into 1-inch cubes
- 2 tablespoons avocado
- oil, divided
- 1 cup low-sodium beef or vegetable broth
- 1 medium red onion, cut into wedges
- 8 garlic cloves, minced
- 1 (28-ounce) carton or can no-salt-added diced tomatoes
- 2 pounds butternut squash, peeled and cut into 1-inch pieces
- Chopped fresh cilantro or parsley, for serving

1. In a zip-top bag or medium bowl, combine the paprika, cinnamon, salt, ginger, red pepper, and black pepper. Add the beef and toss to coat. 2. Set the electric pressure cooker to the Sauté setting. When the pot is hot, pour in 1 tablespoon of avocado oil. 3. Add half of the beef to the pot and cook, stirring occasionally, for 3 to 5 minutes or until the beef is no longer pink. Transfer it to a plate, then add the remaining 1 tablespoon of avocado oil and brown the remaining beef. Transfer to the plate. Hit Cancel. 4. Stir in the broth and scrape up any brown bits from the bottom of the pot. Return the beef to the pot and add the onion, garlic, tomatoes and their juices, and squash. Stir well. 5. Close and lock lid of pressure cooker. Set the valve to sealing. 6. Cook on high pressure for 30 minutes. 7. When cooking is complete, hit Cancel. Allow the pressure to release naturally for 10 minutes, then quick release any remaining pressure. 8. Unlock and remove lid. 9. Spoon into serving bowls, sprinkle with cilantro or parsley, and serve.

Cardamom Beef Stew Meat with Broccoli

Prep time: 10 minutes | Cook time: 50 minutes | Serves 2

- 9 ounces (255 g) beef stew meat, chopped
- 1 teaspoon ground cardamom
- ½ teaspoon salt
- 1 cup chopped broccoli
- 1 cup water

1. Start by preheating the Instant Pot on the Sauté mode. 2. Once the display shows "Hot," add the chopped beef stew meat to the pot and cook for 4 minutes, turning it to brown each side for 2 minutes. 3. Next, add the ground cardamom, salt, and broccoli to the pot, stirring to combine. 4. Pour in the water, then securely close the lid of the Instant Pot. 5. Set the Instant Pot to Sauté mode and cook the stew for 45 minutes to achieve a tender consistency. 6. Once done, enjoy your delicious beef stew!

French Dip Chuck Roast

Prep time: 5 minutes | Cook time: 70 minutes | Serves 6

- 2 tablespoons avocado oil
- 2 to 2½ pounds (907 g to 1.1 kg) chuck roast
- 2 cups beef broth
- 2 tablespoons dried rosemary
- 3 cloves garlic, minced
- 1 teaspoon salt
- ½ teaspoon black pepper
- ¼ teaspoon dried thyme
- ½ onion, quartered
- 2 bay leaves

1. Set your pot to Sauté mode and wait until it's hot. Once heated, pour in the avocado oil. Sear the roast on both sides until browned, which should take about 5 minutes. Press Cancel to stop the sautéing. 2. Pour the broth into the pot around the roast. 3. Sprinkle the top of the roast with rosemary, minced garlic, salt, black pepper, and thyme. Add the chopped onion and bay leaves to the pot as well. 4. Secure the lid tightly and ensure the vent is sealed. Cook on High Pressure for 50 minutes. After cooking, allow the steam to release naturally for 15 minutes before manually releasing any remaining pressure. 5. Carefully transfer the roast to a plate and use two forks to shred the meat. Strain the cooking liquid through a fine-mesh sieve to create a smooth jus. Serve the shredded roast with the jus on the side for dipping.

Balsamic-Glazed Roast Beef

Prep time: 5 minutes | Cook time: 20 minutes | Serves 4

- 1 pound (454 g) chuck roast
- 2 cloves garlic, minced
- 1 cup grass-fed bone broth
- ½ teaspoon ground rosemary
- ½ teaspoon freshly ground black pepper
- ½ teaspoon kosher salt
- ½ teaspoon ground thyme
- ½ teaspoon crushed red pepper
- ¼ cup balsamic vinegar
- 4 tablespoons grass-fed butter, softened
- 1 cup chopped broccoli

1. Pour ½ cup filtered water into the Instant Pot, then add the chuck roast. Close the lid, set the pressure release to Sealing, and select Manual. Set the Instant Pot to 20 minutes on High Pressure, and let cook. 2. In a large bowl, combine the garlic, bone broth, rosemary, black pepper, salt, thyme, red pepper, vinegar, and 2 tablespoons of butter. Mix thoroughly. 3. Once cooked, let the pressure naturally disperse from the Instant Pot for about 10 minutes, then carefully switch the pressure release to Venting. 4. Open the Instant Pot, and remove the dish. Set the Instant Pot to Sauté mode, add in the broccoli, and mix in 2 additional tablespoons of grass-fed butter. Cook the broccoli, stirring continuously, until cooked. 5. Remove the broccoli, and serve alongside the roast. Spoon your prepared sauce over both, to taste.

Beef Shawarma Salad Bowls with Veggies

Prep time: 10 minutes | Cook time: 19 minutes | Serves 4

- 2 teaspoons olive oil
- 1½ pounds (680 g) beef flank steak, thinly sliced
- Sea salt and freshly ground black pepper, to taste
- 1 teaspoon cayenne pepper
- ½ teaspoon ground bay leaf
- ½ teaspoon ground allspice
- ½ teaspoon cumin,
- divided
- ½ cup Greek yogurt
- 2 tablespoons sesame oil
- 1 tablespoon fresh lime juice
- 2 English cucumbers, chopped
- 1 cup cherry tomatoes, halved
- 1 red onion, thinly sliced
- ½ head romaine lettuce, chopped

1. Press the Sauté button to heat up the Instant Pot. Then, heat the olive oil and cook the beef for about 4 minutes. 2. Add all seasonings, 1½ cups of water, and secure the lid. 3. Choose Manual mode. Set the cook time for 15 minutes on High Pressure. 4. Once cooking is complete, use a natural pressure release. Carefully remove the lid. 5. Allow the beef to cool completely. 6. To make the dressing, whisk Greek yogurt, sesame oil, and lime juice in a mixing bowl. 7. Then, divide cucumbers, tomatoes, red onion, and romaine lettuce among four serving bowls. Dress the salad and top with the reserved beef flank steak. Serve warm.

Savory Pork Cubes with Fennel

Prep time: 8 minutes | Cook time: 30 minutes | Serves 2

- 1 teaspoon lemon juice
- 10 ounces (283 g) pork loin, chopped
- ½ cup water
- 1 ounce (28 g) fennel, chopped
- 1 teaspoon salt
- ½ teaspoon peppercorns

1. Sprinkle the chopped pork loin with the lemon juice. 2. Then strew the meat with the salt. 3. Place the meat in the meat mold. 4. Insert the meat mold in the instant pot. 5. Add water, fennel, and peppercorns. 6. Close the lid and lock it. 7. Set the Meat/Stew mode and put a timer on 30 minutes. 8. Serve the pork cubes with hot gravy.

Herb-Crusted Rosemary Lamb Chops

Prep time: 25 minutes | Cook time: 2 minutes | Serves 4

- 1½ pounds lamb chops (4 small chops)
- 1 teaspoon kosher salt
- Leaves from 1 (6-inch) rosemary sprig
- 2 tablespoons avocado oil
- 1 shallot, peeled and cut in quarters
- 1 tablespoon tomato paste
- 1 cup beef broth

1. Place the lamb chops on a cutting board. Press the salt and rosemary leaves into both sides of the chops. Let rest at room temperature for 15 to 30 minutes. 2. Set the electric pressure cooker to Sauté/More setting. When hot, add the avocado oil. 3. Brown the lamb chops, about 2 minutes per side. (If they don't all fit in a single layer, brown them in batches.) 4. Transfer the chops to a plate. In the pot, combine the shallot, tomato paste, and broth. Cook for about a minute, scraping up the brown bits from the bottom. Hit Cancel. 5. Add the chops and any accumulated juices back to the pot. 6. Close and lock the lid of the pressure cooker. Set the valve to sealing. 7. Cook on high pressure for 2 minutes. 8. When the cooking is complete, hit Cancel and quick release the pressure. 9. Once the pin drops, unlock and remove the lid. 10. Place the lamb chops on plates and serve immediately.

Creamed Beef Brisket

Prep time: 6 minutes | Cook time: 20 minutes | Serves 3

- ½ teaspoon salt
- 14 ounces (397 g) beef brisket, cut into the strips
- ½ cup water
- ½ cup heavy cream
- ½ teaspoon ground black pepper
- 1 tablespoon avocado oil

1. Begin by preheating the Instant Pot on Sauté mode.2. When the display shows "Hot," pour in the avocado oil and let it heat up.3. Add the meat to the pot.4. Season the meat with ground black pepper and salt.5. Sauté the meat for 5 minutes, stirring once during the cooking time.6. Pour in the water and heavy cream, mixing to combine.7. Secure the lid on the Instant Pot and set it to Manual mode.8. Adjust the timer to 15 minutes at High Pressure.9. Once the cooking time is complete, perform a quick pressure release to open the lid.

Beef Tenderloin with Red Wine Sauce

Prep time: 30 minutes | Cook time: 10 minutes | Serves 5

- 2 pounds (907 g) beef tenderloin
- Salt and black pepper, to taste
- 2 tablespoons avocado oil
- ½ cup beef broth
- ½ cup dry red wine
- 2 cloves garlic, minced
- 1 teaspoon Worcestershire sauce
- 1½ teaspoons dried rosemary
- ¼ teaspoon xanthan gum
- Chopped fresh rosemary, for garnish (optional)

1. About thirty minutes before you start cooking, take the tenderloin out of the refrigerator and allow it to reach room temperature. Generously coat the surface of the tenderloin with salt and pepper. 2. Set your pot to Sauté mode and pour in the avocado oil. Once the oil is shimmering, add the tenderloin and sear it on all sides for approximately 5 minutes. Press the Cancel button when finished. 3. Pour in the broth, red wine, minced garlic, Worcestershire sauce, and fresh rosemary around the beef in the pot. 4. Secure the lid and ensure the vent is sealed. Cook at High Pressure for 8 minutes, then perform a quick release of the steam. 5. Transfer the tenderloin to a serving platter, cover it loosely with aluminum foil, and allow it to rest for 10 minutes. Press Cancel on the pot. 6. Switch back to Sauté mode. Once the broth reaches a gentle boil, sprinkle in the xanthan gum and whisk continuously until a thin sauce forms, which should take about 2 to 3 minutes. 7. Cut the tenderloin into thin slices against the grain. Drizzle the red wine glaze over each slice and, if you like, garnish with additional rosemary for a touch of elegance.

Pork Blade Steaks with Sauerkraut

Prep time: 15 minutes | Cook time: 37 minutes | Serves 6

- 2 pounds (907 g) blade pork steaks
- Sea salt and ground black pepper, to taste
- ½ teaspoon cayenne pepper
- ½ teaspoon dried parsley flakes
- 1 tablespoon butter
- 1½ cups water
- 2 cloves garlic, thinly sliced
- 2 pork sausages, casing removed and sliced
- 4 cups sauerkraut

1. Season the blade pork steaks with salt, black pepper, cayenne pepper, and dried parsley. 2. Press the Sauté button to heat up the Instant Pot. Melt the butter and sear blade pork steaks for 5 minutes or until browned on all sides. 3. Clean the Instant Pot. Add water and trivet to the bottom of the Instant Pot. 4. Place the blade pork steaks on the trivet. Make small slits over entire pork with a knife. Insert garlic pieces into each slit. 5. Secure the lid. Choose the Meat/Stew mode and set cooking time for 30 minutes on High pressure. 6. Once cooking is complete, use a natural pressure release for 15 minutes, then release any remaining pressure. Carefully remove the lid. 7. Add the sausage and sauerkraut. Press the Sauté button and cook for 2 minutes more or until heated through. 8. Serve immediately

Greek Lamb Leg

Prep time: 10 minutes | Cook time: 50 minutes | Serves 4

- 1 pound (454 g) lamb leg
- ½ teaspoon dried thyme
- 1 teaspoon paprika powder
- ¼ teaspoon cumin seeds
- 1 tablespoon softened butter
- 2 garlic cloves
- ¼ cup water

1. On a clean work surface, rub the lamb leg with dried thyme, paprika powder, and cumin seeds until well coated.2. Brush the leg with softened butter, then transfer it to the Instant Pot. Add the garlic cloves and pour in the water.3. Secure the lid on the Instant Pot. Select Manual mode and set the cooking time for 50 minutes at High Pressure.4. Once the timer beeps, perform a quick pressure release and carefully open the lid.5. Serve the lamb warm for a flavorful dish.

Creamy Pork Liver Delight

Prep time: 5 minutes | Cook time: 7 minutes | Serves 3

- 14 ounces (397 g) pork liver, chopped
- 1 teaspoon salt
- 1 teaspoon butter
- ½ cup heavy cream
- 3 tablespoons scallions, chopped

1. Rub the liver with the salt on a clean work surface. 2. Put the butter in the Instant Pot and melt on the Sauté mode. 3. Add the heavy cream, scallions, and liver. 4. Stir and close the lid. Select Manual mode and set cooking time for 12 minutes on High Pressure. 5. When timer beeps, perform a natural pressure release for 5 minutes, then release any remaining pressure. Open the lid. 6. Serve immediately.

Savory Salisbury Steaks with Sautéed Cauliflower

Prep time: 5 minutes | Cook time: 30 minutes | Serves 4

- Salisbury Steaks
- 1 pound 95 percent lean ground beef
- ⅓ cup almond flour
- 1 large egg
- ½ teaspoon fine sea salt
- ¼ teaspoon freshly ground black pepper
- 2 tablespoons cold-pressed avocado oil
- 1 small yellow onion, sliced
- 1 garlic clove, chopped
- 8 ounces cremini or button mushrooms, sliced
- ½ teaspoon fine sea salt
- 2 tablespoons tomato paste
- 1½ teaspoons yellow mustard
- 1 cup low-sodium roasted beef bone broth
- Seared Cauliflower
- 1 tablespoon olive oil
- 1 head cauliflower, cut into bite-size florets
- 2 tablespoons chopped fresh flat-leaf parsley
- ¼ teaspoon fine sea salt
- 2 teaspoons cornstarch
- 2 teaspoons water

1. To make the steaks: In a bowl, combine the beef, almond flour, egg, salt, and pepper and mix with your hands until all of the ingredients are evenly distributed. Divide the mixture into four equal portions, then shape each portion into an oval patty about ½ inch thick. 2. Select the Sauté setting on the Instant Pot and heat the oil for 2 minutes. Swirl the oil to coat the bottom of the pot, then add the patties and sear for 3 minutes, until browned on one side. Using a thin, flexible spatula, flip the patties and sear the second side for 2 to 3 minutes, until browned. Transfer the patties to a plate.

3. Add the onion, garlic, mushrooms, and salt to the pot and sauté for 4 minutes, until the onion is translucent and the mushrooms have begun to give up their liquid. Add the tomato paste, mustard, and broth and stir with a wooden spoon, using it to nudge any browned bits from the bottom of the pot. Return the patties to the pot in a single layer and spoon a bit of the sauce over each one. 4. Secure the lid and set the Pressure Release to Sealing. Press the Cancel button to reset the cooking program, then select the Pressure Cook or Manual setting and set the cooking time for 10 minutes at high pressure. (The pot will take about 5 minutes to come up to pressure before the cooking program begins.) 5. When the cooking program ends, let the pressure release naturally for at least 10 minutes, then move the Pressure Release to Venting to release any remaining steam. 6. To make the cauliflower: While the pressure is releasing, in a large skillet over medium heat, warm the oil. Add the cauliflower and stir or toss to coat with the oil, then cook, stirring every minute or two, until lightly browned, about 8 minutes. Turn off the heat, sprinkle in the parsley and salt, and stir to combine. Leave in the skillet, uncovered, to keep warm. 7. Open the pot and, using a slotted spatula, transfer the patties to a serving plate. In a small bowl, stir together the cornstarch and water. Press the Cancel button to reset the cooking program, then select the Sauté setting. When the sauce comes to a simmer, stir in the cornstarch mixture and let the sauce boil for about 1 minute, until thickened. Press the Cancel button to turn off the Instant Pot. 8. Spoon the sauce over the patties. Serve right away, with the cauliflower.

Savory Braised Pork Belly

Prep time: 15 minutes | Cook time: 37 minutes | Serves 4

- 1 pound (454 g) pork belly
- 1 tablespoon olive oil
- Salt and ground black
- pepper to taste
- 1 clove garlic, minced
- 1 cup dry white wine
- Rosemary sprig

1. Select the Sauté mode on the Instant Pot and heat the oil. 2. Add the pork belly and sauté for 2 minutes per side, until starting to brown. 3. Season the meat with salt and pepper, add the garlic. 4. Pour in the wine and add the rosemary sprig. Bring to a boil. 5. Select the Manual mode and set the cooking time for 35 minutes at High pressure. 6. Once cooking is complete, use a natural pressure release for 10 minutes, then release any remaining pressure. Open the lid. 7. Slice the meat and serve.

Pork Meatballs with Thyme

Prep time: 15 minutes | Cook time: 16 minutes | Serves 8

- 2 cups ground pork
- 1 teaspoon dried thyme
- ½ teaspoon chili flakes
- ½ teaspoon garlic powder
- 1 tablespoon coconut oil
- ¼ teaspoon ground ginger
- 3 tablespoons almond flour
- ¼ cup water

1. In a mixing bowl, combine the ground pork with dried thyme, chili flakes, garlic powder, ground ginger, and almond flour until well mixed. 2. Shape the mixture into meatballs of your desired size. 3. Set the Instant Pot to Sauté mode and melt the coconut oil. 4. Once the oil is hot, place the meatballs in the Instant Pot in a single layer and cook for 3 minutes on each side until browned. 5. After browning, pour in the water and cook the meatballs under pressure for 10 minutes.

Herbed Pork Loin Roast with Asparagus

Prep time: 25 minutes | Cook time: 17 minutes | Serves 6

- 1 teaspoon dried thyme
- ½ teaspoon garlic powder
- ½ teaspoon onion powder
- ½ teaspoon dried oregano
- 1½ teaspoons smoked paprika
- ½ teaspoon ground black pepper
- 1 teaspoon sea salt
- 2 tablespoons olive oil, divided
- 2 pounds (907 g)
- boneless pork loin roast
- ½ medium white onion, chopped
- 2 garlic cloves, minced
- ⅔ cup chicken broth
- 2 tablespoons Worcestershire sauce
- 1 cup water
- 20 fresh asparagus spears, cut in half and woody ends removed

1. In a small bowl, combine the thyme, garlic powder, onion powder, oregano, smoked paprika, black pepper, and sea salt. Mix until well combined and then add 1½ tablespoons olive oil. Stir until blended. 2. Brush all sides of the pork roast with the oil and spice mixture. Place the roast in a covered dish and transfer to the refrigerator to marinate for 30 minutes. 3. Select Sauté mode and brush the Instant Pot with remaining olive oil. Once the oil is hot, add the pork roast and sear for 5 minutes per side or until browned. Remove the roast from the pot and set aside. 4. Add the onions and garlic to the pot and Sauté for 2 minutes, or until the onions soften and garlic becomes fragrant. 5. Add the chicken broth and Worcestershire sauce. 6. Lock the lid. Select Manual mode and set cooking time for 15 minutes on High pressure. 7. When cooking is complete, allow the pressure release naturally for 10 minutes and then release the remaining pressure. 8. Open the lid. Transfer the roast to a cutting board, cover with aluminum foil, and set aside to rest. Transfer the broth to a measuring cup. Set aside. 9. Place the trivet in the Instant Pot and add the water to the bottom of the pot. 10. Place the asparagus in an ovenproof bowl that will fit in the Instant Pot and place the bowl on top of the trivet. 11. Lock the lid. Select Steam mode and set cooking time for 2 minutes. Once the cook time is complete, quick release the pressure. 12. Open the lid and transfer the asparagus to a large serving platter. Thinly slice the roast and transfer to the serving platter with the asparagus. Drizzle the reserved broth over top. Serve warm.

Sinaloa-Style Meatballs (Albóndigas Sinaloenses)

Prep time: 15 minutes | Cook time: 10 minutes | Serves 6

- 1 pound (454 g) ground pork
- ½ pound (227 g) Italian sausage, crumbled
- 2 tablespoons yellow onion, finely chopped
- ½ teaspoon dried oregano
- 1 sprig fresh mint, finely minced
- ½ teaspoon ground cumin
- 2 garlic cloves, finely minced
- ¼ teaspoon fresh ginger, grated
- Seasoned salt and ground black pepper, to taste
- 1 tablespoon olive oil
- ½ cup yellow onions, finely chopped
- 2 chipotle chilies in adobo
- 2 tomatoes, puréed
- 2 tablespoons tomato passata
- 1 cup chicken broth

1. In a mixing bowl, combine the pork, sausage, 2 tablespoons of yellow onion, oregano, mint, cumin, garlic, ginger, salt, and black pepper. 2. Roll the mixture into meatballs and reserve. 3. Press the Sauté button to heat up the Instant Pot. Heat the olive oil and cook the meatballs for 4 minutes, stirring continuously. 4. Stir in ½ cup of yellow onions, chilies in adobo, tomatoes passata, and broth. Add reserved meatballs. 5. Secure the lid. Choose the Manual mode and set cooking time for 6 minutes at High pressure. 6. Once cooking is complete, use a quick pressure release. Carefully remove the lid. 7. Serve immediately.

Chapter 4

Fish and Seafood

Tuna Salad with Tomatoes and Peppers

Prep time: 10 minutes | Cook time: 4 minutes | Serves 4

- 1½ cups water
- 1 pound (454 g) tuna steaks
- 1 green bell pepper, sliced
- 1 red bell pepper, sliced
- 2 Roma tomatoes, sliced
- 1 head lettuce
- 1 red onion, chopped
- 2 tablespoons Kalamata olives, pitted and halved
- 2 tablespoons extra-virgin olive oil
- 2 tablespoons balsamic vinegar
- ½ teaspoon chili flakes
- Sea salt, to taste

1. Begin by pouring water into the Instant Pot and placing a steamer basket inside. 2. Arrange the tuna steaks in the basket, then layer the bell pepper slices and tomato slices on top of the fish. 3. Secure the lid on the Instant Pot. Choose Manual mode and set the cooking time for 4 minutes at High Pressure. 4. When the timer goes off, perform a quick release of the pressure and carefully lift the lid off. 5. Use a fork to flake the tuna into bite-sized pieces. 6. On four serving plates, divide the lettuce leaves to create a base for your salad. Top with sliced onions and olives, then drizzle with olive oil and balsamic vinegar. 7. Season the salad with chili flakes and salt, then add the flaked fish, tomatoes, and bell peppers on top. 8. Serve the salad right away for a fresh, delightful meal.

Lemon-Dill Foil-Packet Salmon

Prep time: 2 minutes | Cook time: 7 minutes | Serves 2

- 2 (3-ounce / 85-g) salmon fillets
- ¼ teaspoon garlic powder
- 1 teaspoon salt
- ¼ teaspoon pepper
- ¼ teaspoon dried dill
- ½ lemon
- 1 cup water

1. Place each filet of salmon on a square of foil, skin-side down. 2. Season with garlic powder, salt, and pepper and squeeze the lemon juice over the fish. 3. Cut the lemon into four slices and place two on each filet. Close the foil packets by folding over edges. 4. Add the water to the Instant Pot and insert a trivet. Place the foil packets on the trivet. 5. Secure the lid. Select the Steam mode and set the cooking time for 7 minutes at Low Pressure. 6. Once cooking is complete, do a quick pressure release. Carefully open the lid. 7. Check the internal temperature with a meat thermometer to ensure the thickest part of the filets reached at least 145ºF (63ºC). Salmon should easily flake when fully cooked. Serve immediately.

Herb-Infused Mahi-Mahi with Sautéed Peppers

Prep time: 10 minutes | Cook time: 3 minutes | Serves 3

- 2 sprigs fresh rosemary
- 2 sprigs dill, tarragon
- 1 sprig fresh thyme
- 1 cup water
- 1 lemon, sliced
- 3 mahi-mahi fillets
- 2 tablespoons coconut oil, melted
- Sea salt and ground black pepper, to taste
- 1 serrano pepper, seeded and sliced
- 1 green bell pepper, sliced
- 1 red bell pepper, sliced

1. Add the herbs, water, and lemon slices to the Instant Pot and insert a steamer basket. 2. Arrange the mahi-mahi fillets in the steamer basket. 3. Drizzle the melted coconut oil over the top and season with the salt and black pepper. 4. Lock the lid. Select the Manual mode and set the cooking time for 3 minutes at Low Pressure. 5. When the timer beeps, perform a natural pressure release for 10 minutes, then release any remaining pressure. Carefully remove the lid. 6. Place the peppers on top. Select the Sauté mode and let it simmer for another 1 minute. 7. Serve immediately.

Salmon Steaks with Garlic Herb Yogurt

Prep time: 2 minutes | Cook time: 4 minutes | Serves 4

- 1 cup water
- 2 tablespoons olive oil
- 4 salmon steaks
- Coarse sea salt and ground black pepper, to taste
- Garlicky Yogurt:
- 1 (8-ounce / 227-g)
- container full-fat Greek yogurt
- 2 cloves garlic, minced
- 2 tablespoons mayonnaise
- ⅓ teaspoon Dijon mustard

1. Pour the water into the Instant Pot and insert a trivet. 2. Rub the olive oil into the fish and sprinkle with the salt and black pepper on all sides. Put the fish on the trivet. 3. Lock the lid. Select the Manual mode and set the cooking time for 4 minutes at High Pressure. 4. When the timer beeps, perform a quick pressure release. Carefully remove the lid. 5. Meanwhile, stir together all the ingredients for the garlicky yogurt in a bowl. 6. Serve the salmon steaks alongside the garlicky yogurt.

Cayenne Cod

Prep time: 10 minutes | Cook time: 10 minutes | Serves 2

- 2 cod fillets
- ¼ teaspoon chili powder
- ½ teaspoon cayenne pepper
- ½ teaspoon dried oregano
- 1 tablespoon lime juice
- 2 tablespoons avocado oil

1. Begin by seasoning the cod fillets with chili powder, cayenne pepper, and dried oregano, then drizzle with fresh lime juice for added flavor. 2. Pour avocado oil into the Instant Pot and heat it on Sauté mode for 2 minutes until hot. 3. Carefully place the seasoned cod fillets into the hot oil and cook them for 5 minutes without moving them. 4. Flip the fillets to the other side and continue cooking for an additional 5 minutes until the fish is cooked through and flaky.

Cod with Warm Beet and Arugula Salad

Prep time: 15 minutes | Cook time: 8 minutes | Serves 4

- ¼ cup extra-virgin olive oil, divided, plus extra for drizzling
- 1 shallot, sliced thin
- 2 garlic cloves, minced
- 1½ pounds (680 g) small beets, scrubbed, trimmed, and cut into ½-inch wedges
- ½ cup chicken or
- vegetable broth
- 1 tablespoon dukkah, plus extra for sprinkling
- ¼ teaspoon table salt
- 4 (6-ounce / 170-g) skinless cod fillets, 1½ inches thick
- 1 tablespoon lemon juice
- 2 ounces (57 g) baby arugula

1. Set the Instant Pot to the highest sauté setting and heat 1 tablespoon of oil until it shimmers. Add the chopped shallot and cook for about 2 minutes until softened. Stir in the minced garlic and cook for an additional 30 seconds until fragrant. Then, add the beets and broth to the pot. Secure the lid and close the pressure release valve. Select the high-pressure cooking function and set it to cook for 3 minutes. Once done, turn off the Instant Pot and perform a quick release of the pressure. Carefully remove the lid, ensuring the steam escapes away from you. 2. Create a sling by folding a sheet of aluminum foil into a 16 by 6-inch shape. In a bowl, mix together 2 tablespoons of oil, dukkah, and salt. Brush this oil mixture generously over the cod fillets, then place the cod skin-side down in the center of the sling. Using the sling, lower the cod into the Instant Pot, allowing the narrow edges to rest against the sides of the insert.

Secure the lid again and close the pressure release valve. Select the high-pressure cooking function and set it to cook for 2 minutes. 3. Once the cooking time is complete, turn off the Instant Pot and quick-release the pressure. Carefully remove the lid, making sure to allow steam to escape away from you. Using the sling, transfer the cod to a large plate and cover it with foil to keep it warm while you prepare the beet salad. 4. In a large bowl, combine lemon juice and the remaining 1 tablespoon of oil. Using a slotted spoon, transfer the cooked beets to the bowl with the oil mixture. Add the fresh arugula and gently toss everything together. Season the salad with salt and pepper to taste. 5. Serve the cod alongside the beet salad, sprinkling extra dukkah on each portion and drizzling with additional oil for enhanced flavor.

Spicy Louisiana Shrimp Gumbo

Prep time: 10 minutes | Cook time: 4 minutes | Serves 6

- 1 pound (454 g) shrimp
- ¼ cup chopped celery stalk
- 1 chili pepper, chopped
- ¼ cup chopped okra
- 1 tablespoon coconut oil
- 2 cups chicken broth
- 1 teaspoon sugar-free tomato paste

1. Put all ingredients in the instant pot and stir until you get a light red color. 2. Then close and seal the lid. 3. Cook the meal on Manual mode (High Pressure) for 4 minutes. 4. When the time is finished, allow the natural pressure release for 10 minutes.

Lemon Shrimp Skewers

Prep time: 10 minutes | Cook time: 2 minutes | Serves 4

- 1 tablespoon lemon juice
- 1 teaspoon coconut aminos
- 12 ounces (340 g)
- shrimp, peeled
- 1 teaspoon olive oil
- 1 cup water

1. Begin by placing the shrimp into a mixing bowl. 2. Add lemon juice, coconut aminos, and olive oil to the bowl and toss to combine. 3. Next, thread the shrimp onto skewers, ensuring they are securely placed. 4. Pour water into the Instant Pot. 5. Insert the trivet into the pot to hold the skewers above the water. 6. Carefully lay the shrimp skewers on top of the trivet. 7. Close the lid securely and set the Instant Pot to Manual mode, cooking on High Pressure for 2 minutes. 8. Once the cooking time is complete, perform a quick release of the pressure.

Asian-Inspired Cod with Brown Rice and Vegetables

Prep time: 5 minutes | Cook time: 25 minutes | Serves 2

- ¾ cup Minute brand brown rice
- ½ cup water
- Two 5-ounce skinless cod fillets
- 1 tablespoon soy sauce or tamari
- 1 tablespoon fresh lemon juice
- ½ teaspoon peeled and grated fresh ginger
- 1 tablespoon extra-virgin olive oil or 1 tablespoon unsalted butter, cut into 8 pieces
- 2 green onions, white and green parts, thinly sliced
- 12 ounces asparagus, trimmed
- 4 ounces shiitake mushrooms, stems removed and sliced
- ⅛ teaspoon fine sea salt
- ⅛ teaspoon freshly ground black pepper
- Lemon wedges for serving

1. Pour 1 cup water into the Instant Pot. Have ready two-tier stackable stainless-steel containers. 2. In one of the containers, combine the rice and ½ cup water, then gently shake the container to spread the rice into an even layer, making sure all of the grains are submerged. Place the fish fillets on top of the rice. In a small bowl, stir together the soy sauce, lemon juice, and ginger. Pour the soy sauce mixture over the fillets. Drizzle 1 teaspoon olive oil on each fillet (or top with two pieces of the butter), and sprinkle the green onions on and around the fish. 3. In the second container, arrange the asparagus in the center in as even a layer as possible. Place the mushrooms on either side of the asparagus. Drizzle with the remaining 2 teaspoons olive oil (or put the remaining six pieces butter on top of the asparagus, spacing them evenly). Sprinkle the salt and pepper evenly over the vegetables. 4. Place the container with the rice and fish on the bottom and the vegetable container on top. Cover the top container with its lid and then latch the containers together. Grasping the handle, lower the containers into the Instant Pot. 5. Secure the lid and set the Pressure Release to Sealing. Select the Pressure Cook or Manual setting and set the cooking time for 15 minutes at high pressure. (The pot will take about 10 minutes to come up to pressure before the cooking program begins.) 6. When the cooking program ends, let the pressure release naturally for 5 minutes, then move the Pressure Release to Venting to release any remaining steam. Open the pot and, wearing heat-resistant mitts, lift out the stacked containers. Unlatch, unstack, and open the containers, taking care not to get burned by the steam. 7. Transfer the vegetables, rice, and fish to plates and serve right away, with the lemon wedges on the side.

Coconut-Braised Squid in Spicy Gravy

Prep time: 10 minutes | Cook time: 20 minutes | Serves 3

- 1 pound (454 g) squid, sliced
- 1 teaspoon sugar-free tomato paste
- 1 cup coconut milk
- 1 teaspoon cayenne pepper
- ½ teaspoon salt

1. Put all ingredients from the list above in the instant pot. 2. Close and seal the lid and cook the squid on Manual (High Pressure) for 20 minutes. 3. When the cooking time is finished, do the quick pressure release. 4. Serve the squid with coconut milk gravy.

Curried Cod in Almond Milk

Prep time: 10 minutes | Cook time: 3 minutes | Serves 2

- 8 ounces (227 g) cod fillet, chopped
- 1 teaspoon curry paste
- 1 cup organic almond milk

1. Mix up curry paste and almond milk and pour the liquid in the instant pot. 2. Add chopped cod fillet and close the lid. 3. Cook the fish curry on Manual mode (High Pressure) for 3 minutes. 4. Then make the quick pressure release for 5 minutes.

Baked Flounder with Artichoke

Prep time: 10 minutes | Cook time: 10 minutes | Serves 2

- 8 ounces (227 g) flounder fillet
- 1 lemon slice, chopped
- 1 teaspoon ground black pepper
- ¼ teaspoon salt
- ½ large artichoke, chopped
- 1 tablespoon sesame oil
- 1 cup water, for cooking

1. Start by brushing a round baking pan with sesame oil to prevent sticking. 2. Next, add the chopped artichokes to the baking pan, spreading them out evenly across the bottom. 3. Season the flounder fillet with ground black pepper and salt, then place it on top of the artichokes. 4. Scatter the chopped lemon over the fish for added flavor. 5. Pour water into the Instant Pot and insert the steamer rack inside. 6. Carefully position the baking pan with the fish onto the steamer rack. Secure the lid and seal the vent. 7. Set the Instant Pot to Manual mode and cook on High Pressure for 10 minutes. Once the time is up, perform a quick release of the pressure.

Shrimp Louie Salad with Thousand Island Dressing

Prep time: 5 minutes | Cook time: 20 minutes | Serves 4

- 2 cups water
- 1½ teaspoons fine sea salt
- 1 pound medium shrimp, peeled and deveined
- 4 large eggs
- Thousand island Dressing
- ¼ cup no-sugar-added ketchup
- ¼ cup mayonnaise
- 1 tablespoon fresh lemon juice
- 1 teaspoon Worcestershire sauce
- ⅛ teaspoon cayenne pepper
- Freshly ground black pepper
- 2 green onions, white and green parts, sliced thinly
- 2 hearts romaine lettuce or 1 head iceberg lettuce, shredded
- 1 English cucumber, sliced
- 8 radishes, sliced
- 1 cup cherry tomatoes, sliced
- 1 large avocado, pitted, peeled, and sliced

1. Begin by combining water and salt in the Instant Pot, stirring until the salt is fully dissolved. 2. Secure the lid and set the Pressure Release valve to Sealing. Select the Steam setting and set the cooking time to 0 (zero) minutes at low pressure. (The pot will take approximately 10 minutes to come up to pressure before the cooking program starts.) 3. While waiting, prepare an ice bath in a large bowl. 4. When the cooking time is complete, perform a quick release by switching the Pressure Release valve to Venting. Open the pot and gently stir in the shrimp, using a wooden spoon to ensure they are fully submerged in the water. Cover the pot and let the shrimp sit for 2 minutes on the Keep Warm setting, allowing them to gently poach. After 2 minutes, uncover the pot, and using heat-resistant mitts, carefully lift the inner pot out and drain the shrimp in a colander. Transfer them to the ice bath to cool for 5 minutes, then drain again and place them in the refrigerator. 5. Rinse the inner pot and return it to the Instant Pot housing. Pour in 1 cup of water and position the wire metal steam rack inside. Place the eggs on top of the steam rack. 6. Secure the lid again and set the Pressure Release valve to Sealing. Press Cancel to reset the cooking program, then select the Egg, Pressure Cook, or Manual setting and set the cooking time for 5 minutes at high pressure. (The pot will take about 5 minutes to come up to pressure before starting the cooking program.) 7. While the eggs are cooking, prepare another ice bath. 8. Once the cooking program finishes, let the pressure release naturally for 5 minutes before switching the Pressure Release valve to Venting to release any remaining steam. Using tongs, carefully transfer the eggs to the ice bath and allow them to cool for 5 minutes. 9. To prepare the dressing, combine ketchup, mayonnaise, lemon juice, Worcestershire sauce, cayenne, ¼ teaspoon black pepper, and green onions in a small bowl, stirring well to mix. 10. On individual plates or in large shallow bowls, arrange lettuce, cucumber, radishes, tomatoes, and avocado. Place a mound of the cooked shrimp in the center of each salad. Peel the cooled eggs, quarter them lengthwise, and arrange the quarters around the shrimp. 11. Drizzle the dressing over the salads and sprinkle with additional black pepper. Serve immediately for a fresh and delicious meal.

Rosemary Catfish

Prep time: 10 minutes | Cook time: 20 minutes | Serves 4

- 16 ounces (454 g) catfish fillet
- 1 tablespoon dried rosemary
- 1 teaspoon garlic powder
- 1 tablespoon avocado oil
- 1 teaspoon salt
- 1 cup water, for cooking

1. Begin by cutting the catfish fillet into 4 evenly sized steaks. 2. Next, season the catfish steaks with dried rosemary, garlic powder, avocado oil, and salt, ensuring each piece is well coated. 3. Arrange the seasoned fish steaks in a single layer in a baking mold. 4. Pour water into the Instant Pot and place the steamer rack inside. 5. Set the baking mold with the fish on top of the steamer rack. Secure the lid and seal the vent. 6. Select Manual mode and set the cooking time to 20 minutes on High Pressure. Once the cooking time is complete, perform a quick release of the pressure.

Lemon Butter Tuna Fillets

Prep time: 5 minutes | Cook time: 3 minutes | Serves 4

- 1 cup water
- ⅓ cup lemon juice
- 2 sprigs fresh thyme
- 2 sprigs fresh parsley
- 2 sprigs fresh rosemary
- 1 pound (454 g) tuna fillets
- 4 cloves garlic, pressed
- Sea salt, to taste
- ¼ teaspoon black pepper, or more to taste
- 2 tablespoons butter, melted
- 1 lemon, sliced

1. Pour the water into your Instant Pot. Add the lemon juice, thyme, parsley, and rosemary and insert a steamer basket. 2. Put the tuna fillets in the basket. Top with the garlic and season with the salt and black pepper. 3. Drizzle the melted butter over the fish fillets and place the lemon slices on top. 4. Lock the lid. Select the Manual mode and set the cooking time for 3 minutes at Low Pressure. 5. When the timer beeps, perform a quick pressure release. Carefully remove the lid. Serve immediately.

Parmesan Salmon Loaf

Prep time: 15 minutes | Cook time: 25 minutes | Serves 6

- 12 ounces (340 g) salmon, boiled and shredded
- 3 eggs, beaten
- ½ cup almond flour
- 1 teaspoon garlic powder
- ¼ cup grated Parmesan
- 1 teaspoon butter, softened
- 1 cup water, for cooking

1. Start by pouring water into the Instant Pot. 2. In a mixing bowl, combine the remaining ingredients and stir until the mixture is smooth and well-blended. 3. Next, transfer the salmon mixture into a loaf pan, flattening it out evenly, and then place the pan inside the Instant Pot. Secure the lid and seal the vent. 4. Set the Instant Pot to Manual mode and cook on High Pressure for 25 minutes. 5. Once the cooking time is complete, perform a quick release of the pressure, and allow the loaf to cool completely before serving.

Fish Tagine

Prep time: 25 minutes | Cook time: 12 minutes | Serves 4

- 2 tablespoons extra-virgin olive oil, plus extra for drizzling
- 1 large onion, halved and sliced ¼ inch thick
- 1 pound (454 g) carrots, peeled, halved lengthwise, and sliced ¼ inch thick
- 2 (2-inch) strips orange zest, plus 1 teaspoon grated zest
- ¾ teaspoon table salt, divided
- 2 tablespoons tomato paste
- 4 garlic cloves, minced, divided
- 1¼ teaspoons paprika
- 1 teaspoon ground cumin
- ¼ teaspoon red pepper flakes
- ¼ teaspoon saffron threads, crumbled
- 1 (8-ounce / 227-g) bottle clam juice
- 1½ pounds (680 g) skinless halibut fillets, 1½ inches thick, cut into 2-inch pieces
- ¼ cup pitted oil-cured black olives, quartered
- 2 tablespoons chopped fresh parsley
- 1 teaspoon sherry vinegar

1. Set the Instant Pot to the highest sauté function and heat the oil until it shimmers. Add the chopped onion, diced carrots, strips of orange zest, and ¼ teaspoon of salt. Cook the mixture for about 10 to 12 minutes, or until the vegetables are softened and lightly browned. Stir in the tomato paste, three-quarters of the minced garlic, paprika, cumin, red pepper flakes, and saffron, cooking for about 30 seconds until fragrant. Pour in the clam juice, scraping up any browned bits from the bottom of the pot. 2. Season the halibut fillets with the remaining ½ teaspoon of salt. Nestle the halibut pieces into the onion mixture, spooning some of the cooking liquid over the top. Secure the lid and close the pressure release valve. Select the high-pressure cooking function and set the timer for 0 minutes. Once the Instant Pot reaches pressure, immediately turn it off and perform a quick release of the pressure. 3. Remove and discard the orange zest. Gently stir in the olives, chopped parsley, vinegar, grated orange zest, and the remaining minced garlic. Adjust the seasoning with salt and pepper to taste. Drizzle additional oil over each serving just before serving for a finishing touch.

Cod Fillets with Olive Topping

Prep time: 15 minutes | Cook time: 10 minutes | Serves 2

- 8 ounces (227 g) cod fillet
- ¼ cup sliced olives
- 1 teaspoon olive oil
- ¼ teaspoon salt
- 1 cup water, for cooking

1. Pour water and insert the steamer rack in the instant pot. 2. Then cut the cod fillet into 2 servings and sprinkle with salt and olive oil. 3. Then place the fish on the foil and top with the sliced olives. Wrap the fish and transfer it in the steamer rack. 4. Close and seal the lid. Cook the fish on Manual mode (High Pressure) for 10 minutes. 5. Allow the natural pressure release for 5 minutes.

Foil-Pack Haddock with Spinach

Prep time: 15 minutes | Cook time: 15 minutes | Serves 4

- 12 ounces (340 g) haddock fillet
- 1 cup spinach
- 1 tablespoon avocado oil
- 1 teaspoon minced garlic
- ½ teaspoon ground coriander
- 1 cup water, for cooking

1. Start by blending the spinach until it reaches a smooth consistency, then mix in avocado oil, ground coriander, and minced garlic until well combined. 2. Cut the haddock into 4 fillets and place them on a sheet of aluminum foil. 3. Spread the spinach mixture evenly over the top of each fish fillet, then transfer the foil with the fillets onto the rack. 4. Pour water into the Instant Pot and carefully insert the rack with the fish on it. 5. Secure the lid and seal the pressure valve, then cook the haddock on Manual mode at High Pressure for 15 minutes. 6. Once cooking is complete, perform a quick release of the pressure.

Lemon-Butter Mahi Mahi Fillets

Prep time: 10 minutes | Cook time: 9 minutes | Serves 4

- 1 pound (454 g) mahi-mahi fillet
- 1 teaspoon grated lemon zest
- 1 tablespoon lemon juice
- 1 tablespoon butter, softened
- ½ teaspoon salt
- 1 cup water, for cooking

1. Cut the fish on 4 servings and sprinkle with lemon zest, lemon juice, salt, and rub with softened butter. 2. Then put the fish in the baking pan in one layer. 3. Pour water and insert the steamer rack in the instant pot. 4. Put the mold with fish on the rack. Close and seal the lid. 5. Cook the Mahi Mahi on Manual mode (High Pressure) for 9 minutes. Make a quick pressure release.

Garlic Salmon with Broccoli Rabe and White Beans

Prep time: 20 minutes | Cook time: 10 minutes | Serves 4

- 2 tablespoons extra-virgin olive oil, plus extra for drizzling
- 4 garlic cloves, sliced thin
- ½ cup chicken or vegetable broth
- ¼ teaspoon red pepper flakes
- 1 lemon, sliced ¼ inch thick, plus lemon wedges
- for serving
- 4 (6-ounce / 170-g) skinless salmon fillets, 1½ inches thick
- ½ teaspoon table salt
- ¼ teaspoon pepper
- 1 pound (454 g) broccoli rabe, trimmed and cut into 1-inch pieces
- 1 (15-ounce / 425-g) can cannellini beans, rinsed

1. Using highest sauté function, cook oil and garlic in Instant Pot until garlic is fragrant and light golden brown, about 3 minutes. Using slotted spoon, transfer garlic to paper towel–lined plate and season with salt to taste; set aside for serving. Turn off Instant Pot, then stir in broth and pepper flakes. 2. Fold sheet of aluminum foil into 16 by 6-inch sling. Arrange lemon slices widthwise in 2 rows across center of sling. Sprinkle flesh side of salmon with salt and pepper, then arrange skinned side down on top of lemon slices. Using sling, lower salmon into Instant Pot; allow narrow edges of sling to rest along sides of insert. Lock lid in place and close pressure release valve. Select high pressure cook function and cook for 3 minutes. 3. Turn off Instant Pot and quick-release pressure. Carefully remove lid, allowing steam to escape away from you. Using sling,

transfer salmon to large plate. Tent with foil and let rest while preparing broccoli rabe mixture. 4. Stir broccoli rabe and beans into cooking liquid, partially cover, and cook, using highest sauté function, until broccoli rabe is tender, about 5 minutes. Season with salt and pepper to taste. Gently lift and tilt salmon fillets with spatula to remove lemon slices. Serve salmon with broccoli rabe mixture and lemon wedges, sprinkling individual portions with garlic chips and drizzling with extra oil.

Thyme-Infused Steamed Lobster Tails

Prep time: 10 minutes | Cook time: 4 minutes | Serves 4

- 4 lobster tails
- 1 tablespoon butter, softened
- 1 teaspoon dried thyme
- 1 cup water

1. Pour water and insert the steamer rack in the instant pot. 2. Put the lobster tails on the rack and close the lid. 3. Cook the meal on Manual mode (High Pressure) for 4 minutes. Make a quick pressure release. 4. After this, mix up butter and dried thyme. Peel the lobsters and rub them with thyme butter.

Herb-Infused Ahi Tuna and Cherry Tomato Salad

Prep time: 5 minutes | Cook time: 4 minutes | Serves 4

- 1 cup water
- 2 sprigs thyme
- 2 sprigs rosemary
- 2 sprigs parsley
- 1 lemon, sliced
- 1 pound (454 g) ahi tuna
- ⅓ teaspoon ground black pepper
- 1 head lettuce
- 1 cup cherry tomatoes, halved
- 1 red bell pepper, julienned
- 2 tablespoons extra-virgin olive oil
- 1 teaspoon Dijon mustard
- Sea salt, to taste

1. Pour the water into your Instant Pot. Add the thyme, rosemary, parsley, and lemon and insert a trivet. 2. Lay the fish on the trivet and season with the ground black pepper. 3. Lock the lid. Select the Manual mode and set the cooking time for 4 minutes at High Pressure. 4. When the timer beeps, perform a quick pressure release. Carefully remove the lid. 5. In a salad bowl, place the remaining ingredients and toss well. Add the flaked tuna and toss again. 6. Serve chilled.

Crispy Fish Nuggets

Prep time: 15 minutes | Cook time: 9 minutes | Serves 4

- 1 pound (454 g) tilapia fillet
- ½ cup almond flour
- 3 eggs, beaten
- ¼ cup avocado oil
- 1 teaspoon salt

1. Begin by cutting the fish into small pieces, resembling nuggets, and sprinkle them with salt to season. 2. Next, dip each fish nugget into beaten eggs, ensuring they are well coated, and then roll them in almond flour to create a crispy exterior. 3. Heat avocado oil in the Instant Pot on Sauté mode for 3 minutes until it's hot. 4. Carefully place the coated fish nuggets into the hot oil and cook them on Sauté mode for 3 minutes on each side, or until they turn golden brown and crispy.

Lemon Pepper Tilapia with Steamed Broccoli and Carrots

Prep time: 0 minutes | Cook time: 15 minutes | Serves 4

- 1 pound tilapia fillets
- 1 teaspoon lemon pepper seasoning
- ¼ teaspoon fine sea salt
- 2 tablespoons extra-virgin olive oil
- 2 garlic cloves, minced
- 1 small yellow onion, sliced
- ½ cup low-sodium vegetable broth
- 2 tablespoons fresh lemon juice
- 1 pound broccoli crowns, cut into bite-size florets
- 8 ounces carrots, cut into ¼-inch thick rounds

1. Sprinkle the tilapia fillets all over with the lemon pepper seasoning and salt. 2. Select the Sauté setting on the Instant Pot and heat the oil and garlic for 2 minutes, until the garlic is bubbling but not browned. Add the onion and sauté for about 3 minutes more, until it begins to soften. 3. Pour in the broth and lemon juice, then use a wooden spoon to nudge any browned bits from the bottom of the pot. Using tongs, add the fish fillets to the pot in a single layer; it's fine if they overlap slightly. Place the broccoli and carrots on top. 4. Secure the lid and set the Pressure Release to Sealing. Press the Cancel button to reset the cooking program, then select the Pressure Cook or Manual setting and set the cooking time for 1 minute at low pressure. (The pot will take about 10 minutes to come up to pressure before the cooking program begins.) 5. When the cooking program ends, let the pressure release naturally for 10 minutes (don't open the pot before the 10 minutes are up, even if the float valve

has gone down), then move the Pressure Release to Venting to release any remaining steam. Open the pot. Use a fish spatula to transfer the vegetables and fillets to plates. Serve right away.

Mediterranean Salmon with Whole-Wheat Couscous

Prep time: 5 minutes | Cook time: 30 minutes | Serves 4

- Couscous
- 1 cup whole-wheat couscous
- 1 cup water
- 1 tablespoon extra-virgin olive oil
- 1 teaspoon dried basil
- ¼ teaspoon fine sea salt
- 1 pint cherry or grape tomatoes, halved
- 8 ounces zucchini, halved lengthwise, then sliced crosswise ¼ inch thick
- Salmon
- 1 pound skinless salmon fillet
- 2 teaspoons extra-virgin olive oil
- 1 tablespoon fresh lemon juice
- 1 garlic clove, minced
- ¼ teaspoon dried oregano
- ¼ teaspoon fine sea salt
- ¼ teaspoon freshly ground black pepper
- 1 tablespoon capers, drained
- Lemon wedges for serving

1. Start by pouring 1 cup of water into the Instant Pot and prepare two-tier stackable stainless-steel containers. 2. For the couscous, combine the couscous, water, oil, basil, and salt in one of the containers. Then, layer the tomatoes and zucchini on top. 3. In the second container, place the salmon fillet. In a small bowl, whisk together the oil, lemon juice, minced garlic, oregano, salt, pepper, and capers. Drizzle this mixture over the salmon fillet. 4. Position the container with the couscous and vegetables on the bottom and place the salmon container on top. Secure the lid on the top container and latch the two containers together. Grasp the handle and carefully lower them into the Instant Pot. 5. Close the lid of the Instant Pot and set the Pressure Release valve to Sealing. Select the Pressure Cook or Manual setting and set the cooking time for 20 minutes at high pressure. (Note that the pot will take about 10 minutes to come up to pressure before the cooking program begins.) 6. When the cooking program is complete, allow the pressure to release naturally for 5 minutes, then switch the Pressure Release to Venting to release any remaining steam. Open the pot and, using heat-resistant mitts, carefully lift out the stacked containers. Unlatch, unstack, and open the containers, being cautious of the hot steam. 7. Using a fork, fluff the couscous and mix in the vegetables. Spoon the couscous onto plates and cut the salmon into four pieces with a spatula, placing a piece on top of each serving of couscous. Serve immediately, accompanied by lemon wedges on the side.

Cod with Warm Tabbouleh Salad

Prep time: 10 minutes | Cook time: 6 minutes | Serves 4

- 1 cup medium-grind bulgur, rinsed
- 1 teaspoon table salt, divided
- 1 lemon, sliced ¼ inch thick, plus 2 tablespoons juice
- 4 (6-ounce / 170-g) skinless cod fillets, 1½ inches thick
- 3 tablespoons extra-virgin olive oil, divided, plus extra for drizzling
- ¼ teaspoon pepper
- 1 small shallot, minced
- 10 ounces (283 g) cherry tomatoes, halved
- 1 cup chopped fresh parsley
- ½ cup chopped fresh mint

1. Begin by placing the trivet that came with your Instant Pot at the bottom of the insert and adding ½ cup of water. Fold a sheet of aluminum foil into a 16 by 6-inch sling, and rest a 1½-quart round soufflé dish in the center of the sling. In the soufflé dish, combine 1 cup of water, bulgur, and ½ teaspoon of salt. Using the sling, carefully lower the soufflé dish onto the trivet in the pot, allowing the narrow edges of the sling to rest against the sides of the insert. 2. Secure the lid on the Instant Pot and close the pressure release valve. Select the high-pressure cooking function and set the timer for 3 minutes. Once the cooking time is complete, turn off the Instant Pot and perform a quick release of the pressure. Carefully remove the lid, ensuring the steam escapes away from you. Using the sling, transfer the soufflé dish to a wire rack and set it aside to cool. Remove the trivet, but do not discard the sling or the water in the pot. 3. Arrange lemon slices widthwise in two rows across the center of the sling. Brush the cod fillets with 1 tablespoon of oil and season with the remaining ½ teaspoon of salt and pepper. Place the cod, skin-side down, in an even layer on top of the lemon slices. Using the sling, lower the cod into the Instant Pot, allowing the narrow edges of the sling to rest against the sides of the insert. Lock the lid in place and close the pressure release valve. Select the high-pressure cooking function and set the timer for 3 minutes. 4. While the cod is cooking, whisk together the remaining 2 tablespoons of oil, lemon juice, and shallot in a large bowl. Add the cooked bulgur, chopped tomatoes, parsley, and mint, and gently toss to combine. Season the salad with salt and pepper to taste. 5. Once the cooking time for the cod is complete, turn off the Instant Pot and perform a quick release of the pressure. Carefully remove the lid, allowing steam to escape away from you. Using the sling, transfer the cod to a large plate. Gently lift and tilt the fillets with a spatula to remove the lemon slices. Serve the cod alongside the salad, drizzling individual portions with extra oil for enhanced flavor.

Turmeric Salmon

Prep time: 10 minutes | Cook time: 4 minutes | Serves 3

- 1 pound (454 g) salmon fillet
- 1 teaspoon ground black pepper
- ½ teaspoon salt
- 1 teaspoon ground turmeric
- 1 teaspoon lemon juice
- 1 cup water

1. In a shallow bowl, combine salt, ground black pepper, and ground turmeric to create a spice mixture. 2. Sprinkle lemon juice over the salmon fillet and rub it with the spice mixture to ensure it is well coated. 3. Pour water into the Instant Pot and insert the steamer rack. 4. Wrap the seasoned salmon fillet tightly in aluminum foil and place it on the steamer rack. 5. Secure the lid on the Instant Pot and seal the pressure release valve. 6. Set the pot to Manual mode and cook the fish at High Pressure for 4 minutes. 7. Once the cooking time is complete, perform a quick release of the pressure, then carefully unwrap the foil and cut the fish into serving portions.

Flavorful Monkfish Stew with Herbs and Spices

Prep time: 5 minutes | Cook time: 6 minutes | Serves 6

- Juice of 1 lemon
- 1 tablespoon fresh basil
- 1 tablespoon fresh parsley
- 1 tablespoon olive oil
- 1 teaspoon garlic, minced
- 1½ pounds (680 g) monkfish
- 1 tablespoon butter
- 1 bell pepper, chopped
- 1 onion, sliced
- ½ teaspoon cayenne pepper
- ½ teaspoon mixed peppercorns
- ¼ teaspoon turmeric powder
- ¼ teaspoon ground cumin
- Sea salt and ground black pepper, to taste
- 2 cups fish stock
- ½ cup water
- ¼ cup dry white wine
- 2 bay leaves
- 1 ripe tomato, crushed

1. Stir together the lemon juice, basil, parsley, olive oil, and garlic in a ceramic dish. Add the monkfish and marinate for 30 minutes. 2. Set your Instant Pot to Sauté. Add and melt the butter. Once hot, cook the bell pepper and onion until fragrant. 3. Stir in the remaining ingredients. 4. Lock the lid. Select the Manual mode and set the cooking time for 6 minutes at High Pressure. 5. When the timer beeps, perform a quick pressure release. Carefully remove the lid. 6. Discard the bay leaves and divide your stew into serving bowls. Serve hot.

Fish Bake with Veggies

Prep time: 10 minutes | Cook time: 5 minutes | Serves 4

- 1½ cups water
- Cooking spray
- 2 ripe tomatoes, sliced
- 2 cloves garlic, minced
- 1 teaspoon dried oregano
- 1 teaspoon dried basil
- ½ teaspoon dried rosemary
- 1 red onion, sliced
- 1 head cauliflower, cut into florets
- 1 pound (454 g) tilapia fillets, sliced
- Sea salt, to taste
- 1 tablespoon olive oil
- 1 cup crumbled feta cheese
- ⅓ cup Kalamata olives, pitted and halved

1. Start by pouring water into your Instant Pot and inserting a trivet. 2. Lightly coat a casserole dish with cooking spray, then layer the tomato slices evenly in the dish. Sprinkle the minced garlic, oregano, basil, and rosemary over the tomatoes. 3. Add the chopped onion and cauliflower to the dish, mixing everything together. Place the fish fillets on top, then sprinkle with salt and drizzle with olive oil. 4. Finish by adding the feta cheese and Kalamata olives on top of the fish. Carefully lower the casserole dish onto the trivet in the Instant Pot. 5. Secure the lid on the Instant Pot, select the Manual mode, and set the cooking time to 5 minutes at High Pressure. 6. When the cooking time ends, perform a quick release of the pressure and carefully remove the lid. 7. Allow the dish to cool for 5 minutes before serving to let the flavors settle.

Pesto and Cheese Fish Parcels

Prep time: 8 minutes | Cook time: 6 minutes | Serves 4

- 1½ cups cold water.
- 4 (4-ounce / 113-g) white fish fillets, such as cod or haddock
- 1 teaspoon fine sea salt
- ½ teaspoon ground black pepper
- 1 (4-ounce / 113-g) jar pesto
- ½ cup shredded Parmesan cheese (about 2 ounces / 57 g)
- Halved cherry tomatoes, for garnish

1. Pour the water into your Instant Pot and insert a steamer basket. 2. Sprinkle the fish on all sides with the salt and pepper. Take four sheets of parchment paper and place a fillet in the center of each sheet. 3. Dollop 2 tablespoons of the pesto on top of each fillet and sprinkle with 2 tablespoons of the Parmesan cheese. 4. Wrap the fish in the parchment by folding in the edges and folding down the top like an envelope to close tightly. 5. Stack the packets in the steamer basket, seam-side down. 6. Lock the lid. Select the Manual mode and set the cooking time for 6 minutes at Low

Pressure. 7. Once cooking is complete, do a natural pressure release for 10 minutes, then release any remaining pressure. Carefully open the lid. 8. Remove the fish packets from the pot. Transfer to a serving plate and garnish with the cherry tomatoes. 9. Serve immediately.

Herb-Seasoned Italian Salmon

Prep time: 10 minutes | Cook time: 4 minutes | Serves 2

- 10 ounces (283 g) salmon fillet
- 1 teaspoon Italian
- seasoning
- 1 cup water

1. Pour water and insert the trivet in the instant pot. 2. Then rub the salmon fillet with Italian seasoning and wrap in the foil. 3. Place the wrapped fish on the trivet and close the lid. 4. Cook the meal on Manual mode (High Pressure) for 4 minutes. 5. Make a quick pressure release and remove the fish from the foil. 6. Cut it into servings.

Cod Fillets with Cherry Tomatoes

Prep time: 2 minutes | Cook time: 15 minutes | Serves 4

- 2 tablespoons butter
- ¼ cup diced onion
- 1 clove garlic, minced
- 1 cup cherry tomatoes, halved
- ¼ cup chicken broth
- ¼ teaspoon dried thyme
- ¼ teaspoon salt
- ⅛ teaspoon pepper
- 4 (4-ounce / 113-g) cod fillets
- 1 cup water
- ¼ cup fresh chopped Italian parsley

1. Begin by setting your Instant Pot to the Sauté function and melting the butter. Once it's hot, add the chopped onions and sauté until they become softened. Then, add the minced garlic and cook for an additional 30 seconds. 2. Incorporate the tomatoes, chicken broth, thyme, salt, and pepper into the pot. Continue to cook for 5 to 7 minutes, or until the tomatoes begin to soften and release their juices. 3. Transfer the sauce into a glass bowl and gently place the fish fillets inside. Cover the bowl with aluminum foil to retain moisture. 4. Pour water into the Instant Pot and insert a trivet. Carefully set the bowl with the fish on top of the trivet. 5. Secure the lid on the Instant Pot, select Manual mode, and set the cooking time to 3 minutes at Low Pressure. 6. Once the cooking time is complete, perform a quick release of the pressure. Carefully open the lid, ensuring to avoid the steam. 7. Finally, sprinkle the dish with fresh parsley and serve immediately for a delicious meal.

Creamy Shrimp Zoodles Alfredo

Prep time: 10 minutes | Cook time: 10 minutes | Serves 4

- 10 ounces (283 g) salmon fillet (2 fillets)
- 4 ounces (113 g) Mozzarella, sliced
- 4 cherry tomatoes, sliced
- 1 teaspoon erythritol
- 1 teaspoon dried basil
- ½ teaspoon ground black pepper
- 1 tablespoon apple cider vinegar
- 1 tablespoon butter
- 1 cup water, for cooking

1. Melt the butter on Sauté mode and add shrimp. 2. Sprinkle them with seafood seasoning and sauté then for 2 minutes. 3. After this, spiralizer the zucchini with the help of the spiralizer and add in the shrimp. 4. Add coconut cream and close the lid. Cook the meal on Sauté mode for 8 minutes.

Creamy Shrimp and Asparagus Risott

Prep time: 15 minutes | Cook time: 20 minutes | Serves 4

- ¼ cup extra-virgin olive oil, divided
- 8 ounces (227 g) asparagus, trimmed and cut on bias into 1-inch lengths
- ½ onion, chopped fine
- ¼ teaspoon table salt
- 1½ cups Arborio rice
- 3 garlic cloves, minced
- ½ cup dry white wine
- 3 cups chicken or
- vegetable broth, plus extra as needed
- 1 pound (454 g) large shrimp (26 to 30 per pound), peeled and deveined
- 2 ounces (57 g) Parmesan cheese, grated (1 cup)
- 1 tablespoon lemon juice
- 1 tablespoon minced fresh chives

1. Using highest sauté function, heat 1 tablespoon oil in Instant Pot until shimmering. Add asparagus, partially cover, and cook until just crisp-tender, about 4 minutes. Using slotted spoon, transfer asparagus to bowl; set aside. 2. Add onion, 2 tablespoons oil, and salt to now-empty pot and cook, using highest sauté function, until onion is softened, about 5 minutes. Stir in rice and garlic and cook until grains are translucent around edges, about 3 minutes. Stir in wine and cook until nearly evaporated, about 1 minute. 3. Stir in broth, scraping up any rice that sticks to bottom of pot. Lock lid in place and close pressure release valve. Select high pressure cook function and cook for 7 minutes. 4. Turn off Instant Pot and quick-release pressure. Carefully remove lid, allowing steam to escape away from you. Stir shrimp and asparagus into risotto, cover, and let sit until shrimp are opaque throughout, 5 to 7 minutes. Add Parmesan and remaining 1 tablespoon oil, and stir vigorously until risotto becomes creamy. Adjust consistency with extra hot broth as needed. Stir in lemon juice and season with salt and pepper to taste. Sprinkle individual portions with chives before serving.

Braised Striped Bass with Zucchini and Tomatoes

Prep time: 20 minutes | Cook time: 16 minutes | Serves 4

- 2 tablespoons extra-virgin olive oil, divided, plus extra for drizzling
- 3 zucchini (8 ounces / 227 g each), halved lengthwise and sliced ¼ inch thick
- 1 onion, chopped
- ¾ teaspoon table salt, divided
- 3 garlic cloves, minced
- 1 teaspoon minced fresh oregano or ¼ teaspoon dried
- ¼ teaspoon red pepper
- flakes
- 1 (28-ounce / 794-g) can whole peeled tomatoes, drained with juice reserved, halved
- 1½ pounds (680 g) skinless striped bass, 1½ inches thick, cut into 2-inch pieces
- ¼ teaspoon pepper
- 2 tablespoons chopped pitted kalamata olives
- 2 tablespoons shredded fresh mint

1. Start by setting the Instant Pot to the highest sauté function and heating 1 tablespoon of oil for about 5 minutes, or until it's just starting to smoke. Add the zucchini and sauté until it becomes tender, which should take around 5 minutes. Once done, transfer the zucchini to a bowl and set it aside. 2. In the now-empty pot, add the remaining tablespoon of oil, along with the chopped onion and ¼ teaspoon of salt. Continue to sauté on the highest setting until the onion is softened, approximately 5 minutes. Stir in the minced garlic, oregano, and red pepper flakes, cooking for about 30 seconds until fragrant. Then, add the tomatoes and any reserved juice to the pot. 3. Season the bass fillets with the remaining ½ teaspoon of salt and pepper. Nestle the bass into the tomato mixture and spoon some of the cooking liquid over the fillets. Secure the lid, ensuring the pressure release valve is closed. Select the high-pressure cooking function and set the timer for 0 minutes. Once the Instant Pot reaches pressure, immediately turn it off and perform a quick release of the pressure. Carefully remove the lid, allowing the steam to escape away from your face. 4. Transfer the bass to a plate and cover it with aluminum foil to keep it warm while you finish preparing the vegetables. Stir the zucchini back into

the pot and let it sit until heated through, about 5 minutes. Add the olives and season the mixture with salt and pepper to taste. 5. Serve the bass alongside the vegetable mixture, garnishing individual portions with fresh mint and drizzling with extra oil for added flavor.

Snapper in Spicy Tomato Sauce

Prep time: 5 minutes | Cook time: 5 minutes | Serves 6

- 2 teaspoons coconut oil, melted
- 1 teaspoon celery seeds
- ½ teaspoon fresh grated ginger
- ½ teaspoon cumin seeds
- 1 yellow onion, chopped
- 2 cloves garlic, minced
- 1½ pounds (680 g) snapper fillets
- ¾ cup vegetable broth
- 1 (4-ounce / 113-g) can fire-roasted diced tomatoes
- 1 bell pepper, sliced
- 1 jalapeño pepper, minced
- Sea salt and ground black pepper, to taste
- ¼ teaspoon chili flakes
- ½ teaspoon turmeric powder

1. Begin by setting the Instant Pot to the Sauté function and heating the sesame oil until it becomes hot. Add the celery seeds, fresh ginger, and cumin seeds, and sauté them briefly. 2. Next, add the chopped onion and continue to sauté until it becomes softened and aromatic. 3. Stir in the minced garlic and cook for an additional 30 seconds to release its fragrance. Then, add the remaining ingredients and mix thoroughly. 4. Secure the lid on the Instant Pot, select the Manual mode, and set the cooking time to 3 minutes at Low Pressure. 5. Once the timer goes off, perform a quick release of the pressure and carefully remove the lid. 6. Serve the dish warm for the best flavor.

Mackerel and Broccoli Casserole

Prep time: 15 minutes | Cook time: 15 minutes | Serves 5

- 1 cup shredded broccoli
- 10 ounces (283 g) mackerel, chopped
- ½ cup shredded Cheddar
- cheese
- 1 cup coconut milk
- 1 teaspoon ground cumin
- 1 teaspoon salt

1. Start by sprinkling the chopped mackerel fillets with ground cumin and salt, then transfer them to the Instant Pot. 2. Layer the shredded broccoli and Cheddar cheese on top of the fish. 3. Pour the coconut milk over the layered ingredients. Secure the lid on the Instant Pot. 4. Set the pot

to Manual mode and cook at High Pressure for 15 minutes. 5. After cooking, allow the pressure to release naturally for 10 minutes before carefully opening the lid.

Turmeric-Spiced Haddock with Chili

Prep time: 10 minutes | Cook time: 5 minutes | Serves 4

- 1 chili pepper, minced
- 1 pound (454 g) haddock, chopped
- ½ teaspoon ground
- turmeric
- ½ cup fish stock
- 1 cup water

1. In the mixing bowl mix up chili pepper, ground turmeric, and fish stock. 2. Then add chopped haddock and transfer the mixture in the baking mold. 3. Pour water in the instant pot and insert the trivet. 4. Place the baking mold with fish on the trivet and close the lid. 5. Cook the meal on Manual (High Pressure) for 5 minutes. Make a quick pressure release.

Rainbow Trout with Mixed Greens

Prep time: 5 minutes | Cook time: 12 minutes | Serves 4

- 1 cup water
- 1½ (680 g) pounds rainbow trout fillets
- 4 tablespoons melted butter, divided
- Sea salt and ground black pepper, to taste
- 1 pound (454 g) mixed
- greens, trimmed and torn into pieces
- 1 bunch of scallions
- ½ cup chicken broth
- 1 tablespoon apple cider vinegar
- 1 teaspoon cayenne pepper

1. Begin by pouring water into your Instant Pot and inserting a steamer basket. 2. Place the fish into the basket, then drizzle it with 1 tablespoon of melted butter and season with salt and black pepper to taste. 3. Secure the lid on the Instant Pot, select the Manual mode, and set the cooking time for 12 minutes at Low pressure. 4. Once the timer goes off, perform a quick release of the pressure and carefully remove the lid. 5. Using a damp cloth, wipe down the Instant Pot to clean any residue. 6. Add the remaining 3 tablespoons of butter to the pot and warm it up. Once the butter is hot, add the greens, chopped scallions, broth, vinegar, and cayenne pepper. Cook, stirring occasionally, until the greens are wilted and tender. 7. Serve the cooked trout fillets alongside the sautéed greens for a delicious meal.

Chapter 5

Snacks and Appetizers

Cheddar Cauliflower Rice

Prep time: 3 minutes | Cook time: 1 minute | Serves 4

- 1 head fresh cauliflower, chopped into florets
- 1 cup water
- 3 tablespoons butter
- 1 tablespoon heavy cream
- 1 cup shredded sharp Cheddar cheese
- ½ teaspoon salt
- ¼ teaspoon pepper
- ¼ teaspoon garlic powder

1. Start by placing the cauliflower florets in the steamer basket. Pour water into the Instant Pot and carefully lower the steamer basket into the pot. Secure the lid in place. Press the Steam button and set the cooking time to 1 minute. Once the timer beeps, perform a quick release of the pressure. 2. Carefully remove the steamer basket and transfer the cooked cauliflower to a food processor. Pulse the cauliflower until it is broken down into small, pearl-like pieces. Transfer the processed cauliflower into a large bowl and add the remaining ingredients. Gently fold everything together until fully combined.

Hummus with Chickpeas and Tahini Sauce

Prep time: 10 minutes | Cook time: 55 minutes | Makes 4 cups

- 4 cups water
- 1 cup dried chickpeas
- 2½ teaspoons fine sea salt
- ½ cup tahini
- 3 tablespoons fresh lemon juice
- 1 garlic clove
- ¼ teaspoon ground cumin

1. Begin by combining water, chickpeas, and 1 teaspoon of salt in the Instant Pot, stirring to dissolve the salt completely. 2. Secure the lid on the pot and set the Pressure Release valve to Sealing. Select the Bean/Chili, Pressure Cook, or Manual setting and set the cooking time for 40 minutes at high pressure. (Note that the pot will take about 15 minutes to build up pressure before the cooking starts.) 3. Once the cooking program ends, allow the pressure to release naturally for 15 minutes, then switch the Pressure Release to Venting to release any remaining steam. 4. Place a colander over a bowl, then carefully open the pot. Wearing heat-resistant mitts, lift the inner pot out and drain the chickpeas in the colander. Return the drained chickpeas to the inner pot and place it back in the Instant Pot housing on the Keep Warm setting. Reserve the cooking liquid for later use. 5. In a blender or food processor, combine 1 cup of the reserved cooking liquid, tahini, lemon juice, garlic, cumin, and 1 teaspoon of salt. Blend on high speed for about 30 seconds, stopping to scrape down the sides as necessary, until the mixture is smooth and slightly fluffy. Set aside ½ cup of this sauce for topping later. 6. Reserve ½ cup of the chickpeas for the topping, then add the remaining chickpeas to the tahini sauce in the blender or food processor along with ½ cup of the cooking liquid and the remaining ½ teaspoon of salt. Blend on high speed for about 1 minute, stopping to scrape down the sides as needed, until the mixture is very smooth. 7. Transfer the hummus to a shallow serving bowl. Drizzle the reserved tahini sauce over the top and sprinkle the reserved chickpeas for garnish. The hummus can be stored in an airtight container in the refrigerator for up to 3 days. Serve it at room temperature or chilled for the best flavor.

Bacon-Cheddar Stuffed Jalapeños

Prep time: 10 minutes | Cook time: 6 minutes | Serves 2

- 1 ounce (28 g) bacon, chopped, fried
- 2 ounces (57 g) Cheddar cheese, shredded
- 1 tablespoon coconut
- cream
- 1 teaspoon chopped green onions
- 2 jalapeños, trimmed and seeded

1. Mix together the chopped bacon, cheese, coconut cream, and green onions in a mixing bowl and stir until well incorporated. 2. Stuff the jalapeños evenly with the bacon mixture. 3. Press the Sauté button to heat your Instant Pot. 4. Place the stuffed jalapeños in the Instant Pot and cook each side for 3 minutes until softened. 5. Transfer to a paper towel-lined plate and serve.

Lemon-Butter Mushrooms

Prep time: 10 minutes | Cook time: 4 minutes | Serves 2

- 1 cup cremini mushrooms, sliced
- ½ cup water
- 1 tablespoon lemon juice
- 1 teaspoon almond butter
- 1 teaspoon grated lemon zest
- ½ teaspoon salt
- ½ teaspoon dried thyme

.1. Begin by combining all the ingredients in the Instant Pot, mixing them well. 2. Secure the lid tightly on the pot. Select the Manual mode and set the cooking time to 4 minutes at High Pressure. 3. Once the cooking time is complete, allow for a natural pressure release for 5 minutes before releasing any remaining pressure. Carefully open the lid, ensuring to avoid the steam. 4. Serve the dish warm for the best flavor.

Crispy Brussels Sprouts with Bacon

Prep time: 5 minutes | Cook time: 10 minutes | Serves 4

- ½ pound (227 g) bacon
- 1 pound (454 g) Brussels sprouts
- 4 tablespoons butter
- 1 teaspoon salt
- ½ teaspoon pepper
- ½ cup water

1. Start by pressing the Sauté button on your Instant Pot and then press the Adjust button to lower the heat to Less. Add the bacon to the pot and fry it for 3 to 5 minutes, or until the fat begins to render. After this, press the Cancel button to stop the sautéing. 2. Next, press the Sauté button again, setting the heat to Normal, and continue frying the bacon until it becomes crispy. While the bacon is frying, wash the Brussels sprouts, removing any damaged outer leaves, and cut them in half or quarters as desired. 3. Once the bacon is crispy, remove it from the pot and set it aside. Add the Brussels sprouts to the hot bacon grease along with the butter. Sprinkle the mixture with salt and pepper. Sauté the Brussels sprouts for 8 to 10 minutes until they are caramelized and crispy, adding a few tablespoons of water as needed to deglaze the pan. Serve the dish warm for a delicious side.

Tuna-Stuffed Deviled Eggs

Prep time: 10 minutes | Cook time: 8 minutes | Serves 3

- 1 cup water
- 6 eggs
- 1 (5 ounces / 142 g) can tuna, drained
- 4 tablespoons mayonnaise
- 1 teaspoon lemon juice
- 1 celery stalk, diced finely
- ¼ teaspoon Dijon mustard
- ¼ teaspoon chopped fresh dill
- ¼ teaspoon salt
- ⅛ teaspoon garlic powder

1. Add water to Instant Pot. Place steam rack or steamer basket inside pot. Carefully put eggs into steamer basket. Click lid closed. Press the Manual button and adjust time for 8 minutes. 2. Add remaining ingredients to medium bowl and mix. 3. When timer beeps, quick-release the steam and remove eggs. Place in bowl of cool water for 10 minutes, then remove shells. 4. Cut eggs in half and remove hard-boiled yolks, setting whites aside. Place yolks in food processor and pulse until smooth, or mash with fork. Add yolks to bowl with tuna and mayo, mixing until smooth. 5. Spoon mixture into egg-white halves. Serve chilled.

Creamy Cheese-Stuffed Mushrooms

Prep time: 15 minutes | Cook time: 8 minutes | Serves 4

- 1 cup cremini mushroom caps
- 1 tablespoon chopped scallions
- 1 tablespoon chopped chives
- 1 teaspoon cream cheese
- 1 teaspoon sour cream
- 1 ounce (28 g) Monterey Jack cheese, shredded
- 1 teaspoon butter, softened
- ½ teaspoon smoked paprika
- 1 cup water, for cooking

1. Trim the mushroom caps if needed and wash them well. 2. After this, in the mixing bowl, mix up scallions, chives, cream cheese, sour cream, butter, and smoked paprika. 3. Then fill the mushroom caps with the cream cheese mixture and top with shredded Monterey Jack cheese. 4. Pour water and insert the trivet in the instant pot. 5. Arrange the stuffed mushrooms caps on the trivet and close the lid. 6. Cook the meal on Manual (High Pressure) for 8 minutes. 7. Then make a quick pressure release.

Buffalo Chicken Meatballs

Prep time: 5 minutes | Cook time: 10 minutes | Serves 4

- 1 pound (454 g) ground chicken
- ½ cup almond flour
- 2 tablespoons cream cheese
- 1 packet dry ranch dressing mix
- ½ teaspoon salt
- ¼ teaspoon pepper
- ¼ teaspoon garlic powder
- 1 cup water
- 2 tablespoons butter, melted
- ⅓ cup hot sauce
- ¼ cup crumbled feta cheese
- ¼ cup sliced green onion

1. In a large bowl, combine ground chicken, almond flour, cream cheese, ranch seasoning, salt, pepper, and garlic powder. Mix until well blended, then roll the mixture into 16 balls. 2. Place the meatballs on the steam rack inside the Instant Pot and add 1 cup of water to the pot. Secure the lid, click it closed, and press the Meat/Stew button, setting the timer for 10 minutes. 3. While the meatballs are cooking, mix together the melted butter and hot sauce in a separate bowl. Once the timer beeps, carefully remove the meatballs and transfer them to a clean large bowl. Toss the meatballs in the hot sauce mixture until well coated. Serve topped with crumbled feta and sliced green onions for garnish.

Pressure-Roasted Garlic Bulbs

Prep time: 2 minutes | Cook time: 25 minutes | Serves 4

- 4 bulbs garlic
- 1 tablespoon avocado oil
- 1 teaspoon salt
- Pinch of black pepper
- 1 cup water

1. Slice the pointy tops off the bulbs of garlic to expose the cloves. 2. Drizzle the avocado oil on top of the garlic and sprinkle with the salt and pepper. 3. Place the bulbs in the steamer basket, cut-side up. Alternatively, you may place them on a piece of aluminum foil with the sides pulled up and resting on top of the trivet. Place the steamer basket in the pot. 4. Close the lid and seal the vent. Cook on High Pressure for 25 minutes. Quick release the steam. 5. Let the garlic cool completely before removing the bulbs from the pot. 6. Hold the stem end (bottom) of the bulb and squeeze out all the garlic. Mash the cloves with a fork to make a paste.

Herbed Green Goddess White Bean Dip

Prep time: 1 minutes | Cook time: 45 minutes | Makes 3 cups

- 1 cup dried navy, great Northern, or cannellini beans
- 4 cups water
- 2 teaspoons fine sea salt
- 3 tablespoons fresh lemon juice
- ¼ cup extra-virgin olive oil, plus 1 tablespoon
- ¼ cup firmly packed fresh flat-leaf parsley leaves
- 1 bunch chives, chopped
- Leaves from 2 tarragon sprigs
- Freshly ground black pepper

1. Combine the beans, water, and 1 teaspoon of the salt in the Instant Pot and stir to dissolve the salt. 2. Secure the lid and set the Pressure Release to Sealing. Select the Bean/Chili, Pressure Cook, or Manual setting and set the cooking time for 30 minutes at high pressure if using navy or Great Northern beans or 40 minutes at high pressure if using cannellini beans. (The pot will take about 15 minutes to come up to pressure before the cooking program begins.) 3. When the cooking program ends, let the pressure release naturally for 15 minutes, then move the Pressure Release to Venting to release any remaining steam. Open the pot and scoop out and reserve ½ cup of the cooking liquid. Wearing heat-resistant mitts, lift out the inner pot and drain the beans in a colander. 4. In a food processor or blender, combine the beans, ½ cup cooking liquid, lemon juice, ¼ cup olive oil, ½ teaspoon parsley, chives, tarragon, remaining 1 teaspoon salt, and ½ teaspoon pepper. Process or blend on medium speed, stopping to scrape down the sides of the container as needed, for about 1 minute, until the mixture is smooth. 5. Transfer the dip to a serving bowl. Drizzle with the remaining 1 tablespoon olive oil and sprinkle with a few grinds of pepper. The dip will keep in an airtight container in the refrigerator for up to 1 week. Serve at room temperature or chilled.

Broccoli Cheese Dip

Prep time: 5 minutes | Cook time: 10 minutes | Serves 6

- 4 tablespoons butter
- ½ medium onion, diced
- 1½ cups chopped broccoli
- 8 ounces (227 g) cream
- cheese
- ½ cup mayonnaise
- ½ cup chicken broth
- 1 cup shredded Cheddar cheese

1. Begin by pressing the Sauté button on your Instant Pot, then press the Adjust button to lower the heat to Less. Add the butter to the pot and let it melt. Once melted, add the chopped onion and sauté until softened, about 5 minutes. Afterward, press the Cancel button to stop sautéing. 2. Add the broccoli, cream cheese, mayonnaise, and broth to the pot, stirring to combine. Next, press the Manual button and adjust the cooking time to 4 minutes. 3. When the timer beeps, perform a quick release of the pressure. Once the pressure is released, stir in the Cheddar cheese until melted and creamy. Serve the dish warm for a delicious meal.

Oregano Sausage Balls

Prep time: 10 minutes | Cook time: 16 minutes | Serves 10

- 15 ounces (425 g) ground pork sausage
- 1 teaspoon dried oregano
- 4 ounces (113 g) Mozzarella, shredded
- 1 cup coconut flour
- 1 garlic clove, grated
- 1 teaspoon coconut oil, melted

1. In a bowl, combine ground pork sausages, dried oregano, shredded Mozzarella, coconut flour, and minced garlic, mixing until the mixture is well combined and homogenous. 2. Once mixed, form the mixture into small balls of your desired size. 3. Next, pour coconut oil into the Instant Pot and heat it on Sauté mode. 4. Arrange the meatballs in the hot coconut oil and cook them for 8 minutes on each side until they are golden brown and cooked through.

Sautéed Italian-Seasoned Tomatillos

Prep time: 10 minutes | Cook time: 10 minutes | Serves 4

- 1 tablespoon Italian seasoning
- 4 tomatillos, sliced
- 4 teaspoons olive oil
- 4 tablespoons water

1. Sprinkle the tomatillos with Italian seasoning. 2. Then pour the olive oil in the instant pot and heat it up on Sauté mode for 1 minute. 3. Put the tomatillos in the instant pot in one layer and cook them for 2 minutes from each side. 4. Then add water and close the lid. 5. Sauté the vegetables for 3 minutes more.

Garlic Herb Shrimp

Prep time: 5 minutes | Cook time: 5 minutes | Serves 4

- 2 tablespoons olive oil
- ¾ pound (340 g) shrimp, peeled and deveined
- 1 teaspoon paprika
- 1 teaspoon garlic powder
- 1 teaspoon onion powder
- 1 teaspoon dried parsley flakes
- ½ teaspoon dried oregano
- ½ teaspoon dried thyme
- ½ teaspoon dried basil
- ½ teaspoon dried rosemary
- ¼ teaspoon red pepper flakes
- Coarse sea salt and ground black pepper, to taste
- 1 cup chicken broth

1. Set your Instant Pot to Sauté and heat the olive oil. 2. Add the shrimp and sauté for 2 to 3 minutes. 3. Add the remaining ingredients to the Instant Pot and stir to combine. 4. Secure the lid. Select the Manual mode and set the cooking time for 2 minutes at Low Pressure. 5. When the timer beeps, perform a quick pressure release. Carefully remove the lid. 6. Transfer the shrimp to a plate and serve.

Garlic Meatballs

Prep time: 20 minutes | Cook time: 15 minutes | Serves 6

- 7 ounces (198 g) ground beef
- 7 ounces (198 g) ground pork
- 1 teaspoon minced garlic
- 3 tablespoons water
- 1 teaspoon chili flakes
- 1 teaspoon dried parsley
- 1 tablespoon coconut oil
- ¼ cup beef broth

1. In a mixing bowl, combine the ground beef, ground pork, minced garlic, water, chili flakes, and dried parsley, mixing well to create a uniform mixture. 2. Form the mixture into medium-sized meatballs. 3. Next, heat coconut oil in the Instant Pot using the Sauté mode until hot. 4. Place the meatballs in the hot coconut oil in a single layer and cook them for 2 minutes on each side until browned. 5. After browning, pour in the beef broth and close the lid securely. 6. Set the Instant Pot to Manual mode and cook the meatballs at High Pressure for 10 minutes. 7. Once the cooking time is complete, perform a quick release of the pressure, then carefully transfer the meatballs to a plate for serving.

Crispy Parmesan Zucchini Fries

Prep time: 15 minutes | Cook time: 5 minutes | Serves 4

- 1 zucchini
- 1 ounce (28 g) Parmesan, grated
- 1 tablespoon almond
- flour
- ½ teaspoon Italian seasoning
- 1 tablespoon coconut oil

1. Trim the zucchini and cut it into the French fries. 2. Then sprinkle them with grated Parmesan, almond flour, and Italian seasoning. 3. Put coconut oil in the instant pot and melt it on Sauté mode. 4. Put the zucchini in the hot oil in one layer and cook for 2 minutes from each side or until they are golden brown. 5. Dry the zucchini fries with paper towels.

Tomato-Braised Porcupine Meatballs

Prep time: 20 minutes | Cook time: 15 minutes | Serves 8

- 1 pound ground sirloin or turkey
- ½ cup raw brown rice, parboiled
- 1 egg
- ¼ cup finely minced onion
- 1 or 2 cloves garlic,
- minced
- ¼ teaspoon dried basil and/or oregano, optional
- 10¾-ounce can reduced-fat condensed tomato soup
- ½ soup can of water

1. Mix all ingredients, except tomato soup and water, in a bowl to combine well. 2. Form into balls about 1½-inch in diameter. 3. Mix tomato soup and water in the inner pot of the Instant Pot, then add the meatballs. 4. Secure the lid and make sure the vent is turned to sealing. 5. Press the Meat button and set for 15 minutes on high pressure. 6. Allow the pressure to release naturally after cook time is up.

Sesame Mushrooms

Prep time: 2 minutes | Cook time: 10 minutes | Serves 6

- 3 tablespoons sesame oil
- ¾ pound (340 g) small button mushrooms
- 1 teaspoon minced garlic
- ½ teaspoon smoked
- paprika
- ½ teaspoon cayenne pepper
- Salt and ground black pepper, to taste

1. Start by setting your Instant Pot to the Sauté function and heating the sesame oil. 2. Add the mushrooms to the pot and sauté them for about 4 minutes, stirring occasionally, until they are just tender. 3. Next, add the remaining ingredients to the Instant Pot and stir well to combine everything thoroughly. 4. Secure the lid on the Instant Pot, select the Manual mode, and set the cooking time to 5 minutes at High Pressure. 5. Once the timer beeps, perform a quick release of the pressure, then carefully remove the lid. 6. Serve the dish warm for a delightful meal.

Garlic Rosemary Chicken Wings

Prep time: 10 minutes | Cook time: 16 minutes | Serves 4

- 4 boneless chicken wings
- 1 tablespoon olive oil
- 1 teaspoon dried
- rosemary
- ½ teaspoon garlic powder
- ¼ teaspoon salt

1. In the mixing bowl, mix up olive oil, dried rosemary, garlic powder, and salt. 2. Then rub the chicken wings with the rosemary mixture and leave for 10 minutes to marinate. 3. After this, put the chicken wings in the instant pot, add the remaining rosemary marinade and cook them on Sauté mode for 8 minutes from each side.

Curried Broccoli Skewers

Prep time: 15 minutes | Cook time: 1 minute | Serves 2

- 1 cup broccoli florets
- ½ teaspoon curry paste
- 2 tablespoons coconut
- cream
- 1 cup water, for cooking

1. In a shallow bowl, combine the curry paste and coconut cream, mixing well to create a smooth mixture. 2. Next, coat the broccoli florets with the curry paste mixture and thread them onto skewers. 3. Pour water into the Instant Pot and insert the steamer rack. 4. Carefully place the broccoli skewers on the steamer rack. Close the lid and seal the

pressure valve. 5. Set the Instant Pot to Manual mode and cook on High Pressure for 1 minute. 6. Once the cooking time is complete, perform a quick release of the pressure.

Crispy Cauliflower Cheese Bites

Prep time: 5 minutes | Cook time: 21 minutes | Serves 8

- 1 cup water
- 1 head cauliflower, broken into florets
- 1 cup shredded Asiago cheese
- ½ cup grated Parmesan cheese
- 2 eggs, beaten
- 2 tablespoons butter
- 2 tablespoons minced fresh chives
- 1 garlic clove, minced
- ½ teaspoon cayenne pepper
- Coarse sea salt and white pepper, to taste

1. Pour the water into the Instant Pot and insert a steamer basket. Place the cauliflower in the basket. 2. Lock the lid. Select the Manual mode and set the cooking time for 3 minutes at High Pressure. 3. When the timer beeps, perform a quick pressure release. Carefully remove the lid. 4. Transfer the cauliflower to a food processor, along with the remaining ingredients. Pulse until everything is well combined. 5. Form the mixture into bite-sized balls and place them on a baking sheet. 6. Bake in the preheated oven at 400°F (205°C) for 18 minutes until golden brown. Flip the balls halfway through the cooking time. Cool for 5 minutes before serving.

Spicy Parmesan Chicken Chive Bites

Prep time: 10 minutes | Cook time: 15 minutes | Serves 4

- 1 teaspoon coconut oil, softened
- 1 cup ground chicken
- ¼ cup chicken broth
- 1 tablespoon chopped
- chives
- 1 teaspoon cayenne pepper
- 3 ounces (85 g) Parmesan cheese, grated

1. Set your Instant Pot to Sauté and heat the coconut oil. 2. Add the remaining ingredients except the cheese to the Instant Pot and stir to mix well. 3. Secure the lid. Select the Manual mode and set the cooking time for 15 minutes at High Pressure. 4. Once cooking is complete, do a quick pressure release. Carefully open the lid. 5. Add the grated cheese and stir until combined. Form the balls from the cooked chicken mixture and allow to cool for 10 minutes, then serve.

Steamed Asparagus with Herbed Creamy Dip

Prep time: 5 minutes | Cook time: 1 minute | Serves 6

- 1 cup water
- 1½ pounds (680 g) asparagus spears, trimmed
- Dipping Sauce:
- ½ cup mayonnaise
- ½ cup sour cream
- 2 tablespoons chopped scallions
- 2 tablespoons fresh chervil
- 1 teaspoon minced garlic
- Salt, to taste

1. Pour the water into the Instant Pot and insert a steamer basket. Place the asparagus in the basket. 2. Lock the lid. Select the Manual mode and set the cooking time for 1 minute at High Pressure. 3. When the timer beeps, perform a quick pressure release. Carefully remove the lid. Transfer the asparagus to a plate. 4. Whisk together the remaining ingredients to make your dipping sauce. Serve the asparagus with the dipping sauce on the side.

Thyme Sautéed Radishes

Prep time: 5 minutes | Cook time: 15 minutes | Serves 4

- 1 pound (454 g) radishes, quartered (remove leaves and ends)
- 2 tablespoons butter
- ¼ teaspoon dried thyme
- ¼ teaspoon minced garlic
- ⅛ teaspoon salt
- ⅛ teaspoon garlic powder
- ⅛ teaspoon dried rosemary

1. Begin by pressing the Sauté button on your Instant Pot, then use the Adjust button to lower the heat to Less. 2. Add the radishes to the Instant Pot along with the butter and your chosen seasonings. 3. Sauté the radishes, stirring occasionally, until they become tender, which should take about 10 to 15 minutes. If the radishes start to stick to the pot, add a couple of teaspoons of water to prevent this.

Creole Pancetta and Cheese Balls

Prep time: 5 minutes | Cook time: 5 minutes | Serves 6

- 1 cup water
- 6 eggs
- 4 slices pancetta, chopped
- ⅓ cup grated Cheddar cheese
- ¼ cup cream cheese
- ¼ cup mayonnaise
- 1 teaspoon Creole seasonings
- Sea salt and ground black pepper, to taste

1. Start by pouring water into the Instant Pot and inserting a steamer basket. Place the eggs in the basket. 2. Secure the lid on the Instant Pot, select the Manual mode, and set the cooking time to 5 minutes at Low Pressure. 3. Once the timer beeps, perform a quick release of the pressure and carefully remove the lid. 4. Allow the eggs to cool for 10 to 15 minutes. Once cooled, peel the eggs, chop them, and transfer them to a mixing bowl. Add the remaining ingredients and stir until well combined. 5. Shape the mixture into balls using your hands. Serve chilled for a refreshing snack.

Sautéed Brussels Sprouts with Lemon Garlic Aioli

Prep time: 5 minutes | Cook time: 7 minutes | Serves 4

- 1 tablespoon butter
- ½ cup chopped scallions
- ¾ pound (340 g) Brussels sprouts
- Aioli Sauce:
- ¼ cup mayonnaise
- 1 tablespoon fresh lemon juice
- 1 garlic clove, minced
- ½ teaspoon Dijon mustard

1. Set your Instant Pot to Sauté and melt the butter. 2. Add the scallions and sauté for 2 minutes until softened. Add the Brussels sprouts and cook for another 1 minute. 3. Lock the lid. Select the Manual mode and set the cooking time for 4 minutes at High Pressure. 4. Meanwhile, whisk together all the ingredients for the Aioli sauce in a small bowl until well incorporated. 5. When the timer beeps, perform a quick pressure release. Carefully remove the lid. 6. Serve the Brussels sprouts with the Aioli sauce on the side.

Coconut Cajun Shrimp

Prep time: 10 minutes | Cook time: 6 minutes | Serves 2

- 4 Royal tiger shrimps
- 3 tablespoons coconut shred
- 2 eggs, beaten
- ½ teaspoon Cajun seasoning
- 1 teaspoon olive oil

1. Begin by heating olive oil in the Instant Pot on Sauté mode until it's hot. 2. While the oil is heating, mix together Cajun seasoning and shredded coconut in a bowl. 3. Dip each shrimp into beaten eggs, ensuring they are well coated, then roll them in the coconut mixture to coat thoroughly. 4. Once the oil is hot, place the coated shrimp in the pot and cook them on Sauté mode for 3 minutes on each side, or until they are golden brown and cooked through.

Spicy Baked Feta in Foil

Prep time: 10 minutes | Cook time: 6 minutes | Serves 6

- 12 ounces (340 g) feta cheese
- ½ tomato, sliced
- 1 ounce (28 g) bell pepper, sliced
- 1 teaspoon ground paprika
- 1 tablespoon olive oil
- 1 cup water, for cooking

1. Begin by sprinkling the cheese with olive oil and ground paprika, then place it on a sheet of aluminum foil. 2. Top the feta cheese with sliced tomatoes and bell peppers, then wrap it tightly in the foil to seal it well. 3. Next, pour water into the Instant Pot and insert the steamer rack. 4. Place the wrapped cheese on the rack inside the pot. Secure the lid and seal the pressure release valve. 5. Cook the cheese on Manual mode at High Pressure for 6 minutes, then perform a quick release of the pressure. 6. Carefully discard the foil and transfer the cheese to serving plates for presentation.

Steamed Parmesan Artichoke with a Spicy Kick

Prep time: 1 minute | Cook time: 30 minutes | Serves 2

- 1 large artichoke
- 1 cup water
- ¼ cup grated Parmesan cheese
- ¼ teaspoon salt
- ¼ teaspoon red pepper flakes

1. Trim artichoke. Remove stem, outer leaves and top. Gently spread leaves. 2. Add water to Instant Pot and place steam rack on bottom. Place artichoke on steam rack and sprinkle with Parmesan, salt, and red pepper flakes. Click lid closed. Press the Steam button and adjust time for 30 minutes. 3. When timer beeps, allow a 15-minute natural release and then quick-release the remaining pressure. Enjoy warm topped with additional Parmesan.

Mayo Chicken Celery

Prep time: 15 minutes | Cook time: 15 minutes | Serves 4

- 14 ounces (397 g) chicken breast, skinless, boneless
- 1 cup water
- 4 celery stalks
- 1 teaspoon salt
- ½ teaspoon onion powder
- 1 teaspoon mayonnaise

1. Begin by combining all the ingredients, except the mayonnaise, in the Instant Pot. 2. Secure the lid on the pot and select Manual mode, setting the cooking time for 15 minutes at High Pressure. 3. Once the cooking time is complete, allow for a natural pressure release for 6 minutes, then carefully release any remaining pressure. Open the lid cautiously. 4. Remove the chicken from the pot and shred it using two forks. Return the shredded chicken to the Instant Pot. 5. Stir in the mayonnaise and mix well until fully incorporated. Serve immediately for a delicious meal.

Fast Spring Kale Appetizer

Prep time: 5 minutes | Cook time: 2 minutes | Serves 6

- 3 teaspoons butter
- 1 cup chopped spring onions
- 1 pound (454 g) kale, torn into pieces
- 1 cup water
- ½ teaspoon cayenne pepper
- Himalayan salt and ground black pepper, to taste
- ½ cup shredded Colby cheese, for serving

1. Start by setting your Instant Pot to Sauté mode and melting the butter. 2. Once the butter is melted, add the spring onions and sauté for 1 minute until they are wilted. 3. Add the remaining ingredients, except for the cheese, to the Instant Pot and mix everything together well. 4. Secure the lid on the pot, select Manual mode, and set the cooking time for 1 minute at High Pressure. 5. When the timer beeps, perform a quick release of the pressure, then carefully remove the lid. 6. Transfer the kale mixture to a bowl and serve it topped with cheese for a delicious finish.

Creamy Pancetta Pizza Dip

Prep time: 10 minutes | Cook time: 4 minutes | Serves 10

- 10 ounces (283 g) Pepper Jack cheese
- 10 ounces (283 g) cream cheese
- 10 ounces (283 g) pancetta, chopped
- 1 pound (454 g) tomatoes, puréed
- 1 cup green olives, pitted and halved
- 1 teaspoon dried oregano
- ½ teaspoon garlic powder
- 1 cup chicken broth
- 4 ounces (113 g) Mozzarella cheese, thinly sliced

1. Mix together the Pepper Jack cheese, cream cheese, pancetta, tomatoes, olives, oregano, and garlic powder in the Instant Pot. Pour in the chicken broth. 2. Lock the lid. Select the Manual mode and set the cooking time for 4 minutes at High Pressure. 3. When the timer beeps, perform a quick pressure release. Carefully remove the lid. 4. Scatter the Mozzarella cheese on top. Cover and allow to sit in the residual heat. Serve warm.

Garlic Herb Butter

Prep time: 10 minutes | Cook time: 8 minutes | Serves 4

- ⅓ cup butter
- 1 teaspoon dried parsley
- 1 tablespoon dried dill
- ½ teaspoon minced garlic
- ¼ teaspoon dried thyme

1. Start by preheating the Instant Pot on Sauté mode. 2. Once heated, add the butter and allow it to melt completely. 3. Stir in the dried parsley, dill, minced garlic, and thyme, mixing the butter mixture well to combine all the flavors. 4. Transfer the mixture into a butter mold or container and refrigerate until it solidifies.

Cajun Chicken and Cabbage Salad

Prep time: 15 minutes | Cook time: 10 minutes | Serves 4

- 12 ounces (340 g) chicken fillet, chopped
- 1 teaspoon Cajun seasoning
- 1 tablespoon coconut oil
- 1 cup chopped Chinese cabbage
- 1 tablespoon avocado oil
- 1 teaspoon sesame seeds

1. Sprinkle the chopped chicken with the Cajun seasoning. 2. Set your Instant Pot to Sauté and heat the coconut oil. Add the chicken and cook for 10 minutes, stirring occasionally. 3. When the chicken is cooked, transfer to a salad bowl. Add the cabbage, avocado oil, and sesame seeds and gently toss to combine. Serve immediately.

Cauliflower Fritters with Cheese

Prep time: 10 minutes | Cook time: 8 minutes | Serves 4

- 1 cup cauliflower, boiled
- 2 eggs, beaten
- 2 tablespoons almond flour
- 2 ounces (57 g) Cheddar cheese, shredded
- ½ teaspoon garlic powder
- 1 tablespoon avocado oil

1. In a medium bowl, mash the cauliflower until smooth. Then, add the beaten eggs, flour, cheese, and garlic powder, stirring until everything is well incorporated. Form the mixture into fritters. 2. Set your Instant Pot to Sauté mode and heat the avocado oil until hot. 3. Carefully add the fritters to the hot oil and cook for 3 minutes on each side, or until they are golden brown. 4. Serve the fritters hot for the best flavor and texture.

Shrimp Bok Choy Salad Boats with Feta and Herbs

Prep time: 8 minutes | Cook time: 2 minutes | Serves 8

- 26 shrimp, cleaned and deveined
- 2 tablespoons fresh lemon juice
- 1 cup water
- Sea salt and ground black pepper, to taste
- 4 ounces (113 g) feta cheese, crumbled
- 2 tomatoes, diced
- ⅓ cup olives, pitted and sliced
- 4 tablespoons olive oil
- 2 tablespoons apple cider vinegar
- 8 Bok choy leaves
- 2 tablespoons fresh basil leaves, snipped
- 2 tablespoons chopped fresh mint leaves

1. Toss the shrimp and lemon juice in the Instant Pot until well coated. Pour in the water. 2. Lock the lid. Select the Manual mode and set the cooking time for 2 minutes at Low Pressure. 3. When the timer beeps, perform a quick pressure release. Carefully remove the lid. 4. Season the shrimp with salt and pepper to taste, then let them cool completely. 5. Toss the shrimp with the feta cheese, tomatoes, olives, olive oil, and vinegar until well incorporated. 6. Divide the salad evenly onto each Bok choy leaf and place them on a serving plate. Scatter the basil and mint leaves on top and serve immediately.

Spicy Colby Pepper Cheese Dip

Prep time: 5 minutes | Cook time: 5 minutes | Serves 8

- 1 tablespoon butter
- 2 red bell peppers, sliced
- 2 cups shredded Colby cheese
- 1 cup cream cheese, room temperature
- 1 cup chicken broth
- 2 garlic cloves, minced
- 1 teaspoon red Aleppo pepper flakes
- 1 teaspoon sumac
- Salt and ground black pepper, to taste

1. Set your Instant Pot to Sauté and melt the butter. 2. Add the bell peppers and sauté for about 2 minutes until just tender. 3. Add the remaining ingredients to the Instant Pot and gently stir to incorporate. 4. Lock the lid. Select the Manual mode and set the cooking time for 3 minutes at High Pressure. 5. When the timer beeps, perform a quick pressure release. Carefully remove the lid. 6. Allow to cool for 5 minutes and serve warm.

Cheesy Zucchini Tots

Prep time: 15 minutes | Cook time: 10 minutes | Serves 6

- 4 ounces (113 g) Parmesan, grated
- 4 ounces (113 g) Cheddar cheese, grated
- 1 zucchini, grated
- 1 egg, beaten
- 1 teaspoon dried oregano
- 1 tablespoon coconut oil

1. In the mixing bowl, mix up Parmesan, Cheddar cheese, zucchini, egg, and dried oregano. 2. Make the small tots with the help of the fingertips. 3. Then melt the coconut oil in the instant pot on Sauté mode. 4. Put the prepared zucchini tots in the hot coconut oil and cook them for 3 minutes from each side or until they are light brown. Cool the zucchini tots for 5 minutes.

Creamy Scallion Dip

Prep time: 10 minutes | Cook time: 11 minutes | Serves 4

- 5 ounces (142 g) scallions, diced
- 4 tablespoons cream cheese
- 1 tablespoon chopped fresh parsley
- 1 teaspoon garlic powder
- 2 tablespoons coconut cream
- ½ teaspoon salt
- 1 teaspoon coconut oil

1. Start by heating the Instant Pot on Sauté mode. 2. Add coconut oil and let it melt completely. 3. Once melted, add the diced scallions and sauté for 6 to 7 minutes, or until they are lightly browned. 4. Stir in the cream cheese, parsley, garlic powder, salt, and coconut cream, mixing well. 5. Secure the lid on the Instant Pot and cook the scallion dip for 5 minutes on Manual mode at High Pressure. 6. After cooking, perform a quick release of the pressure. If desired, blend the dip until smooth for a creamy texture.

Herbed Mushrooms

Prep time: 5 minutes | Cook time: 10 minutes | Serves 4

- 2 tablespoons butter
- 2 cloves garlic, minced
- 20 ounces (567 g) button mushrooms
- 1 tablespoon coconut aminos
- 1 teaspoon dried rosemary
- 1 teaspoon dried basil
- 1 teaspoon dried sage
- 1 bay leaf
- Sea salt, to taste
- ½ teaspoon freshly ground black pepper
- ½ cup chicken broth
- ½ cup water
- 1 tablespoon roughly chopped fresh parsley leaves, for garnish

1. Begin by setting your Instant Pot to Sauté mode and melting the butter. 2. Add the minced garlic and sliced mushrooms, sautéing for 3 to 4 minutes until the garlic becomes fragrant. 3. Stir in the remaining ingredients, excluding the parsley, and mix well. 4. Secure the lid on the Instant Pot, select Manual mode, and set the cooking time for 5 minutes at High Pressure. 5. Once the timer beeps, perform a quick release of the pressure and carefully open the lid. 6. Transfer the mushrooms to a platter and serve, garnished with fresh parsley leaves for a touch of color and flavor.

Chapter 6

Vegetables and Sides

Lemony Asparagus with Garlic Herb Gremolata

Prep time: 15 minutes | Cook time: 2 minutes | Serves 2 to 4

- Gremolata:
- 1 cup finely chopped fresh Italian flat-leaf parsley leaves
- 3 garlic cloves, peeled and grated
- Zest of 2 small lemons
- Asparagus:
- 1½ pounds (680 g) asparagus, trimmed
- 1 cup water
- Lemony Vinaigrette:
- 1½ tablespoons fresh lemon juice
- 1 teaspoon Swerve
- 1 teaspoon Dijon mustard
- 2 tablespoons extra-virgin olive oil
- Kosher salt and freshly ground black pepper, to taste
- Garnish:
- 3 tablespoons slivered almonds

1. In a small bowl, stir together all the ingredients for the gremolata. 2. Pour the water into the Instant Pot. Arrange the asparagus in a steamer basket. Lower the steamer basket into the pot. 3. Lock the lid. Select the Steam mode and set the cooking time for 2 minutes on Low Pressure. 4. Meanwhile, prepare the lemony vinaigrette: In a bowl, combine the lemon juice, swerve and mustard and whisk to combine. Slowly drizzle in the olive oil and continue to whisk. Season generously with salt and pepper. 5. When the timer goes off, perform a quick pressure release. Carefully open the lid. Remove the steamer basket from the Instant Pot. 6. Transfer the asparagus to a serving platter. Drizzle with the vinaigrette and sprinkle with the gremolata. Serve the asparagus topped with the slivered almonds.

Cauliflower Curry

Prep time: 10 minutes | Cook time: 3 minutes | Serves 6

- 1 pound (454 g) cauliflower, chopped
- 3 ounces (85 g) scallions, chopped
- 1 cup coconut milk
- ¼ cup crushed tomatoes
- 1 tablespoon coconut oil
- 1 teaspoon garam masala
- 1 teaspoon ground turmeric

1. Begin by adding all the ingredients to the Instant Pot and stirring them together until well combined. 2. Secure the lid on the pot and select Manual mode, setting the cooking time for 3 minutes at High Pressure. Once the timer goes off, allow for a natural pressure release for 5 minutes, then release any remaining pressure. Carefully open the lid. 3. Before serving, give the cooked dish a good stir to ensure everything is evenly mixed.

Buttery Whole Cauliflower

Prep time: 5 minutes | Cook time: 8 minutes | Serves 4

- 1 large cauliflower, rinsed and patted dry
- 1 cup water
- 4 tablespoons melted butter
- 2 cloves garlic, minced
- Pinch of sea salt
- Pinch of fresh ground black pepper
- 1 tablespoon chopped fresh flat leaf parsley, for garnish

1. Begin by pouring water into the Instant Pot and placing the trivet inside. Set the cauliflower on top of the trivet. 2. Secure the lid and select Manual mode, adjusting the cooking time to 3 minutes at High Pressure. 3. While the cauliflower cooks, preheat the oven to 550ºF (288ºC) and line a baking sheet with parchment paper. 4. In a small bowl, whisk together the butter, minced garlic, sea salt, and black pepper, then set the mixture aside. 5. When the timer beeps, perform a quick release of the pressure and carefully open the lid. 6. Transfer the cauliflower to the lined baking sheet and gently dab the surface with a clean kitchen towel to dry it. Brush the cauliflower generously with the garlic butter mixture. 7. Place the baking sheet in the preheated oven and roast the cauliflower for 5 minutes, or until it is golden brown. Drizzle any remaining garlic butter over the cauliflower and sprinkle with chopped parsley. Serve immediately for the best flavor.

Italian Sautéed Wild Mushrooms with Peppers

Prep time: 30 minutes | Cook time: 3 minutes | Serves 10

- 2 tablespoons canola oil
- 2 large onions, chopped
- 4 garlic cloves, minced
- 3 large red bell peppers, chopped
- 3 large green bell peppers, chopped
- 12 ounces package oyster mushrooms, cleaned and chopped
- 3 fresh bay leaves
- 10 fresh basil leaves, chopped
- 1 teaspoon salt
- 1½ teaspoons pepper
- 28 ounces can Italian plum tomatoes, crushed or chopped

1. Press Sauté on the Instant Pot and add in the oil. Once the oil is heated, add the onions, garlic, peppers, and mushroom to the oil. Sauté just until mushrooms begin to turn brown. 2. Add remaining ingredients. Stir well. 3. Secure the lid and make sure vent is set to sealing. Press Manual and set time for 3 minutes. 4. When cook time is up, release the pressure manually. Discard bay leaves.

Cauliflower Falafel with Fresh Lettuce Salad

Prep time: 10 minutes | Cook time: 6 to 8 minutes | Serves 4

- 1 cup shredded cauliflower
- ⅓ cup coconut flour
- 1 teaspoon grated lemon zest
- 1 egg, beaten
- 2 tablespoons coconut oil
- 2 cups chopped lettuce
- 1 cucumber, chopped
- 1 tablespoon olive oil
- 1 teaspoon lemon juice
- ½ teaspoon cayenne pepper

1. In a bowl, combine the cauliflower, coconut flour, grated lemon zest and egg. Form the mixture into small balls. 2. Set the Instant Pot to the Sauté mode and melt the coconut oil. Place the balls in the pot in a single layer. Cook for 3 to 4 minutes per side, or until they are golden brown. 3. In a separate bowl, stir together the remaining ingredients. 4. Place the cooked balls on top and serve.

North African Spiced Braised Cauliflower

Prep time: 15 minutes | Cook time: 10 minutes | Serves 4

- 2 tablespoons extra-virgin olive oil
- 6 garlic cloves, minced
- 3 anchovy fillets, rinsed and minced (optional)
- 2 teaspoons ras el hanout
- ⅛ teaspoon red pepper flakes
- 1 (28-ounce / 794-g) can whole peeled tomatoes,
- drained with juice reserved, chopped coarse
- 1 large head cauliflower (3 pounds / 1.4 kg)
- ½ cup pitted brine-cured green olives, chopped coarse
- ¼ cup golden raisins
- ¼ cup fresh cilantro leaves
- ¼ cup pine nuts, toasted

1. Using highest sauté function, cook oil, garlic, anchovies (if using), ras el hanout, and pepper flakes in Instant Pot until fragrant, about 3 minutes. Turn off Instant Pot, then stir in tomatoes and reserved juice. 2. Trim outer leaves of cauliflower and cut stem flush with bottom florets. Using paring knife, cut 4-inch-deep cross in stem. Nestle cauliflower stem side down into pot and spoon some of sauce over top. Lock lid in place and close pressure release valve. Select high pressure cook function and cook for 3 minutes. 3. Turn off Instant Pot and quick-release pressure. Carefully remove lid, allowing steam to escape away from you. Using tongs and slotted spoon, transfer cauliflower to serving dish and tent with aluminum foil. Stir olives and raisins into sauce and cook, using highest sauté function, until sauce has thickened slightly, about 5 minutes. Season with salt and pepper to taste. Cut cauliflower into wedges and spoon some of sauce over top. Sprinkle with cilantro and pine nuts. Serve, passing remaining sauce separately.

Chinese-Style Sautéed Pe-Tsai with Onion and Szechuan Pepper

Prep time: 5 minutes | Cook time: 8 minutes | Serves 4

- 2 tablespoons sesame oil
- 1 yellow onion, chopped
- 1 pound (454 g) pe-tsai cabbage, shredded
- ¼ cup rice wine vinegar
- 1 tablespoon coconut
- aminos
- 1 teaspoon finely minced garlic
- ½ teaspoon salt
- ¼ teaspoon Szechuan pepper

1. Set the Instant Pot on the Sauté mode and heat the sesame oil. Add the onion to the pot and sauté for 5 minutes, or until tender. Stir in the remaining ingredients. 2. Lock the lid. Select the Manual mode and set the cooking time for 3 minutes on High Pressure. When the timer goes off, perform a quick pressure release. Carefully open the lid. 3. Transfer the cabbage mixture to a bowl and serve immediately.

Parmesan Cauliflower Mash

Prep time: 7 minutes | Cook time: 5 minutes | Serves 4

- 1 head cauliflower, cored and cut into large florets
- ½ teaspoon kosher salt
- ½ teaspoon garlic pepper
- 2 tablespoons plain Greek yogurt
- ¾ cup freshly grated Parmesan cheese
- 1 tablespoon unsalted butter or ghee (optional)
- Chopped fresh chives

1. Start by pouring 1 cup of water into the electric pressure cooker and inserting a steamer basket or wire rack. 2. Place the cauliflower florets into the basket. 3. Securely close and lock the lid of the pressure cooker, ensuring the valve is set to sealing. 4. Cook on high pressure for 5 minutes. 5. Once the cooking time is complete, press Cancel and perform a quick release of the pressure. 6. When the pin drops, carefully unlock and remove the lid. 7. Take the cauliflower out of the pot and pour out the water. Return the cauliflower to the pot, then add salt, garlic pepper, yogurt, and cheese. Use an immersion blender or potato masher to purée or mash the cauliflower until smooth. 8. Transfer the mixture to a serving bowl and garnish with butter (if desired) and chopped chives before serving.

Garlicky Broccoli with Roasted Almonds

Prep time: 10 minutes | Cook time: 4 minutes | Serves 4 to 6

- 6 cups broccoli florets
- 1 cup water
- 1½ tablespoons olive oil
- 8 garlic cloves, thinly sliced
- 2 shallots, thinly sliced
- ½ teaspoon crushed red pepper flakes
- Grated zest and juice of 1

- medium lemon
- ½ teaspoon kosher salt
- Freshly ground black pepper, to taste
- ¼ cup chopped roasted almonds
- ¼ cup finely slivered fresh basil

1. Begin by pouring water into the Instant Pot. Place the broccoli florets in a steamer basket and lower it into the pot. 2. Secure the lid tightly and select the Steam setting, setting the cooking time for 2 minutes at Low Pressure. Once the timer beeps, perform a quick pressure release and carefully open the lid. 3. Immediately transfer the broccoli to a large bowl filled with ice water to stop the cooking process. Once cooled, drain the broccoli and pat it dry with a towel. 4. Select the Sauté mode on the Instant Pot and heat the olive oil. Add the minced garlic to the pot and sauté for 30 seconds while tossing constantly. Then, add the shallots and red pepper flakes, sautéing for an additional minute. 5. Stir in the cooked broccoli along with lemon juice, salt, and black pepper. Toss everything together and cook for 1 minute. 6. Finally, transfer the broccoli to a serving platter and garnish with chopped almonds, lemon zest, and fresh basil. Serve immediately for the best flavor.

Braised Cabbage with Ginger

Prep time: 10 minutes | Cook time: 8 minutes | Serves 6

- 1 tablespoon avocado oil
- 1 tablespoon butter or ghee (or more avocado oil)
- ½ medium onion, diced
- 1 medium bell pepper (any color), diced
- 1 teaspoon sea salt
- ½ teaspoon ground black

- pepper
- 1 clove garlic, minced
- 1-inch piece fresh ginger, grated
- 1 pound (454 g) green or red cabbage, cored and leaves chopped
- ½ cup bone broth or vegetable broth

1. Begin by setting the Instant Pot to Sauté mode and heating the oil and butter together. Once the butter stops foaming, add the chopped onion, diced bell pepper, salt, and black pepper. Sauté while stirring frequently until the vegetables are just softened, about 3 minutes. Then, add the minced garlic and ginger, cooking for an additional minute before adding the shredded cabbage and stirring to combine. Pour in the broth. 2. Secure the lid on the Instant Pot and set the steam release valve to Sealing. Press the Manual button and set the cooking time to 2 minutes. 3. When the Instant Pot beeps, carefully switch the steam release valve to Venting to quick-release the pressure. Once the pressure is fully released, open the lid. Stir the cabbage mixture and transfer it to a serving dish. Serve warm for a delicious side dish.

Lemon Garlic Asparagus

Prep time: 6 minutes | Cook time: 5 minutes | Serves 4

- 1 large bunch asparagus, woody ends cut off (medium-thick spears if possible)
- 1 cup water
- 2 tablespoons salted butter
- 2 large cloves garlic,

- minced
- 2 teaspoons fresh lemon juice (from ½ lemon)
- ¾ cup finely shredded Parmesan cheese (optional)
- Salt, to taste

1. Begin by cutting the asparagus spears on a diagonal into 3 equal pieces, or trim the whole spears to fit your Instant Pot. 2. Pour water into the Instant Pot and place a metal steaming basket inside. Arrange the asparagus in the basket. Secure the lid and set the steam release valve to Sealing. Press the Manual button and set the cooking time to 1 minute for tender asparagus (for softer asparagus, increase to 2 minutes; for crisp asparagus, decrease to 0 minutes). While the asparagus cooks, prepare a bowl of ice water. 3. When the Instant Pot beeps, carefully switch the steam release valve to Venting to quick-release the pressure. Once the pressure is fully released, open the lid and use tongs to transfer the asparagus to the ice bath. Let it sit for a minute, then drain and place the asparagus on a clean kitchen towel to pat dry. 4. Carefully remove the pot insert from the Instant Pot, take out the steaming basket, drain the water, and wipe the pot insert dry. 5. Return the pot insert to the Instant Pot and press the Sauté button. Add the butter to the pot. Once the butter has melted and begins to foam, add the minced garlic and sauté while stirring for 1 minute. 6. Add the asparagus back to the pot, stirring well to coat it with the garlic-butter mixture. Drizzle in the lemon juice and sauté until the asparagus reaches your desired doneness, about 1 minute more. 7. Transfer the asparagus to a serving bowl and stir in the Parmesan cheese. Taste and add salt as needed. Serve warm for a delightful side dish.

Wild Rice Salad with Cranberries and Almonds

Prep time: 10 minutes | Cook time: 25 minutes | Serves 18

- For the rice
- 2 cups wild rice blend, rinsed
- 1 teaspoon kosher salt
- 2½ cups Vegetable Broth or Chicken Bone Broth
- For the dressing
- ¼ cup extra-virgin olive oil
- ¼ cup white wine vinegar
- 1½ teaspoons grated orange zest
- Juice of 1 medium orange (about ¼ cup)
- 1 teaspoon honey or pure maple syrup
- For the salad
- ¾ cup unsweetened dried cranberries
- ½ cup sliced almonds, toasted
- Freshly ground black pepper

1. Start by placing the rice, salt, and broth in the electric pressure cooker. 2. Secure the lid tightly and set the valve to the sealing position. 3. Set the cooker to high pressure and cook for 25 minutes. 4. After the cooking time ends, press Cancel and allow the pressure to naturally release for 15 minutes before quick releasing any remaining pressure. 5. Once the pressure pin drops, unlock the lid and remove it carefully. 6. Let the rice cool for a moment, then fluff it gently with a fork. 7. While the rice is cooking, prepare the dressing by mixing olive oil, vinegar, lemon zest, lemon juice, and honey in a small jar with a screw-top lid. (If you don't have a jar, use a small bowl to whisk the ingredients together.) Shake or whisk until well combined. 8. In a large mixing bowl, combine the fluffed rice with cranberries and almonds. 9. Pour the dressing over the mixture and season with freshly ground pepper to taste. 10. You can serve the salad warm or store it in the refrigerator for later enjoyment.

Quick Cauliflower Gnocchi

Prep time: 5 minutes | Cook time: 2 minutes | Serves 4

- 2 cups cauliflower, boiled
- ½ cup almond flour
- 1 tablespoon sesame oil
- 1 teaspoon salt
- 1 cup water

1. In a bowl, mash the cauliflower until puréed. Mix it up with the almond flour, sesame oil and salt. 2. Make the log from the cauliflower dough and cut it into small pieces. 3. Pour the water in the Instant Pot and add the gnocchi. 4. Lock the lid. Select the Manual mode and set the cooking time for 2 minutes on High Pressure. Once the timer goes off, perform a natural pressure release for 5 minutes, then release any remaining pressure. Carefully open the lid. 5. Remove the cooked gnocchi from the water and serve.

Mushroom Stroganoff with Vodka

Prep time: 8 minutes | Cook time: 8 minutes | Serves 4

- 2 tablespoons olive oil
- ½ teaspoon crushed caraway seeds
- ½ cup chopped onion
- 2 garlic cloves, smashed
- ¼ cup vodka
- ¾ pound (340 g) button
- mushrooms, chopped
- 1 celery stalk, chopped
- 1 ripe tomato, puréed
- 1 teaspoon mustard seeds
- Sea salt and freshly ground pepper, to taste
- 2 cups vegetable broth

1. Begin by pressing the Sauté button on your Instant Pot to heat it up. Once hot, add the oil and sauté the caraway seeds until they become fragrant, about 40 seconds. 2. Next, add the chopped onion and minced garlic, continuing to sauté for an additional 1 to 2 minutes while stirring frequently. 3. After that, incorporate the remaining ingredients and stir everything together until well combined. 4. Secure the lid on the Instant Pot, select Manual mode, and set it to High Pressure; cook for 5 minutes. When the cooking time is complete, perform a quick pressure release and carefully remove the lid. 5. Ladle the mixture into individual bowls and serve warm. Enjoy your meal!

Green Cabbage Turmeric Stew

Prep time: 5 minutes | Cook time: 4 minutes | Serves 4

- 2 tablespoons olive oil
- ½ cup sliced yellow onion
- 1 teaspoon crushed garlic
- Sea salt and freshly ground black pepper, to taste
- 1 teaspoon turmeric powder
- 1 serrano pepper, chopped
- 1 pound (454 g) green cabbage, shredded
- 1 celery stalk, chopped
- 2 tablespoons rice wine
- 1 cup roasted vegetable broth

1. Begin by placing all of the listed ingredients into the Instant Pot. 2. Secure the lid tightly, select Manual mode, and set it to High Pressure, cooking for 4 minutes. Once the cooking time is complete, perform a quick pressure release and carefully remove the lid. 3. Portion the contents into individual bowls and serve warm. Enjoy your meal!

Moroccan Spiced Zucchini with Tomatoes

Prep time: 10 minutes | Cook time: 6 minutes | Serves 4

- 2 tablespoons avocado oil
- ½ medium onion, diced
- 1 clove garlic, minced
- ¼ teaspoon cayenne pepper
- ¼ teaspoon ground coriander
- ¼ teaspoon ground cumin
- ¼ teaspoon ground ginger
- Pinch of ground cinnamon
- 1 Roma (plum) tomato, diced
- 2 medium zucchini, cut into 1-inch pieces
- ½ tablespoon fresh lemon juice
- ¼ cup bone broth or vegetable stock

1. Set the Instant Pot to Sauté. When hot, add the oil. Add the onion and sauté, stirring frequently, until translucent, about 2 minutes. Add the garlic, cayenne, coriander, cumin, ginger, and cinnamon and cook until fragrant, about 1 minute. Stir in the tomato and zucchini and cook 2 minutes longer. 2. Press Cancel. Add the lemon juice and broth. Secure the lid and set the steam release valve to Sealing. Press the Manual button, adjust the pressure to Low, and set the cook time to 1 minute. 3. When the Instant Pot beeps, carefully switch the steam release valve to Venting to quick-release the pressure. When fully released, open the lid. Stir and serve warm.

Braised Fennel with Radicchio, Pear, and Pecorino Salad

Prep time: 20 minutes | Cook time: 12 minutes | Serves 4

- 6 tablespoons extra-virgin olive oil, divided
- 2 fennel bulbs (12 ounces / 340 g each), 2 tablespoons fronds chopped, stalks discarded, bulbs halved, each half cut into 1-inch-thick wedges
- ¾ teaspoon table salt, divided
- ½ teaspoon grated lemon zest plus 4 teaspoons
- juice
- 5 ounces (142 g) baby arugula
- 1 small head radicchio (6 ounces/ 170 g), shredded
- 1 Bosc or Bartlett pear, quartered, cored, and sliced thin
- ¼ cup whole almonds, toasted and chopped
- Shaved Pecorino Romano cheese

1. Using highest sauté function, heat 2 tablespoons oil in Instant Pot for 5 minutes (or until just smoking). Brown half of fennel, about 3 minutes per side; transfer to plate.

Repeat with 1 tablespoon oil and remaining fennel; do not remove from pot. 2. Return first batch of fennel to pot along with ½ cup water and ½ teaspoon salt. Lock lid in place and close pressure release valve. Select high pressure cook function and cook for 2 minutes. Turn off Instant Pot and quick-release pressure. Carefully remove lid, allowing steam to escape away from you. Using slotted spoon, transfer fennel to plate; discard cooking liquid. 3. Whisk remaining 3 tablespoons oil, lemon zest and juice, and remaining ¼ teaspoon salt together in large bowl. Add arugula, radicchio, and pear and toss to coat. Transfer arugula mixture to serving dish and arrange fennel wedges on top. Sprinkle with almonds, fennel fronds, and Pecorino. Serve.

Steamed Zucchini Sticks with Olive Oil and Pepper

Prep time: 5 minutes | Cook time: 8 minutes | Serves 2

- 2 zucchinis, trimmed and cut into sticks
- 2 teaspoons olive oil
- ½ teaspoon white pepper
- ½ teaspoon salt
- 1 cup water

1. Place the zucchini sticks in the Instant Pot pan and sprinkle with the olive oil, white pepper and salt. 2. Pour the water and put the trivet in the pot. Place the pan on the trivet. 3. Lock the lid. Select the Manual setting and set the cooking time for 8 minutes at High Pressure. Once the timer goes off, use a quick pressure release. Carefully open the lid. 4. Remove the zucchinis from the pot and serve.

Almond Butter Zucchini Noodles with Cabbage

Prep time: 10 minutes | Cook time: 4 minutes | Serves 4

- 2 tablespoons coconut oil
- 1 yellow onion, chopped
- 2 zucchini, julienned
- 1 cup shredded Chinese cabbage
- 2 garlic cloves, minced
- 2 tablespoons almond
- butter
- Sea salt and freshly ground black pepper, to taste
- 1 teaspoon cayenne pepper

1. Press the Sauté button to heat up your Instant Pot. Heat the coconut oil and sweat the onion for 2 minutes. 2. Add the other ingredients. 3. Secure the lid. Choose Manual mode and High Pressure; cook for 2 minutes. Once cooking is complete, use a quick pressure release; carefully remove the lid. Bon appétit!

Vegan Broccoli and Mushroom Bake with Nutty Béchamel

Prep time: 10 minutes | Cook time: 3 minutes | Serves 4

- ½ cup sunflower seeds, soaked overnight
- 2 tablespoons sesame seeds
- 1 cup water
- 1 cup unsweetened almond milk
- ¼ teaspoon grated nutmeg
- ½ teaspoon sea salt
- 1 tablespoon nutritional yeast
- 2 tablespoons rice vinegar
- 1 pound (454 g) broccoli, broken into florets
- ½ cup chopped spring onions
- 10 ounces (283 g) white fresh mushrooms, sliced
- Sea salt and white pepper, to taste
- 1 tablespoon cayenne pepper
- ¼ teaspoon dried dill
- ¼ teaspoon ground bay leaf

1. Add sunflower seeds, sesame seeds, water, milk, nutmeg, ½ teaspoon of sea salt, nutritional yeast, and vinegar to your blender. 2. Blend until smooth and uniform. 3. Spritz a casserole dish with a nonstick cooking spray. Add broccoli, spring onions and mushrooms. 4. Sprinkle with salt, white pepper, cayenne pepper, dill, and ground bay leaf. Pour the prepared vegan béchamel over your casserole. 5. Add 1 cup of water and a metal rack to your Instant Pot. Place the dish on the rack. 6. Secure the lid. Choose Manual mode and High Pressure; cook for 3 minutes. Once cooking is complete, use a quick pressure release; carefully remove the lid. 7. Allow the dish to stand for 5 to 10 minutes before slicing and serving. Bon appétit!

Asparagus with Copoundy Cheese

Prep time: 5 minutes | Cook time: 1 minute | Serves 4

- 1½ pounds (680 g) fresh asparagus
- 1 cup water
- 2 tablespoons olive oil
- 4 garlic cloves, minced
- Sea salt, to taste
- ¼ teaspoon ground black pepper
- ½ cup shredded Copoundy cheese

1. Start by pouring water into the Instant Pot and placing the steamer basket inside. 2. Arrange the asparagus in the steamer basket, then drizzle with olive oil and sprinkle minced garlic on top. Season with salt and black pepper to taste. 3. Secure the lid and select Manual mode, setting the cooking time to 1 minute at High Pressure. Once the cooking time is complete, perform a quick pressure release and carefully open the lid. 4. Transfer the asparagus to a platter and serve it topped with shredded cheese for added flavor.

Gobi Masala

Prep time: 5 minutes | Cook time: 4 to 5 minutes | Serves 4 to 6

- 1 tablespoon olive oil
- 1 teaspoon cumin seeds
- 1 white onion, diced
- 1 garlic clove, minced
- 1 head cauliflower, chopped
- 1 tablespoon ground coriander
- 1 teaspoon ground cumin
- ½ teaspoon garam masala
- ½ teaspoon salt
- 1 cup water

1. Begin by setting the Instant Pot to Sauté mode and heating the olive oil. Once hot, add the cumin seeds and sauté for 30 seconds, stirring constantly. Then, add the chopped onion and continue to sauté for 2 to 3 minutes, stirring frequently. Add the minced garlic and sauté for another 30 seconds, continuing to stir. 2. Next, stir in the remaining ingredients until well combined. 3. Secure the lid on the Instant Pot, select Manual mode, and set the cooking time to 1 minute at High Pressure. When the timer beeps, perform a quick pressure release and carefully open the lid. 4. Serve the dish immediately for the best flavor and warmth.

Satarash with Eggs

Prep time: 10 minutes | Cook time: 5 minutes | Serves 4

- 2 tablespoons olive oil
- 1 white onion, chopped
- 2 cloves garlic
- 2 ripe tomatoes, puréed
- 1 green bell pepper, deseeded and sliced
- 1 red bell pepper, deseeded and sliced
- 1 teaspoon paprika
- ½ teaspoon dried oregano
- ½ teaspoon turmeric
- Kosher salt and ground black pepper, to taste
- 1 cup water
- 4 large eggs, lightly whisked

1. Start by pressing the Sauté button on the Instant Pot to heat the olive oil. Add the chopped onion and minced garlic to the pot, sautéing for 2 minutes or until they become fragrant. Next, stir in the remaining ingredients, excluding the eggs. 2. Secure the lid on the Instant Pot, select Manual mode, and set the cooking time for 3 minutes at High Pressure. When the timer sounds, perform a quick pressure release and carefully open the lid. 3. Gently fold in the eggs and stir everything to combine. Secure the lid again and let the mixture sit in the residual heat for 5 minutes. Serve warm for the best flavor.

Sesame Zoodles with Scallions and Chili Flakes

Prep time: 10 minutes | Cook time: 3 minutes | Serves 6

- 2 large zucchinis, trimmed and spiralized
- ¼ cup chicken broth
- 1 tablespoon chopped scallions
- 1 tablespoon coconut aminos
- 1 teaspoon sesame oil
- 1 teaspoon sesame seeds
- ¼ teaspoon chili flakes

1. Set the Instant Pot on the Sauté mode. Add the zucchini spirals to the pot and pour in the chicken broth. Sauté for 3 minutes and transfer to the serving bowls. 2. Sprinkle with the scallions, coconut aminos, sesame oil, sesame seeds and chili flakes. Gently stir the zoodles. 3. Serve immediately.

Thyme Cabbage

Prep time: 10 minutes | Cook time: 5 minutes | Serves 4

- 1 pound (454 g) white cabbage
- 2 tablespoons butter
- 1 teaspoon dried thyme
- ½ teaspoon salt
- 1 cup water

1. Start by cutting the white cabbage into medium-sized petals and sprinkling them with butter, dried thyme, and salt. Place the cabbage petals in the Instant Pot pan. 2. Pour water into the Instant Pot and insert the trivet. Set the pan with the cabbage on top of the trivet. 3. Secure the lid in place, select Manual mode, and set the cooking time for 5 minutes at High Pressure. Once the timer beeps, perform a quick pressure release and carefully open the lid. 4. Serve the cabbage immediately for the best flavor and texture.

Perfectly Steamed Sweet Potatoes

Prep time: 5 minutes | Cook time: 15 minutes | Serves 4 to 6

- 4–6 medium sweet potatoes
- 1 cup of water

1. Scrub skin of sweet potatoes with a brush until clean. Pour water into inner pot of the Instant Pot. Place steamer basket in the bottom of the inner pot. Place sweet potatoes on top of steamer basket. 2. Secure the lid and turn valve to seal. 3. Select the Manual mode and set to pressure cook on high for 15 minutes. 4. Allow pressure to release naturally (about 10 minutes). 5. Once the pressure valve lowers, remove lid and serve immediately.

Curried Cauliflower and Tomatoes

Prep time: 10 minutes | Cook time: 2 minutes | Serves 4 to 6

- 1 medium head cauliflower, cut into bite-size pieces
- 1 (14-ounce / 397-g) can sugar-free diced tomatoes, undrained
- 1 bell pepper, thinly sliced
- 1 (14-ounce / 397-g) can full-fat coconut milk
- ½ to 1 cup water
- 2 tablespoons red curry paste
- 1 teaspoon salt
- 1 teaspoon garlic powder
- ½ teaspoon onion powder
- ½ teaspoon ground ginger
- ¼ teaspoon chili powder
- Freshly ground black pepper, to taste

1. Begin by adding all the ingredients, except for the black pepper, to the Instant Pot and stirring to combine thoroughly. 2. Secure the lid on the pot and select the Manual setting, setting the cooking time for 2 minutes at High Pressure. When the timer goes off, perform a quick release of the pressure and carefully open the lid. 3. Once opened, sprinkle in the black pepper and stir well to incorporate. Serve the dish immediately for the best flavor.

Spiced Masala Cauliflower with Almond Yogurt

Prep time: 6 minutes | Cook time: 5 minutes | Serves 4

- 2 tablespoons olive oil
- ½ cup chopped scallions
- 2 cloves garlic, pressed
- 1 tablespoon garam masala
- 1 teaspoon curry powder
- 1 red chili pepper, minced
- ½ teaspoon ground cumin
- Sea salt and ground black
- pepper, to taste
- 1 tablespoon chopped fresh coriander
- 2 tomatoes, puréed
- 1 pound (454 g) cauliflower, broken into florets
- ½ cup water
- ½ cup almond yogurt

1. Press the Sauté button to heat up your Instant Pot. Now, heat the oil and sauté the scallions for 1 minute. 2. Add garlic and continue to cook an additional 30 seconds or until aromatic. 3. Add garam masala, curry powder, chili pepper, cumin, salt, black pepper, coriander, tomatoes, cauliflower, and water. 4. Secure the lid. Choose Manual mode and High Pressure; cook for 3 minutes. Once cooking is complete, use a quick pressure release; carefully remove the lid. 5. Pour in the almond yogurt, stir well and serve warm. Bon appétit!

Hearty Vegetable Curry

Prep time: 25 minutes | Cook time: 3 minutes | Serves 10

- 16-ounce package baby carrots
- 3 medium potatoes, unpeeled, cubed
- 1 pound fresh or frozen green beans, cut in 2-inch pieces
- 1 medium green pepper, chopped
- 1 medium onion, chopped
- 1–2 cloves garlic, minced
- 15-ounce can garbanzo beans, drained
- 28-ounce can crushed tomatoes
- 3 teaspoons curry powder
- 1½ teaspoons chicken bouillon granules
- 1¾ cups boiling water
- 3 tablespoons minute tapioca

1. Combine carrots, potatoes, green beans, pepper, onion, garlic, garbanzo beans, crushed tomatoes, and curry powder in the Instant Pot. 2. Dissolve bouillon in boiling water, then stir in tapioca. Pour over the contents of the Instant Pot and stir. 3. Secure the lid and make sure vent is set to sealing. Press Manual and set for 3 minutes. 4. When cook time is up, manually release the pressure.

Spiced Butternut Squash with Halloumi and Shaved Brussels Sprouts

Prep time: 20 minutes | Cook time: 15 minutes | Serves 4

- 3 tablespoons extra-virgin olive oil, divided
- 2 tablespoons lemon juice
- 2 garlic cloves, minced, divided
- ⅛ teaspoon plus ½ teaspoon table salt, divided
- 8 ounces (227 g) Brussels sprouts, trimmed, halved, and sliced very thin
- 1 (8-ounce / 227-g) block halloumi cheese, sliced crosswise into ¾-inch-thick slabs
- 4 scallions, white parts minced, green parts sliced
- thin on bias
- ½ teaspoon ground cardamom
- ¼ teaspoon ground cumin
- ⅛ teaspoon cayenne pepper
- 2 pounds (907 g) butternut squash, peeled, seeded, and cut into 1-inch pieces
- ½ cup chicken or vegetable broth
- 2 teaspoons honey
- ¼ cup dried cherries
- 2 tablespoons roasted pepitas

1. Whisk 1 tablespoon oil, lemon juice, ¼ teaspoon garlic, and ⅛ teaspoon salt together in bowl. Add Brussels sprouts and toss to coat; let sit until ready to serve. 2. Using highest sauté function, heat remaining 2 tablespoons oil in Instant Pot until shimmering. Arrange halloumi around edges of pot and cook until browned, about 3 minutes per side; transfer to plate. Add scallion whites to fat left in pot and cook until softened, about 2 minutes. Stir in remaining garlic, cardamom, cumin, and cayenne and cook until fragrant, about 30 seconds. Stir in squash, broth, and remaining ½ teaspoon salt. Lock lid in place and close pressure release valve. Select high pressure cook function and cook for 6 minutes. 3. Turn off Instant Pot and quick-release pressure. Carefully remove lid, allowing steam to escape away from you. Using highest sauté function, continue to cook squash mixture, stirring occasionally until liquid is almost completely evaporated, about 5 minutes. Turn off Instant Pot. Using potato masher, mash squash until mostly smooth. Season with salt and pepper to taste. 4. Spread portion of squash over bottom of individual serving plates. Top with Brussels sprouts and halloumi. Drizzle with honey and sprinkle with cherries, pepitas, and scallion greens. Serve.

Best Brown Rice

Prep time: 5 minutes | Cook time: 22 minutes | Serves 6 to 12

- 2 cups brown rice
- 2½ cups water

1. Begin by rinsing the brown rice in a fine-mesh strainer to remove excess starch. 2. Add the rinsed rice and the appropriate amount of water to the inner pot of the Instant Pot. 3. Secure the lid tightly and ensure that the vent is set to sealing. 4. Select the Manual setting and set the cooking time for 22 minutes at high pressure. 5. Once the cooking time is complete, allow the pressure to release naturally for 10 minutes, then press Cancel and manually release any remaining pressure.

Steamed Tomatoes with Halloumi and Basil

Prep time: 5 minutes | Cook time: 3 minutes | Serves 4

- 8 tomatoes, sliced
- 1 cup water
- ½ cup crumbled Halloumi cheese
- 2 tablespoons extra-virgin
- olive oil
- 2 tablespoons snipped fresh basil
- 2 garlic cloves, smashed

1. Pour the water into the Instant Pot and put the trivet in the pot. Place the tomatoes in the trivet. 2. Lock the lid. Select the Manual mode and set the cooking time for 3 minutes on High Pressure. When the timer goes off, perform a quick pressure release. Carefully open the lid. 3. Toss the tomatoes with the remaining ingredients and serve.

Parmesan Zoodles

Prep time: 5 minutes | Cook time: 5 minutes | Serves 2

- 1 large zucchini, trimmed and spiralized
- 1 tablespoon butter
- 1 garlic clove, diced
- ½ teaspoon chili flakes
- 3 ounces (85 g) Parmesan cheese, grated

1. Start by setting the Instant Pot to Sauté mode and melting the butter. Add the minced garlic and chili flakes to the pot, sautéing for 2 minutes or until fragrant. 2. Next, stir in the zucchini spirals and sauté for an additional 2 minutes, or until they become tender. 3. Add the grated Parmesan cheese to the pot and stir thoroughly. Continue to cook for 1 minute, or until the cheese has melted completely. 4. Transfer the mixture to a plate and serve immediately for the best flavor.

Braised Radishes with Sugar Snap Peas and Dukkah

Prep time: 20 minutes | Cook time: 5 minutes | Serves 4

- ¼ cup extra-virgin olive oil, divided
- 1 shallot, sliced thin
- 3 garlic cloves, sliced thin
- 1½ pounds (680 g) radishes, 2 cups greens reserved, radishes trimmed and halved if small or quartered if large
- ½ cup water
- ½ teaspoon table salt
- 8 ounces (227 g) sugar
- snap peas, strings removed, sliced thin on bias
- 8 ounces (227 g) cremini mushrooms, trimmed and sliced thin
- 2 teaspoons grated lemon zest plus 1 teaspoon juice
- 1 cup plain Greek yogurt
- ½ cup fresh cilantro leaves
- 3 tablespoons dukkah

1. Start by using the highest sauté function to heat 2 tablespoons of oil in the Instant Pot until it shimmers. Add the chopped shallot and sauté until softened, about 2 minutes. Stir in the minced garlic and cook until fragrant, about 30 seconds. Then, add the radishes, water, and salt to the pot. Secure the lid in place and close the pressure release valve. Select the high-pressure cooking function and set the timer for 1 minute. 2. After the cooking time is complete, turn off the Instant Pot and perform a quick release of the pressure. Carefully remove the lid, allowing the steam to escape away from you. Stir in the snap peas, cover the pot, and let the mixture sit until heated through, about 3 minutes. Then, add the radish greens, mushrooms, lemon zest and

juice, along with the remaining 2 tablespoons of oil, and gently toss to combine. Season with salt and pepper to taste. 3. To serve, spread ¼ cup of yogurt over the bottom of 4 individual serving plates. Using a slotted spoon, arrange the vegetable mixture on top of the yogurt and sprinkle with cilantro and dukkah. Enjoy your dish!

Simple Instant Pot Spaghetti Squash

Prep time: 5 minutes | Cook time: 7 minutes | Serves 4

- 1 spaghetti squash (about 2 pounds)

1. Cut the spaghetti squash in half crosswise and use a large spoon to remove the seeds. 2. Pour 1 cup of water into the electric pressure cooker and insert a wire rack or trivet. 3. Place the squash halves on the rack, cut-side up. 4. Close and lock the lid of the pressure cooker. Set the valve to sealing. 5. Cook on high pressure for 7 minutes. 6. When the cooking is complete, hit Cancel and quick release the pressure. 7. Once the pin drops, unlock and remove the lid. 8. With tongs, remove the squash from the pot and transfer it to a plate. When it is cool enough to handle, scrape the squash with the tines of a fork to remove the strands. Discard the skin.

Cauliflower Rice Curry

Prep time: 5 minutes | Cook time: 2 minutes | Serves 4

- 1 (9-ounce / 255-g) head cauliflower, chopped
- ½ teaspoon garlic powder
- ½ teaspoon freshly ground black pepper
- ½ teaspoon ground
- turmeric
- ½ teaspoon curry powder
- ½ teaspoon kosher salt
- ½ teaspoon fresh paprika
- ¼ small onion, thinly sliced

1. Begin by pouring 1 cup of filtered water into the inner pot of the Instant Pot, then insert the trivet. In a well-greased dish suitable for the Instant Pot, add the cauliflower. Sprinkle the garlic powder, black pepper, turmeric, curry powder, salt, paprika, and onion evenly over the cauliflower. 2. Carefully place the dish onto the trivet and cover it loosely with aluminum foil. Secure the lid, set the pressure release valve to Sealing, and select Manual mode. Adjust the cooking time to 2 minutes at High Pressure, then let it cook. 3. Once the cooking is complete, perform a quick release of the pressure. 4. Open the Instant Pot and carefully remove the dish. Serve the cauliflower warm and enjoy your meal!

Crispy Zucchini and Daikon Fritters

Prep time: 10 minutes | Cook time: 8 minutes | Serves 4

- 2 large zucchinis, grated
- 1 daikon, diced
- 1 egg, beaten
- 1 teaspoon ground flax
- meal
- 1 teaspoon salt
- 1 tablespoon coconut oil

1. In the mixing bowl, combine all the ingredients, except for the coconut oil. Form the zucchini mixture into fritters. 2. Press the Sauté button on the Instant Pot and melt the coconut oil. 3. Place the zucchini fritters in the hot oil and cook for 4 minutes on each side, or until golden brown. 4. Transfer to a plate and serve.

Spaghetti Squash Noodles with Tomato and Olive Sauce

Prep time: 15 minutes | Cook time: 14 to 16 minutes | Serves 4

- 1 medium spaghetti squash
- 1 cup water
- 2 tablespoons olive oil
- 1 small yellow onion, diced
- 6 garlic cloves, minced
- 2 teaspoons crushed red pepper flakes
- 2 teaspoons dried oregano
- 1 cup sliced cherry tomatoes
- 1 teaspoon kosher salt
- ½ teaspoon freshly ground black pepper
- 1 (14.5-ounce / 411-g) can sugar-free crushed tomatoes
- ¼ cup capers
- 1 tablespoon caper brine
- ½ cup sliced olives

1. With a sharp knife, halve the spaghetti squash crosswise. Using a spoon, scoop out the seeds and sticky gunk in the middle of each half. 2. Pour the water into the Instant Pot and place the trivet in the pot with the handles facing up. Arrange the squash halves, cut side facing up, on the trivet. 3. Lock the lid. Select the Manual mode and set the cooking time for 7 minutes on High Pressure. When the timer goes off, use a quick pressure release. Carefully open the lid. 4. Remove the trivet and pour out the water that has collected in the squash cavities. Using the tines of a fork, separate the cooked strands into spaghetti-like pieces and set aside in a bowl. 5. Pour the water out of the pot. Select the Sauté mode and heat the oil. 6. Add the onion to the pot and sauté for 3 minutes. Add the garlic, pepper flakes and oregano to the pot and sauté for 1 minute. 7. Stir in the cherry tomatoes, salt and black pepper and cook for 2 minutes, or until the tomatoes are tender. 8. Pour in the crushed tomatoes, capers, caper brine and olives and bring the mixture to a boil. Continue to cook for 2 to 3 minutes to allow the flavors to meld. 9. Stir in the spaghetti squash noodles and cook for 1 to 2 minutes to warm everything through. 10. Transfer the dish to a serving platter and serve.

Caramelized Onions

Prep time: 10 minutes | Cook time: 35 minutes | Serves 8

- 4 tablespoons margarine
- 6 large Vidalia or other sweet onions, sliced into
- thin half rings
- 10-ounce can chicken, or vegetable, broth

1. Start by pressing Sauté on the Instant Pot. Add the margarine and let it melt completely. 2. Once the margarine has melted, stir in the chopped onions and sauté for about 5 minutes until they become translucent. Then, pour in the broth and press Cancel to stop the sautéing. 3. Secure the lid on the Instant Pot and ensure that the vent is set to sealing. Select Manual mode and set the cooking time for 20 minutes. 4. When the cooking time is complete, manually release the pressure and carefully remove the lid. Press Sauté again and stir the onion mixture for about 10 more minutes to allow any excess liquid to evaporate.

Corn on the Cob

Prep time: 5 minutes | Cook time: 12 to 15 minutes | Serves 4

- 2 large ears fresh corn
- Olive oil for misting
- Salt, to taste (optional)

1. Start by shucking the corn, removing the silks, and washing the ears thoroughly. 2. Cut or break each ear of corn in half crosswise. 3. Lightly spray the corn with olive oil to coat. 4. Air fry the corn at 390ºF (199ºC) for 12 to 15 minutes, or until it reaches your desired level of browning. 5. Serve the corn plain or sprinkle with coarsely ground salt for added flavor.

Chapter 7

Desserts

Cardamom Coconut Rolls with Cream Cheese Frosting

Prep time: 20 minutes | Cook time: 18 minutes | Serves 5

- ½ cup coconut flour
- 1 tablespoon ground cardamom
- 2 tablespoon Swerve
- 1 egg, whisked
- ¼ cup almond milk
- 1 tablespoon butter, softened
- 1 tablespoon cream cheese
- ⅓ cup water

1. Combine together coconut flour, almond milk, and softened butter. 2. Knead the smooth dough. 3. Roll up the dough with the help of the rolling pin. 4. Then combine together Swerve and ground cardamom. 5. Sprinkle the surface of the dough with the ground cardamom mixture. 6. Roll the dough into one big roll and cut them into servings. 7. Place the rolls into the instant pot round mold. 8. Pour water in the instant pot (⅓ cup) and insert the mold inside. 9. Set Manual mode (High Pressure) for 18 minutes. 10. Then use the natural pressure release method for 15 minutes. 11. Chill the rolls to the room temperature and spread with cream cheese.

Chocolate Chip Banana Cake

Prep time: 15 minutes | Cook time: 25 minutes | Serves 8

- Nonstick cooking spray
- 3 ripe bananas
- ½ cup buttermilk
- 3 tablespoons honey
- 1 teaspoon vanilla extract
- 2 large eggs, lightly beaten
- 3 tablespoons extra-virgin olive oil
- 1½ cups whole wheat
- pastry flour
- ⅛ teaspoon ground nutmeg
- 1 teaspoon ground cinnamon
- ¼ teaspoon salt
- 1 teaspoon baking soda
- ⅓ cup dark chocolate chips

1. Begin by spraying a 7-inch Bundt pan with nonstick cooking spray to ensure easy removal of the cake. 2. In a large bowl, mash the bananas until smooth. Add the buttermilk, honey, vanilla extract, eggs, and olive oil, mixing well to combine all the ingredients. 3. In a separate medium bowl, whisk together the flour, nutmeg, cinnamon, salt, and baking soda until evenly blended. 4. Gradually add the flour mixture to the banana mixture, stirring until well combined. Fold in the chocolate chips, then pour the batter into the prepared Bundt pan and cover it with foil. 5. Pour 1 cup of water into the electric pressure cooker, then place the Bundt pan on the wire rack and carefully lower it into the pot. 6. Secure the lid of the pressure cooker and set the valve to sealing. 7. Cook on high pressure for 25 minutes. 8. When the cooking time is complete, press Cancel and perform a quick release of the pressure. 9. Once the pressure pin drops, carefully unlock and remove the lid. 10. Transfer the Bundt pan to a cooling rack, remove the foil, and let it cool for about 10 minutes. 11. After cooling, invert the cake onto the rack and allow it to cool for approximately an hour. 12. Once cooled, slice the cake and serve. Enjoy your delicious creation!

Quick Chocolate Coconut Mousse

Prep time: 10 minutes | Cook time: 4 minutes | Serves 1

- 1 egg yolk
- 1 teaspoon erythritol
- 1 teaspoon cocoa powder
- 2 tablespoons coconut
- milk
- 1 tablespoon cream cheese
- 1 cup water, for cooking

1. Pour water and insert the steamer rack in the instant pot. 2. Then whisk the egg yolk with erythritol. 3. When the mixture turns into lemon color, add coconut milk, cream cheese, and cocoa powder. Whisk the mixture until smooth. 4. Then pour it in the glass jar and place it on the steamer rack. 5. Close and seal the lid. 6. Cook the dessert on Manual (High Pressure) for 4 minutes. Make a quick pressure release.

Almond Cinnamon Daikon Cake

Prep time: 10 minutes | Cook time: 45 minutes | Serves 12

- 5 eggs, beaten
- ½ cup heavy cream
- 1 cup almond flour
- 1 daikon, diced
- 1 teaspoon ground
- cinnamon
- 2 tablespoon erythritol
- 1 tablespoon butter, melted
- 1 cup water

1. In the mixing bowl, mix up eggs, heavy cream, almond flour, ground cinnamon, and erythritol. 2. When the mixture is smooth, add daikon and stir it carefully with the help of the spatula. 3. Pour the mixture in the cake pan. 4. Then pour water and insert the trivet in the instant pot. 5. Place the cake in the instant pot. 6. Set the lid in place. Select the Manual mode and set the cooking time for 45 minutes on High Pressure. When the timer goes off, do a quick pressure release. Carefully open the lid. 7. Serve immediately.

Tapioca Berry Parfaits

Prep time: 10 minutes | Cook time: 6 minutes | Serves 4

- 2 cups unsweetened almond milk
- ½ cup small pearl tapioca, rinsed and still wet
- 1 teaspoon almond
- extract
- 1 tablespoon pure maple syrup
- 2 cups berries
- ¼ cup slivered almonds

1. Start by pouring the almond milk into the electric pressure cooker. Stir in the tapioca pearls and almond extract until well combined. 2. Secure the lid of the pressure cooker and set the valve to sealing. 3. Cook on High pressure for 6 minutes. 4. Once the cooking time is complete, press Cancel and allow the pressure to release naturally for 10 minutes before performing a quick release for any remaining pressure. 5. After the pin drops, carefully unlock and remove the lid. Lift the pot out of the cooker and place it on a cooling rack. 6. Stir in the maple syrup and allow the mixture to cool for about an hour. 7. In small glasses, layer the tapioca pudding with berries and almonds to create several beautiful layers. Refrigerate the glasses for 1 hour to chill. 8. Serve the dessert chilled for a refreshing treat!

Chipotle Black Bean Brownies

Prep time: 15 minutes | Cook time: 30 minutes | Serves 8

- Nonstick cooking spray
- ½ cup dark chocolate chips, divided
- ¾ cup cooked calypso beans or black beans
- ½ cup extra-virgin olive oil
- 2 large eggs
- ¼ cup unsweetened dark chocolate cocoa powder
- ⅓ cup honey
- 1 teaspoon vanilla extract
- ⅓ cup white wheat flour
- ½ teaspoon chipotle chili powder
- ½ teaspoon ground cinnamon
- ½ teaspoon baking powder
- ½ teaspoon kosher salt

1. Begin by spraying a 7-inch Bundt pan with nonstick cooking spray to prevent sticking. 2. In a small bowl, place half of the chocolate chips and microwave them for 30 seconds. Stir and continue microwaving in 15-second intervals until the chips are completely melted. 3. Using a food processor, blend the beans and oil together until smooth. Then, add the melted chocolate chips, eggs, cocoa powder, honey, and vanilla extract, blending until the mixture is completely smooth. 4. In a large mixing bowl, whisk together the flour, chili powder, cinnamon, baking powder, and salt. Pour the bean mixture from the food processor into the bowl and stir with a wooden spoon until everything is well combined. Fold in the remaining chocolate chips. 5. Pour the batter into the prepared Bundt pan and cover it loosely with aluminum foil. 6. Add 1 cup of water to the electric pressure cooker. 7. Place the Bundt pan on the wire rack and lower it into the pressure cooker. 8. Secure the lid of the pressure cooker and set the valve to sealing. 9. Cook on high pressure for 30 minutes. 10. When the cooking time is complete, press Cancel and perform a quick release of the pressure. 11. Once the pressure pin drops, unlock and carefully remove the lid. 12. Gently transfer the Bundt pan to a cooling rack and let it sit for about 10 minutes before inverting the cake onto the rack to cool completely. 13. Once cooled, slice the cake and serve. Enjoy!

Pumpkin Walnut Cheesecake

Prep time: 15 minutes | Cook time: 50 minutes | Serves 6

- 2 cups walnuts
- 3 tablespoons melted butter
- 1 teaspoon cinnamon
- 16 ounces (454 g) cream cheese, softened
- 1 cup powdered erythritol
- ⅓ cup heavy cream
- ⅔ cup pumpkin purée
- 2 teaspoons pumpkin spice
- 1 teaspoon vanilla extract
- 2 eggs
- 1 cup water

1. Preheat your oven to 350°F (180°C). In a food processor, combine the walnuts, butter, and cinnamon. Pulse until a ball forms, scraping down the sides as necessary. The dough should hold together when pressed. 2. Press the walnut mixture into a greased 7-inch springform pan and bake for 10 minutes or until it begins to brown. Remove from the oven and set aside while you prepare the cheesecake filling. 3. In a large bowl, stir the cream cheese until completely smooth. Using a rubber spatula, mix in the erythritol, heavy cream, pumpkin purée, pumpkin spice, and vanilla extract until well combined. 4. In a small bowl, whisk the eggs, then slowly add them to the cream cheese mixture, folding gently until just combined. 5. Pour the cheesecake mixture into the prepared crust and cover it with foil. Add water to the Instant Pot and place the steam rack at the bottom. Carefully place the springform pan on the steam rack, close the lid, and select the Cake button. Press the Adjust button to set the heat to More and set the timer for 40 minutes. 6. When the timer beeps, allow for a full natural release of pressure. Once the pressure indicator drops, carefully remove the pan and place it on the counter. Remove the foil and let the cheesecake cool for an additional hour before refrigerating. Serve chilled for the best flavor.

Creamy Pine Nut Mousse with Whipped Topping

Prep time: 5 minutes | Cook time: 35 minutes | Serves 8

- 1 tablespoon butter
- 1¼ cups pine nuts
- 1¼ cups full-fat heavy cream
- 2 large eggs
- 1 teaspoon vanilla extract
- 1 cup Swerve, reserve 1 tablespoon
- 1 cup water
- 1 cup full-fat heavy whipping cream

1. Butter the bottom and the side of a pie pan and set aside. 2. In a food processor, blend the pine nuts and heavy cream. Add the eggs, vanilla extract and Swerve and pulse a few times to incorporate. 3. Pour the batter into the pan and loosely cover with aluminum foil. Pour the water in the Instant Pot and place the trivet inside. Place the pan on top of the trivet. 4. Close the lid. Select Manual mode and set the timer for 35 minutes on High pressure. 5. In a small mixing bowl, whisk the heavy whipping cream and 1 tablespoon of Swerve until a soft peak forms. 6. When timer beeps, use a natural pressure release for 15 minutes, then release any remaining pressure and open the lid. 7. Serve immediately with whipped cream on top.

Almond Butter Chocolate Chip Blondies

Prep time: 10 minutes | Cook time: 20 minutes | Serves 8

- ½ cup creamy natural almond butter, at room temperature
- 4 large eggs
- ¾ cup Lakanto Monkfruit Sweetener Golden
- 1 teaspoon pure vanilla extract
- ½ teaspoon fine sea salt
- 1¼ cups almond flour
- ¾ cup stevia-sweetened chocolate chips

1. Pour 1 cup water into the Instant Pot. Line the base of a 7 by 3-inch round cake pan with a circle of parchment paper. Butter the sides of the pan and the parchment or coat with nonstick cooking spray. 2. Put the almond butter into a medium bowl. One at a time, whisk the eggs into the almond butter, then whisk in the sweetener, vanilla, and salt. Stir in the flour just until it is fully incorporated, followed by the chocolate chips. 3. Transfer the batter to the prepared pan and, using a rubber spatula, spread it in an even layer. Cover the pan tightly with aluminum foil. Place the pan on a long-handled silicone steam rack, then, holding the handles of the steam rack, lower it into the Instant Pot. 4. Secure the lid and set the Pressure Release to Sealing. Select the Cake, Pressure Cook, or Manual setting and set the cooking time for 40 minutes at high pressure. (The pot will take about 10 minutes to come up to pressure before the cooking program begins.) 5. When the cooking program ends, let the pressure release naturally for 10 minutes, then move the Pressure Release to Venting to release any remaining steam. Open the pot and, wearing heat-resistant mitts, grasp the handles of the steam rack and lift it out of the pot. Uncover the pan, taking care not to get burned by the steam or to drip condensation onto the blondies. Let the blondies cool in the pan on a cooling rack for about 5 minutes. 6. Run a butter knife around the edge of pan to make sure the blondies are not sticking to the pan sides. Invert the blondies onto the rack, lift off the pan, and peel off the parchment paper. Let cool for 15 minutes, then invert the blondies onto a serving plate and cut into eight wedges. The blondies will keep, stored in an airtight container in the refrigerator for up to 5 days, or in the freezer for up to 4 months.

Chocolate Cake with Walnuts

Prep time: 10 minutes | Cook time: 20 minutes | Serves 6

- 1 cup almond flour
- ⅔ cup Swerve
- ¼ cup unsweetened cocoa powder
- ¼ cup chopped walnuts
- 1 teaspoon baking powder
- 3 eggs
- ⅓ cup heavy (whipping) cream
- ¼ cup coconut oil
- Nonstick cooking spray

1. In a large bowl, combine the flour, Swerve, cocoa powder, walnuts, baking powder, eggs, cream, and coconut oil. Using a hand mixer on high speed, blend the ingredients until the mixture is well incorporated and fluffy, which helps prevent the cake from becoming too dense. 2. Grease a heatproof pan, such as a 3-cup Bundt pan that fits inside your Instant Pot, with cooking spray. Pour the prepared cake batter into the pan and cover it with aluminum foil. 3. Add 2 cups of water to the inner cooking pot of the Instant Pot, then place a trivet in the pot. Carefully position the pan on top of the trivet. 4. Secure the lid in place, select Manual mode, and set the pressure to High. Cook for 20 minutes. Once cooking is complete, allow the pressure to release naturally for 10 minutes before performing a quick release for any remaining pressure. 5. Carefully remove the pan from the Instant Pot and let it cool for 15 to 20 minutes. Invert the cake onto a plate. It can be enjoyed hot or at room temperature. Serve with a dollop of whipped cream if desired.

Creamy Pumpkin Pie Pudding with Whipped Cream

Prep time: 10 minutes | Cook time: 20 minutes | Serves 6

- Nonstick cooking spray
- 2 eggs
- ½ cup heavy (whipping) cream or almond milk (for dairy-free)
- ¾ cup Swerve
- 1 (15-ounce / 425-g) can pumpkin purée
- 1 teaspoon pumpkin pie spice
- 1 teaspoon vanilla extract
- For Serving:
- ½ cup heavy (whipping) cream

1. Grease a 6-by-3-inch pan extremely well with the cooking spray, making sure it gets into all the nooks and crannies. 2. In a medium bowl, whisk the eggs. Add the cream, Swerve, pumpkin purée, pumpkin pie spice, and vanilla, and stir to mix thoroughly. 3. Pour the mixture into the prepared pan and cover it with a silicone lid or aluminum foil. 4. Pour 2 cups of water into the inner cooking pot of the Instant Pot, then place a trivet in the pot. Place the covered pan on the trivet. 5. Lock the lid into place. Select Manual and adjust the pressure to High. Cook for 20 minutes. When the cooking is complete, let the pressure release naturally for 10 minutes, then quick-release any remaining pressure. Unlock the lid. 6. Remove the pan and place it in the refrigerator. Chill for 6 to 8 hours. 8. When ready to serve, finish by making the whipped cream. Using a hand mixer, beat the heavy cream until it forms soft peaks. Do not overbeat and turn it to butter. Serve each pudding with a dollop of whipped cream.

Classic Low-Carb Cheesecake with Almond Crust

Prep time: 30 minutes | Cook time: 45 minutes | Serves 8

- For Crust:
- 1½ cups almond flour
- 4 tablespoons butter, melted
- 1 tablespoon Swerve
- 1 tablespoon granulated erythritol
- ½ teaspoon ground cinnamon
- For Filling:
- 16 ounces (454 g) cream cheese, softened
- ½ cup granulated erythritol
- 2 eggs
- 1 teaspoon vanilla extract
- ½ teaspoon lemon extract
- 1½ cups water

1. To make the crust: In a medium bowl, combine the almond flour, butter, Swerve, erythritol, and cinnamon. Use a fork to press it all together. When completed, the mixture should resemble wet sand. 2. Spray the springform pan with cooking spray and line the bottom with parchment paper. 3. Press the crust evenly into the pan. Work the crust up the sides of the pan, about halfway from the top, and make sure there are no bare spots on the bottom. 4. Place the crust in the freezer for 20 minutes while you make the filling. 5. To make the filling: In the bowl of a stand mixer using the whip attachment, combine the cream cheese and erythritol on medium speed until the cream cheese is light and fluffy, 2 to 3 minutes. 6. Add the eggs, vanilla extract, and lemon extract. Mix until well combined. 7. Remove the crust from the freezer and pour in the filling. Cover the pan tightly with aluminum foil and place it on the trivet. 8. Add the water to the pot and carefully lower the trivet into the pot. 9. Close the lid. Select Manual mode and set cooking time for 45 minutes on High Pressure. 10. When timer beeps, use a quick pressure release and open the lid. 11. Remove the trivet and cheesecake from the pot. Remove the foil from the pan. The center of the cheesecake should still be slightly jiggly. If the cheesecake is still very jiggly in the center, cook for an additional 5 minutes on High pressure until the appropriate doneness is reached. 12. Let the cheesecake cool for 30 minutes on the counter before placing it in the refrigerator to set. Leave the cheesecake in the refrigerator for at least 6 hours before removing the sides of the pan, slicing, and serving.

Vanilla Poppy Seed Almond Cake

Prep time: 10 minutes | Cook time: 25 minutes | Serves 6

- 1 cup almond flour
- 2 eggs
- ½ cup erythritol
- 2 teaspoons vanilla extract
- 1 teaspoon lemon extract
- 1 tablespoon poppy seeds
- 4 tablespoons melted butter
- ¼ cup heavy cream
- ⅛ cup sour cream
- ½ teaspoon baking powder
- 1 cup water
- ¼ cup powdered erythritol, for garnish

1. In large bowl, mix almond flour, eggs, erythritol, vanilla, lemon, and poppy seeds. 2. Add butter, heavy cream, sour cream, and baking powder. 3. Pour into 7-inch round cake pan. Cover with foil. 4. Pour water into Instant Pot and place steam rack in bottom. Place baking pan on steam rack and click lid closed. Press the Cake button and press the Adjust button to set heat to Less. Set time for 25 minutes. 5. When timer beeps, allow a 15-minute natural release, then quick-release the remaining pressure. Let cool completely. Sprinkle with powdered erythritol for serving.

Almond Pie with Coconut

Prep time: 5 minutes | Cook time: 41 minutes | Serves 8

- 1 cup almond flour
- ½ cup coconut milk
- 1 teaspoon vanilla extract
- 2 tablespoons butter,
- softened
- 1 tablespoon Truvia
- ¼ cup shredded coconut
- 1 cup water

1. In a mixing bowl, combine almond flour, coconut milk, vanilla extract, melted butter, Truvia, and shredded coconut. Mix until the mixture is smooth and well blended. 2. Once smooth, transfer the mixture to a baking pan and flatten it evenly. 3. Pour water into the Instant Pot and insert the trivet inside. 4. Place the baking pan with the cake batter on top of the trivet. 5. Secure the lid of the Instant Pot, select Manual mode, and set the cooking time for 41 minutes at High Pressure. When the timer goes off, allow for a natural pressure release for 10 minutes, then release any remaining pressure. 6. Carefully open the lid and serve the cake immediately for the best flavor.

Lush Chocolate Cake

Prep time: 10 minutes | Cook time: 35 minutes | Serves 8

- For Cake:
- 2 cups almond flour
- ⅓ cup unsweetened cocoa powder
- 1½ teaspoons baking powder
- 1 cup granulated erythritol
- Pinch of salt
- 4 eggs
- 1 teaspoon vanilla extract
- ½ cup butter, melted and cooled
- 6 tablespoons strong
- coffee, cooled
- ½ cup water
- For Frosting:
- 4 ounces (113 g) cream cheese, softened
- ½ cup butter, softened
- ¼ teaspoon vanilla extract
- 2½ tablespoons powdered erythritol
- 2 tablespoons unsweetened cocoa powder

1. To make the cake, start by whisking together the almond flour, cocoa powder, baking powder, granulated erythritol, and salt in a large bowl. Ensure you whisk well to remove any lumps. 2. Add the eggs and vanilla extract to the dry ingredients and mix using a hand mixer until everything is combined. 3. With the mixer still on low speed, gradually pour in the melted butter and mix until fully incorporated. 4. Next, add the coffee and continue mixing on low speed until the batter is thoroughly combined. Be sure to scrape the sides and bottom of the bowl to ensure everything is well mixed. 5. Spray the cake pan with cooking spray to prevent sticking. Pour the batter into the prepared pan and cover it tightly with aluminum foil. 6. Add water to the Instant Pot. Place the cake pan on the trivet and carefully lower it into the pot. 7. Close the lid securely, select Manual mode, and set the cooking time for 35 minutes at High Pressure. 8. When the timer beeps, perform a quick pressure release and carefully open the lid. 9. Gently remove the cake pan from the pot and place it on a wire rack to cool. Once it's cool enough to touch, flip the cake onto a plate and let it cool completely before frosting. 10. To make the frosting, in a medium bowl, use the mixer to whip together the cream cheese, butter, and vanilla until light and fluffy, about 1 to 2 minutes. With the mixer running, slowly add the powdered erythritol and cocoa powder, mixing until everything is well combined. 11. Once the cake has completely cooled, spread the frosting generously over the top and down the sides of the cake.

Slow-Cooked Vanilla Butter Curd

Prep time: 5 minutes | Cook time: 6 hours | Serves 3

- 4 egg yolks, whisked
- 2 tablespoon butter
- 1 tablespoon erythritol
- ½ cup organic almond milk
- 1 teaspoon vanilla extract

1. Set the instant pot to Sauté mode and when the "Hot" is displayed, add butter. 2. Melt the butter but not boil it and add whisked egg yolks, almond milk, and vanilla extract. 3. Add erythritol. Whisk the mixture. 4. Cook the meal on Low for 6 hours.

Chocolate Pecan Clusters

Prep time: 5 minutes | Cook time: 5 minutes | Makes 8 clusters

- 3 tablespoons butter
- ¼ cup heavy cream
- 1 teaspoon vanilla extract
- 1 cup chopped pecans
- ¼ cup low-carb chocolate chips

1. Start by pressing the Sauté button on the Instant Pot and adding butter. Allow the butter to melt and begin to turn golden brown. Once it starts to brown, immediately add the heavy cream and press the Cancel button. 2. Stir in the vanilla extract and chopped pecans, then let the mixture cool for 10 minutes, stirring occasionally. 3. Spoon the mixture onto a parchment-lined baking sheet to form eight clusters, and scatter chocolate chips over the top of each cluster. 4. Place the baking sheet in the fridge to cool and set. Enjoy your delicious clusters!

Maple Goat Cheese–Stuffed Pears with Toasted Pistachios

Prep time: 6 minutes | Cook time: 2 minutes | Serves 4

- 2 ounces goat cheese, at room temperature
- 2 teaspoons pure maple syrup
- 2 ripe, firm pears, halved lengthwise and cored
- 2 tablespoons chopped pistachios, toasted

1. Pour 1 cup of water into the electric pressure cooker and insert a wire rack or trivet. 2. In a small bowl, combine the goat cheese and maple syrup. 3. Spoon the goat cheese mixture into the cored pear halves. Place the pears on the rack inside the pot, cut-side up. 4. Close and lock the lid of the pressure cooker. Set the valve to sealing. 5. Cook on high pressure for 2 minutes. 6. When the cooking is complete, hit Cancel and quick release the pressure. 7. Once the pin drops, unlock and remove the lid. 8. Using tongs, carefully transfer the pears to serving plates. 9. Sprinkle with pistachios and serve immediately.

Lemon-Ricotta Cheesecake

Prep time: 10 minutes | Cook time: 30 minutes | Serves 6

- Unsalted butter or vegetable oil, for greasing the pan
- 8 ounces (227 g) cream cheese, at room temperature
- ¼ cup plus 1 teaspoon Swerve, plus more as needed
- ⅓ cup full-fat or part-skim ricotta cheese, at room temperature
- Zest of 1 lemon
- Juice of 1 lemon
- ½ teaspoon lemon extract
- 2 eggs, at room temperature
- 2 tablespoons sour cream

1. Begin by greasing a 6-inch springform pan thoroughly. Using a silicone basting brush makes it easier to get into all the nooks and crannies. Alternatively, you can line the sides of the pan with parchment paper for easier removal. 2. In the bowl of a stand mixer, beat together the cream cheese, ¼ cup of Swerve, ricotta, lemon zest, lemon juice, and lemon extract on high speed until the mixture is smooth and free of lumps. 3. Taste the mixture to check the sweetness and adjust as needed. 4. Add the eggs to the mixture, then reduce the mixer speed to low. Gently blend until the eggs are just incorporated, being careful not to overbeat, as this can cause a cracked crust. 5. Pour the cream cheese mixture into the prepared springform pan and cover it with aluminum foil or a silicone lid. 6. Pour 2 cups of water into the inner cooking pot of the Instant Pot and insert a trivet. Carefully place the covered pan on the trivet. 7. Secure the lid on the Instant Pot, select Manual mode, and adjust the pressure to High. Cook for 30 minutes. Once cooking is complete, allow the pressure to release naturally, then unlock the lid. 8. Carefully remove the springform pan from the pot and take off the foil. 9. In a small bowl, mix the sour cream with the remaining 1 teaspoon of Swerve, then spread this mixture over the top of the warm cheesecake. 10. Refrigerate the cheesecake for 6 to 8 hours. Patience is key—this time is essential for the cheesecake to set perfectly and achieve its best flavor.

Nutmeg Almond Cupcakes with Creamy Vanilla Frosting

Prep time: 5 minutes | Cook time: 30 minutes | Serves 7

- Cake:
- 2 cups blanched almond flour
- 2 tablespoons grass-fed butter, softened
- 2 eggs
- ½ cup unsweetened almond milk
- ½ cup Swerve, or more to taste
- ½ teaspoon ground nutmeg
- ½ teaspoon baking powder
- Frosting:
- 4 ounces (113 g) full-fat cream cheese, softened
- 4 tablespoons grass-fed butter, softened
- 2 cups heavy whipping cream
- 1 teaspoon vanilla extract
- ½ cup Swerve, or more to taste
- 6 tablespoons sugar-free chocolate chips (optional)

1. Pour 1 cup of filtered water into the inner pot of the Instant Pot, then insert the trivet. In a large bowl, combine the flour, butter, eggs, almond milk, Swerve, nutmeg, and baking powder. Mix thoroughly. Working in batches if needed, transfer this mixture into a well-greased, Instant Pot-friendly muffin (or egg bites) mold. 2. Place the molds onto the trivet, and cover loosely with aluminum foil. Close the lid, set the pressure release to Sealing, and select Manual. Set the Instant Pot to 30 minutes on High Pressure, and let cook. 3. While you wait, in a large bowl, combine the cream cheese, butter, whipping cream, vanilla, Swerve, and chocolate chips. Use an electric hand mixer until you achieve a light and fluffy texture. Place frosting in refrigerator. 4. Once the cupcakes are cooked, let the pressure release naturally, for about 10 minutes. Then, switch the pressure release to Venting. Open the Instant Pot, and remove the food. Let cool, top each cupcake evenly with a scoop of frosting.

Coconut Almond Cream Cake

Prep time: 10 minutes | Cook time: 40 minutes | Serves 8

- Nonstick cooking spray
- 1 cup almond flour
- ½ cup unsweetened shredded coconut
- ⅓ cup Swerve
- 1 teaspoon baking powder
- 1 teaspoon apple pie spice
- 2 eggs, lightly whisked
- ¼ cup unsalted butter, melted
- ½ cup heavy (whipping) cream

1. Start by greasing a 6-inch round cake pan thoroughly with cooking spray. 2. In a medium bowl, combine the almond flour, shredded coconut, Swerve, baking powder, and apple pie spice, mixing well. 3. Add the eggs to the mixture, followed by the melted butter and heavy cream, mixing thoroughly after each addition. 4. Pour the batter into the prepared pan and cover it tightly with aluminum foil. 5. Pour 2 cups of water into the inner cooking pot of the Instant Pot, then place a trivet inside. Carefully place the cake pan on top of the trivet. 6. Secure the lid on the Instant Pot, select Manual mode, and set the pressure to High. Cook for 40 minutes. Once cooking is complete, allow the pressure to release naturally for 10 minutes, then perform a quick release for any remaining pressure. Unlock the lid. 7. Carefully remove the pan from the Instant Pot and let it cool for 15 to 20 minutes. Invert the cake onto a plate and, if desired, sprinkle with shredded coconut, almond slices, or powdered sweetener before serving. Enjoy!

Southern-Style Almond Cinnamon Pie

Prep time: 10 minutes | Cook time: 35 minutes | Serves 12

- 2 cups almond flour
- 1½ cups powdered erythritol
- 1 teaspoon baking powder
- Pinch of salt
- ½ cup sour cream
- 4 tablespoons butter,
- melted
- 1 egg
- 1 teaspoon vanilla extract
- Cooking spray
- 1½ teaspoons ground cinnamon
- 1½ teaspoons Swerve
- 1 cup water

1. In a large bowl, whisk together the almond flour, powdered erythritol, baking powder, and salt. 2. Add the sour cream, butter, egg, and vanilla and whisk until well combined. The batter will be very thick, almost like cookie dough. 3. Grease the baking dish with cooking spray. Line

with parchment paper, if desired. 4. Transfer the batter to the dish and level with an offset spatula. 5. In a small bowl, combine the cinnamon and Swerve. Sprinkle over the top of the batter. 6. Cover the dish tightly with aluminum foil. Add the water to the pot. Set the dish on the trivet and carefully lower it into the pot. 7. Set the lid in place. Select the Manual mode and set the cooking time for 35 minutes on High Pressure. When the timer goes off, do a quick pressure release. Carefully open the lid. 8. Remove the trivet and pie from the pot. Remove the foil from the pan. The pie should be set but soft, and the top should be slightly cracked. 9. Cool completely before cutting.

Warm Apple Crunch with Granola Topping

Prep time: 13 minutes | Cook time: 2 minutes | Serves 4

- 3 apples, peeled, cored, and sliced (about 1½ pounds)
- 1 teaspoon pure maple syrup
- 1 teaspoon apple pie spice or ground cinnamon
- ¼ cup unsweetened apple juice, apple cider, or water
- ¼ cup low-sugar granola

1. In the electric pressure cooker, combine the apples, maple syrup, apple pie spice, and apple juice. 2. Close and lock the lid of the pressure cooker. Set the valve to sealing. 3. Cook on high pressure for 2 minutes. 4. When the cooking is complete, hit Cancel and quick release the pressure. 5. Once the pin drops, unlock and remove the lid. 6. Spoon the apples into 4 serving bowls and sprinkle each with 1 tablespoon of granola.

Mini Strawberry Coconut Cheesecake

Prep time: 20 minutes | Cook time: 10 minutes | Serves 2

- 1 tablespoon gelatin
- 4 tablespoon water (for gelatin)
- 4 tablespoon cream
- cheese
- 1 strawberry, chopped
- ¼ cup coconut milk
- 1 tablespoon Swerve

1. Mix up gelatin and water and leave the mixture for 10 minutes. 2. Meanwhile, pour coconut milk in the instant pot. 3. Bring it to boil on Sauté mode, about 10 minutes. 4. Meanwhile, mash the strawberry and mix it up with cream cheese. 5. Add the mixture in the hot coconut milk and stir until smooth. 6. Cool the liquid for 10 minutes and add gelatin. Whisk it until gelatin is melted. 7. Then pour the cheesecake in the mold and freeze in the freezer for 3 hours.

Lemon and Ricotta Torte

Prep time: 15 minutes | Cook time: 35 minutes | Serves 12

- Cooking spray
- Torte:
- 1⅓ cups Swerve
- ½ cup (1 stick) unsalted butter, softened
- 2 teaspoons lemon or vanilla extract
- 5 large eggs, separated
- 2½ cups blanched almond flour
- 1¼ (10-ounce / 284-g) cups whole-milk ricotta
- cheese
- ¼ cup lemon juice
- 1 cup cold water
- Lemon Glaze:
- ½ cup (1 stick) unsalted butter
- ¼ cup Swerve
- 2 tablespoons lemon juice
- 2 ounces (57 g) cream cheese (¼ cup)
- Grated lemon zest and lemon slices, for garnish

1. Begin by lining a baking pan with parchment paper and spraying it with cooking spray. Set it aside. 2. To make the torte, place the Swerve, butter, and extract in the bowl of a stand mixer and blend for 8 to 10 minutes until well combined, scraping down the sides of the bowl as needed. 3. Add the egg yolks and continue blending until fully incorporated. Then, mix in the almond flour until smooth, followed by the ricotta and lemon juice. 4. In a separate medium bowl, whisk the egg whites until stiff peaks form. Gently fold the egg whites into the batter until well mixed. Pour the batter into the prepared pan and smooth the top. 5. Place a trivet in the bottom of your Instant Pot and add water. Use a foil sling to lower the baking pan onto the trivet, tucking in the sides of the sling. 6. Seal the lid, select Pressure Cook or Manual, and set the timer for 30 minutes. Once cooking is complete, allow the pressure to release naturally. 7. After the natural release, lock the lid again. Select Manual mode and set the cooking time for an additional 30 minutes at High Pressure. 8. When the timer beeps, perform a natural pressure release for 10 minutes, then carefully remove the lid. 9. Use the foil sling to lift the pan out of the Instant Pot and place the torte in the fridge for 40 minutes to chill before glazing. 10. Meanwhile, prepare the glaze by placing butter in a large pan over high heat and cooking for about 5 minutes until browned, stirring occasionally. Remove from heat and, while stirring the browned butter, add the Swerve. 11. Carefully mix in the lemon juice and cream cheese to the butter mixture. Allow the glaze to cool for a few minutes until it begins to thicken. 12. Once chilled, transfer the torte to a serving plate and pour the glaze over the top. Return it to the fridge to chill for an additional 30 minutes. 13. Before serving, scatter lemon zest on top of the torte and arrange lemon slices on the plate around it. 14. Serve and enjoy your delicious torte!

Traditional Kentucky Butter Cake

Prep time: 5 minutes | Cook time: 35 minutes | Serves 4

- 2 cups almond flour
- ¾ cup granulated erythritol
- 1½ teaspoons baking powder
- 4 eggs
- 1 tablespoon vanilla extract
- ½ cup butter, melted
- Cooking spray
- ½ cup water

1. In a medium bowl, whisk together the almond flour, erythritol, and baking powder until well combined and free of lumps. 2. Add the eggs and vanilla extract, whisking until the mixture is fully combined. 3. Incorporate the melted butter and continue whisking until the batter is mostly smooth and well mixed. 4. Grease the pan with cooking spray, then pour the batter into it. Cover the pan tightly with aluminum foil. 5. Pour water into the Instant Pot and place the Bundt pan on the trivet, carefully lowering it into the pot. 6. Secure the lid in place, select Manual mode, and set the cooking time for 35 minutes at High Pressure. When the timer beeps, perform a quick pressure release and carefully open the lid. 7. Remove the Bundt pan from the pot and allow the cake to cool in the pan before flipping it out onto a plate. Enjoy your delicious cake!

Candied Mixed Nuts

Prep time: 5 minutes | Cook time: 15 minutes | Serves 8

- 1 cup pecan halves
- 1 cup chopped walnuts
- ⅓ cup Swerve, or more to taste
- ⅓ cup grass-fed butter
- 1 teaspoon ground cinnamon

1. Preheat your oven to 350°F (180°C) and line a baking sheet with aluminum foil for easy cleanup. 2. While the oven is warming, pour ½ cup of filtered water into the inner pot of the Instant Pot, then add the pecans, walnuts, Swerve, butter, and cinnamon. Stir the nut mixture to combine, close the lid, and set the pressure valve to Sealing. Select Manual mode and cook at High Pressure for 5 minutes. 3. Once the cooking time is complete, perform a quick release by carefully switching the pressure valve to Venting. Strain the nuts and pour them onto the prepared baking sheet, spreading them out in an even layer. 4. Place the baking sheet in the oven and bake for 5 to 10 minutes, or until the nuts are crisp, being careful not to overcook. Allow the nuts to cool before serving. Store any leftovers in the refrigerator or freezer for later enjoyment.

Vanilla Cream Pie

Prep time: 20 minutes | Cook time: 35 minutes | Serves 12

- 1 cup heavy cream
- 3 eggs, beaten
- 1 teaspoon vanilla extract
- ¼ cup erythritol
- 1 cup coconut flour
- 1 tablespoon butter, melted
- 1 cup water, for cooking

1. In a mixing bowl, combine the coconut flour, erythritol, vanilla extract, eggs, and heavy cream, mixing until well combined. 2. Grease the baking pan with melted butter to prevent sticking. 3. Pour the coconut mixture into the prepared baking pan. 4. Add water to the Instant Pot and insert the steamer rack. 5. Carefully place the baking pan on the steamer rack. Close and seal the lid securely. 6. Set the Instant Pot to cook the pie on Manual mode at High Pressure for 35 minutes. 7. Once cooking is complete, allow for a natural pressure release for 10 minutes before opening the lid.

Crustless Key Lime Cheesecake

Prep time: 15 minutes | Cook time: 35 minutes | Serves 8

- Nonstick cooking spray
- 16 ounces light cream cheese (Neufchâtel), softened
- ⅔ cup granulated erythritol sweetener
- ¼ cup unsweetened Key lime juice (I like Nellie & Joe's Famous Key West
- Lime Juice)
- ½ teaspoon vanilla extract
- ¼ cup plain Greek yogurt
- 1 teaspoon grated lime zest
- 2 large eggs
- Whipped cream, for garnish (optional)

1. Start by spraying a 7-inch springform pan with nonstick cooking spray. Line the bottom and partway up the sides with aluminum foil for easy removal. 2. In a large bowl, add the cream cheese and use an electric mixer to whip it until smooth, which should take about 2 minutes. Next, incorporate the erythritol, lime juice, vanilla extract, yogurt, and lime zest, blending until the mixture is completely smooth. Stop the mixer and use a rubber spatula to scrape down the sides of the bowl. With the mixer on low speed, add the eggs one at a time, blending until just combined. Be careful not to overbeat the eggs. 3. Pour the cream cheese mixture into the prepared pan. Drape a paper towel over the top of the pan (ensuring it doesn't touch the mixture), and tightly wrap the top of the pan with foil to minimize moisture exposure. 4. Pour 1 cup of water into the electric pressure cooker. 5. Carefully place the foil-covered pan onto the wire rack and lower it into the pot. 6. Secure the lid of the pressure cooker and set the valve to sealing. 7. Set the cooker to high pressure and cook for 35 minutes. 8. Once the cooking is complete, press Cancel and allow the pressure to release naturally for 20 minutes before performing a quick release for any remaining pressure. 9. After the pin drops, unlock and carefully remove the lid. 10. Using the handles of the wire rack, carefully transfer the pan to a cooling rack. Allow it to cool to room temperature, then refrigerate for at least 3 hours to set. 11. When you're ready to serve, run a thin rubber spatula around the rim of the cheesecake to loosen it, and then remove the ring from the springform pan. 12. Slice the cheesecake into wedges and serve with whipped cream if desired. Enjoy your delicious dessert!

Quick Coconut Butter Squares

Prep time: 15 minutes | Cook time: 4 minutes | Serves 2

- ⅓ cup coconut flakes
- 1 tablespoon butter
- 1 egg, beaten
- 1 cup water, for cooking

1. Mix up together coconut flakes, butter, and egg. 2. Then put the mixture into the square shape mold and flatten well. 3. Pour water and insert the steamer rack in the instant pot. 4. Put the mold with dessert on the rack. Close and seal the lid. 5. Cook the meal on Manual mode (High Pressure) for 4 minutes. Make a quick pressure release. 6. Cool the cooked dessert little and cut into the squares.

Pandan Coconut Custard

Prep time: 10 minutes | Cook time: 30 minutes | Serves 4

- Nonstick cooking spray
- 1 cup unsweetened coconut milk
- 3 eggs
- ⅓ cup Swerve
- 3 to 4 drops pandan extract, or use vanilla extract if you must

1. Grease a 6-inch heatproof bowl with the cooking spray. 2. In a large bowl, whisk together the coconut milk, eggs, Swerve, and pandan extract. Pour the mixture into the prepared bowl and cover it with aluminum foil. 3. Pour 2 cups of water into the inner cooking pot of the Instant Pot, then place a trivet in the pot. Place the bowl on the trivet. 4. Lock the lid into place. Select Manual and adjust the pressure to High. Cook for 30 minutes. When the cooking is complete, let the pressure release naturally. Unlock the lid. 5. Remove the bowl from the pot and remove the foil. A knife inserted into the custard should come out clean. Cool in the refrigerator for 6 to 8 hours, or until the custard is set.

Glazed Pumpkin Bundt Cake

Prep time: 7 minutes | Cook time: 35 minutes | Serves 12

- Cake:
- 3 cups blanched almond flour
- 1 teaspoon baking soda
- ½ teaspoon fine sea salt
- 2 teaspoons ground cinnamon
- 1 teaspoon ground nutmeg
- 1 teaspoon ginger powder
- ¼ teaspoon ground cloves

- 6 large eggs
- 2 cups pumpkin purée
- 1 cup Swerve
- ¼ cup (½ stick) unsalted butter (or coconut oil for dairy-free), softened
- Glaze:
- 1 cup (2 sticks) unsalted butter (or coconut oil for dairy-free), melted
- ½ cup Swerve

1. In a large bowl, combine the almond flour, baking soda, salt, and spices. In another large bowl, whisk together the eggs, pumpkin puree, sweetener, and melted butter until smooth. Pour the wet ingredients into the dry ingredients and stir until well combined. 2. Grease a 6-cup Bundt pan thoroughly. Pour the batter into the prepared pan and cover it first with a paper towel, then with aluminum foil to trap moisture. 3. Place a trivet in the bottom of the Instant Pot and pour in 2 cups of cold water. Carefully set the Bundt pan on the trivet. 4. Secure the lid on the Instant Pot. Select Manual mode and set the cooking time for 35 minutes at High Pressure. 5. Once the timer beeps, allow a natural pressure release for 10 minutes before carefully removing the lid. 6. Let the cake cool in the pot for 10 minutes before removing it from the pan. 7. While the cake is cooling, prepare the glaze by mixing the butter and sweetener in a small bowl until well combined. Spoon the glaze over the warm cake for added flavor. 8. Allow the cake to cool for an additional 5 minutes before slicing and serving. Enjoy your delicious creation!

Coconut Lemon Squares

Prep time: 5 minutes | Cook time: 40 minutes | Serves 5 to 6

- 3 eggs
- 2 tablespoons grass-fed butter, softened
- ½ cup full-fat coconut milk
- ½ teaspoon baking powder

- ½ teaspoon vanilla extract
- ½ cup Swerve, or more to taste
- ¼ cup lemon juice
- 1 cup blanched almond flour

1. In a large bowl, combine the eggs, melted butter, coconut milk, baking powder, vanilla extract, Swerve, lemon juice, and flour. Stir thoroughly until the mixture is smooth and well combined. 2. Pour 1 cup of filtered water into the Instant Pot and insert the trivet. Transfer the batter into a well-greased, Instant Pot-friendly pan or dish. 3. If desired, use a sling to place the dish onto the trivet, then cover it loosely with aluminum foil. Close the lid, set the pressure release valve to Sealing, and select Manual mode. Set the Instant Pot to cook for 40 minutes on High Pressure. 4. After cooking, allow the pressure to naturally release for about 10 minutes, then carefully switch the pressure release to Venting. 5. Open the Instant Pot and remove the dish. Allow it to cool slightly, then cut into 6 squares. Serve and enjoy your delicious creation!

Ultimate Chocolate Cheesecake

Prep time: 10 minutes | Cook time: 50 minutes | Serves 12

- 2 cups pecans
- 2 tablespoons butter
- 16 ounces (454 g) cream cheese, softened
- 1 cup powdered erythritol
- ¼ cup sour cream
- 2 tablespoons cocoa powder

- 2 teaspoons vanilla extract
- 2 cups low-carb chocolate chips
- 1 tablespoon coconut oil
- 2 eggs
- 2 cups water

1. Preheat your oven to 400ºF (205ºC). In a food processor, combine the pecans and butter, pulsing until you achieve a dough-like consistency. Press this mixture into the bottom of a 7-inch springform pan. Bake for 10 minutes, then set aside to cool. 2. While the crust is baking, mix together the cream cheese, erythritol, sour cream, cocoa powder, and vanilla extract in a large bowl using a rubber spatula until well combined. Set this mixture aside. 3. In a medium bowl, combine the chocolate chips and coconut oil. Microwave in 20-second intervals until the chocolate starts to melt, then stir until smooth. Gently fold this melted chocolate mixture into the cheesecake mixture until well incorporated. 4. Add the eggs to the mixture and fold them in gently, taking care not to overmix. Pour the cheesecake batter over the cooled pecan crust and cover the pan with aluminum foil. 5. Pour water into the Instant Pot and place the steam rack at the bottom. Carefully place the cheesecake on the steam rack and secure the lid. 6. Press the Manual button and set the cooking time for 40 minutes. Once the timer beeps, allow for a natural release of pressure. 7. Carefully remove the cheesecake from the Instant Pot and let it cool completely. Once cooled, serve chilled for a delicious dessert!

Coconut Egg Custard Tarts

Prep time: 10 minutes | Cook time: 20 minutes | Serves 2

- ¼ cup almond flour
- 1 tablespoon coconut oil
- 2 egg yolks
- ¼ cup coconut milk
- 1 tablespoon erythritol
- 1 teaspoon vanilla extract
- 1 cup water, for cooking

1. Make the dough: Mix up almond flour and coconut oil. 2. Then place the dough into 2 mini tart molds and flatten well in the shape of cups. 3. Pour water in the instant pot. Insert the steamer rack. 4. Place the tart mold in the instant pot. Close and seal the lid. 5. Cook them for 3 minutes on Manual mode (High Pressure). Make a quick pressure release. 6. Then whisk together vanilla extract, erythritol, coconut milk, and egg yolks. 7. Pour the liquid in the tart molds and close the lid. 8. Cook the dessert for 7 minutes on Manual mode (High Pressure). 9. Then allow the natural pressure release for 10 minutes more.

Deconstructed Espresso Tiramisu Cups

Prep time: 5 minutes | Cook time: 9 minutes | Serves 4

- 1 cup heavy cream (or full-fat coconut milk for dairy-free)
- 2 large egg yolks
- 2 tablespoons brewed decaf espresso or strong brewed coffee
- 2 tablespoons Swerve, or more to taste
- 1 teaspoon rum extract
- 1 teaspoon unsweetened cocoa powder, or more to taste
- Pinch of fine sea salt
- 1 cup cold water
- 4 teaspoons Swerve, for topping

1. Heat the cream in a pan over medium-high heat until hot, about 2 minutes. 2. Place the egg yolks, coffee, sweetener, rum extract, cocoa powder, and salt in a blender and blend until smooth. 3. While the blender is running, slowly pour in the hot cream. Taste and adjust the sweetness to your liking. Add more cocoa powder, if desired. 4. Scoop the mixture into four ramekins with a spatula. Cover the ramekins with aluminum foil. 5. Place a trivet in the bottom of the Instant Pot and pour in the water. Place the ramekins on the trivet. 6. Lock the lid. Select the Manual mode and set the cooking time for 7 minutes at High Pressure. 7. When the timer beeps, use a quick pressure release. Carefully remove the lid. 8. Keep the ramekins covered with the foil and place in the refrigerator for about 2 hours until completely chilled.

9. Sprinkle 1 teaspoon of Swerve on top of each tiramisu. Use the oven broiler to melt the sweetener. 10. Put in the fridge to chill the topping, about 20 minutes. 11. Serve.

Blackberry Crisp

Prep time: 5 minutes | Cook time: 5 minutes | Serves 1

- 10 blackberries
- ½ teaspoon vanilla extract
- 2 tablespoons powdered erythritol
- ⅛ teaspoon xanthan gum
- 1 tablespoon butter
- ¼ cup chopped pecans
- 3 teaspoons almond flour
- ½ teaspoon cinnamon
- 2 teaspoons powdered erythritol
- 1 cup water

1. Start by placing the blackberries, vanilla extract, erythritol, and xanthan gum into a 4-inch ramekin. Stir gently to coat the blackberries evenly. 2. In a small bowl, mix together the remaining ingredients until well combined. Sprinkle this mixture over the blackberries and cover the ramekin with foil. 3. Secure the lid on the Instant Pot, press the Manual button, and set the cooking time for 4 minutes. Once the timer beeps, perform a quick release of the pressure. 4. Serve the dessert warm, and feel free to add a scoop of whipped cream on top for extra deliciousness!

Chai-Spiced Pear and Fig Compote

Prep time: 20 minutes | Cook time: 3 minutes | Serves 4

- 1 vanilla chai tea bag
- 1 (3-inch) cinnamon stick
- 1 strip lemon peel (about 2-by-½ inches)
- 1½ pounds pears, peeled
- and chopped (about 3 cups)
- ½ cup chopped dried figs
- 2 tablespoons raisins

1. Pour 1 cup of water into the electric pressure cooker and hit Sauté/More. When the water comes to a boil, add the tea bag and cinnamon stick. Hit Cancel. Let the tea steep for 5 minutes, then remove and discard the tea bag. 2. Add the lemon peel, pears, figs, and raisins to the pot. 3. Close and lock the lid of the pressure cooker. Set the valve to sealing. 4. Cook on high pressure for 3 minutes. 5. When the cooking is complete, hit Cancel and quick release the pressure. 6. Once the pin drops, unlock and remove the lid. 7. Remove the lemon peel and cinnamon stick. Serve warm or cool to room temperature and refrigerate.

Low-Carb Chocolate Chip Brownies

Prep time: 10 minutes | Cook time: 33 minutes | Serves 8

- 1½ cups almond flour
- ⅓ cup unsweetened cocoa powder
- ¾ cup granulated erythritol
- 1 teaspoon baking powder
- 2 eggs

- 1 tablespoon vanilla extract
- 5 tablespoons butter, melted
- ¼ cup sugar-free chocolate chips
- ½ cup water

1. In a large bowl, add the almond flour, cocoa powder, erythritol, and baking powder. Use a hand mixer on low speed to combine and smooth out any lumps. 2. Add the eggs and vanilla and mix until well combined. 3. Add the butter and mix on low speed until well combined. Scrape the bottom and sides of the bowl and mix again if needed. Fold in the chocolate chips. 4. Grease a baking dish with cooking spray. Pour the batter into the dish and smooth with a spatula. Cover tightly with aluminum foil. 5. Pour the water into the pot. Place the trivet in the pot and carefully lower the baking dish onto the trivet. 6. Close the lid. Select Manual mode and set cooking time for 33 minutes on High Pressure. 7. When timer beeps, use a quick pressure release and open the lid. 8. Use the handles to carefully remove the trivet from the pot. Remove the foil from the dish. 9. Let the brownies cool for 10 minutes before turning out onto a plate.

Fudgy Walnut Brownies

Prep time: 10 minutes | Cook time: 1 hour | Serves 12

- ¾ cup walnut halves and pieces
- ½ cup unsalted butter, melted and cooled
- 4 large eggs
- 1½ teaspoons instant coffee crystals
- 1½ teaspoons vanilla extract

- 1 cup Lakanto Monkfruit Sweetener Golden
- ¼ teaspoon fine sea salt
- ¾ cup almond flour
- ¾ cup natural cocoa powder
- ¾ cup stevia-sweetened chocolate chips

1. Begin by toasting the walnuts in a dry small skillet over medium heat, stirring frequently for about 5 minutes or until they are golden brown. Transfer the toasted walnuts to a bowl and let them cool. 2. Pour 1 cup of water into the Instant Pot. Line the bottom of a 7 by 3-inch round cake pan with a circle of parchment paper. Butter the sides of the pan and the parchment, or coat them with nonstick cooking spray for easy removal. 3. In a medium bowl, pour in the melted butter. Whisk in the eggs one at a time, followed by the coffee crystals, vanilla extract, sweetener, and salt. Finally, sift in the flour and cocoa powder, whisking just until combined. Using a rubber spatula, gently fold in the chocolate chips and toasted walnuts. 4. Transfer the brownie batter to the prepared pan, spreading it evenly with the spatula. Cover the pan tightly with aluminum foil. 5. Place the pan on a long-handled silicone steam rack, then carefully lower it into the Instant Pot. 6. Secure the lid and set the Pressure Release valve to Sealing. Select the Cake, Pressure Cook, or Manual setting and set the cooking time for 45 minutes at high pressure. (Keep in mind that the pot will take about 10 minutes to build pressure before cooking begins.) 7. When the cooking time ends, allow the pressure to release naturally for 10 minutes, then switch the Pressure Release to Venting to release any remaining steam. Carefully open the pot and, using heat-resistant mitts, grasp the handles of the steam rack to lift it out. Uncover the pan, being cautious of the hot steam and condensation. Let the brownies cool in the pan on a cooling rack for about 2 hours until they reach room temperature. 8. Once cooled, run a butter knife around the edge of the pan to ensure the brownies aren't sticking. Invert the brownies onto the cooling rack, remove the pan, and peel off the parchment paper. Finally, invert the brownies onto a serving plate and cut them into twelve wedges. The brownies can be stored in an airtight container in the refrigerator for up to 5 days or in the freezer for up to 4 months. Enjoy!

Chapter 8

Stews and Soups

Slow-Cooked Italian Vegetable and Ham Soup

Prep time: 20 minutes | Cook time: 5 to 9 hours | Serves 6

- 3 small carrots, sliced
- 1 small onion, chopped
- 2 small potatoes, diced
- 2 tablespoons chopped parsley
- 1 garlic clove, minced
- 3 teaspoons sodium-free beef bouillon powder
- 1¼ teaspoons dried basil
- ¼ teaspoon pepper
- 16-ounce can red kidney beans, undrained
- 3 cups water
- 14½-ounce can stewed tomatoes, with juice
- 1 cup diced, extra-lean, lower-sodium cooked ham

1. In the inner pot of the Instant Pot, layer the carrots, onion, potatoes, parsley, garlic, beef bouillon, basil, pepper, and kidney beans. Do not stir. Add water. 2. Secure the lid and cook on the Low Slow Cook mode for 8–9 hours, or on high 4½–5½ hours, until vegetables are tender. 3. Remove the lid and stir in the tomatoes and ham. Secure the lid again and cook on high Slow Cook mode for 10–15 minutes more.

All-Purpose Chicken Broth

Prep time: 10 minutes | Cook time: 1 hour 25 minutes | Makes 3 quarts

- 3 pounds (1.4 kg) chicken wings
- 1 tablespoon vegetable oil
- 1 onion, chopped
- 3 garlic cloves, lightly crushed and peeled
- 12 cups water, divided
- ½ teaspoon table salt
- 3 bay leaves

1. Begin by patting the chicken wings dry with paper towels. Using the highest sauté function, heat oil in the Instant Pot for about 5 minutes, or until it starts to smoke. Add half of the chicken wings to the pot and brown them on all sides for approximately 10 minutes. Once browned, transfer them to a bowl. Repeat the process with the remaining chicken wings and transfer them to the bowl as well. 2. Add the chopped onion to the remaining fat in the pot and cook until softened and well browned, about 8 to 10 minutes. Stir in the garlic and cook until fragrant, which should take about 30 seconds. Next, stir in 1 cup of water, scraping up any browned bits from the bottom of the pot. Then, add the remaining 11 cups of water, along with the salt, bay leaves, and the browned chicken wings along with any accumulated juices. 3. Secure the lid in place and close the pressure release valve. Select the high pressure cook function and set the timer for 1 hour. After cooking, turn off the Instant Pot and let the pressure release naturally for 15 minutes. Then, perform a quick release for any remaining pressure, carefully removing the lid while allowing steam to escape away from you. 4. Strain the broth through a fine-mesh strainer into a large container, pressing on the solids to extract as much liquid as possible; discard the solids. Use a wide, shallow spoon to skim off any excess fat from the surface of the broth. (The broth can be refrigerated for up to 4 days or frozen for up to 2 months.) Enjoy your homemade chicken broth!

Moroccan-Inspired Beef Stew with Eggplant and Potatoes

Prep time: 15 minutes | Cook time: 50 minutes | Serves 6 to 8

- 2 pounds (907 g) boneless short ribs, trimmed and cut into 1-inch pieces
- 1½ teaspoons table salt, divided
- 2 tablespoons extra-virgin olive oil
- 1 onion, chopped fine
- 3 tablespoons tomato paste
- ¼ cup all-purpose flour
- 3 garlic cloves, minced
- 1 tablespoon ground cumin
- 1 teaspoon ground turmeric
- 1 teaspoon ground cardamom
- ¾ teaspoon ground cinnamon
- 4 cups chicken broth
- 1 cup water
- 1 pound (454 g) eggplant, cut into 1-inch pieces
- 1 pound (454 g) Yukon Gold potatoes, unpeeled, cut into 1-inch pieces
- ½ cup chopped fresh mint or parsley

1. Pat beef dry with paper towels and sprinkle with 1 teaspoon salt. Using highest sauté function, heat oil in Instant Pot for 5 minutes (or until just smoking). Brown half of beef on all sides, 7 to 9 minutes; transfer to bowl. Set aside remaining uncooked beef. 2. Add onion to fat left in pot and cook, using highest sauté function, until softened, about 5 minutes. Stir in tomato paste, flour, garlic, cumin, turmeric, cardamom, cinnamon, and remaining ½ teaspoon salt. Cook until fragrant, about 1 minute. Slowly whisk in broth and water, scraping up any browned bits. Stir in eggplant and potatoes. Nestle remaining uncooked beef into pot along with browned beef, and add any accumulated juices. 3. Lock lid in place and close pressure release valve. Select high pressure cook function and cook for 30 minutes. Turn off Instant Pot and quick-release pressure. Carefully remove lid, allowing steam to escape away from you. 4. Using wide, shallow spoon, skim excess fat from surface of stew. Stir in mint and season with salt and pepper to taste. Serve.

Hearty Turkey Barley Vegetable Soup

Prep time: 5 minutes | Cook time: 20 minutes | Serves 8

- 2 tablespoons avocado oil
- 1 pound ground turkey
- 4 cups Chicken Bone Broth, low-sodium store-bought chicken broth, or water
- 1 (28-ounce) carton or can diced tomatoes
- 2 tablespoons tomato paste
- 1 (15-ounce) package
- frozen chopped carrots (about 2½ cups)
- 1 (15-ounce) package frozen peppers and onions (about 2½ cups)
- ⅓ cup dry barley
- 1 teaspoon kosher salt
- ¼ teaspoon freshly ground black pepper
- 2 bay leaves

1. Set the electric pressure cooker to the Sauté/More setting. When the pot is hot, pour in the avocado oil. 2. Add the turkey to the pot and sauté, stirring frequently to break up the meat, for about 7 minutes or until the turkey is no longer pink. Hit Cancel. 3. Add the broth, tomatoes and their juices, and tomato paste. Stir in the carrots, peppers and onions, barley, salt, pepper, and bay leaves. 4. Close and lock the lid of the pressure cooker. Set the valve to sealing. 5. Cook on high pressure for 20 minutes. 6. When the cooking is complete, hit Cancel and allow the pressure to release naturally for 10 minutes, then quick release any remaining pressure. 7. Once the pin drops, unlock and remove the lid. Discard the bay leaves. 8. Spoon into bowls and serve.

Green Chile Corn Chowder

Prep time: 20 minutes | Cook time: 7 to 8 hours | Serves 8

- 16-ounce can cream-style corn
- 3 potatoes, peeled and diced
- 2 tablespoons chopped fresh chives
- 4-ounce can diced green chilies, drained
- 2-ounce jar chopped
- pimentos, drained
- ½ cup chopped cooked ham
- 2 10½-ounce cans 100% fat-free lower-sodium chicken broth
- Pepper to taste
- Tabasco sauce to taste
- 1 cup fat-free milk

1. In the inner pot of the Instant Pot, combine all ingredients except for the milk. 2. Secure the lid and select the Slow Cook function, setting it to low for 7 to 8 hours, or until the potatoes are tender. 3. Once the cooking time is complete, remove the lid and stir in the milk. Cover the pot again and let it simmer for an additional 20 minutes to heat through. Enjoy your dish!

Salmon and Tomatillos Stew

Prep time: 15 minutes | Cook time: 12 minutes | Serves 2

- 10 ounces (283 g) salmon fillet, chopped
- 2 tomatillos, chopped
- ½ teaspoon ground turmeric
- 1 cup coconut cream
- 1 teaspoon ground paprika
- ½ teaspoon salt

1. Add all ingredients to the Instant Pot and stir well to combine. 2. Close the lid securely, select Manual mode, and set the cooking time for 12 minutes at Low Pressure. 3. When the timer beeps, perform a quick pressure release and carefully open the lid. 4. Serve the dish warm and enjoy!

Hearty Venison and Tomato Stew with Mushrooms and Cauliflower

Prep time: 12 minutes | Cook time: 42 minutes | Serves 8

- 1 tablespoon unsalted butter
- 1 cup diced onions
- 2 cups button mushrooms, sliced in half
- 2 large stalks celery, cut into ¼-inch pieces
- Cloves squeezed from 2 heads roasted garlic or 4 cloves garlic, minced
- 2 pounds (907 g) boneless venison or beef roast, cut into 4 large pieces
- 5 cups beef broth
- 1 (14½-ounce / 411-g)
- can diced tomatoes
- 1 teaspoon fine sea salt
- 1 teaspoon ground black pepper
- ½ teaspoon dried rosemary, or 1 teaspoon fresh rosemary, finely chopped
- ½ teaspoon dried thyme leaves, or 1 teaspoon fresh thyme leaves, finely chopped
- ½ head cauliflower, cut into large florets
- Fresh thyme leaves, for garnish

1. Place the butter in the Instant Pot and press Sauté. Once melted, add the onions and sauté for 4 minutes, or until soft. 2. Add the mushrooms, celery, and garlic and sauté for another 3 minutes, or until the mushrooms are golden brown. Press Cancel to stop the Sauté. Add the roast, broth, tomatoes, salt, pepper, rosemary, and thyme. 3. Seal the lid, press Manual, and set the timer for 30 minutes. Once finished, turn the valve to venting for a quick release. 4. Add the cauliflower. Seal the lid, press Manual, and set the timer for 5 minutes. Once finished, let the pressure release naturally. 5. Remove the lid and shred the meat with two forks. Taste the liquid and add more salt, if needed. Ladle the stew into bowls. Garnish with thyme leaves.

Cauliflower Rice Chicken Thigh Soup with Vegetables and Herbs

Prep time: 15 minutes | Cook time: 13 minutes | Serves 5

- 2 cups cauliflower florets
- 1 pound (454 g) boneless, skinless chicken thighs
- 4½ cups chicken broth
- ½ yellow onion, chopped
- 2 garlic cloves, minced
- 1 tablespoon unflavored gelatin powder
- 2 teaspoons sea salt
- ½ teaspoon ground black pepper
- ½ cup sliced zucchini
- ⅓ cup sliced turnips
- 1 teaspoon dried parsley
- 3 celery stalks, chopped
- 1 teaspoon ground turmeric
- ½ teaspoon dried marjoram
- 1 teaspoon dried thyme
- ½ teaspoon dried oregano

1. Add the cauliflower florets to a food processor and pulse until a ricelike consistency is achieved. Set aside. 2. Add the chicken thighs, chicken broth, onions, garlic, gelatin powder, sea salt, and black pepper to the pot. Gently stir to combine. 3. Lock the lid. Select Manual mode and set cooking time for 10 minutes on High Pressure. 4. When cooking is complete, quick release the pressure and open the lid. 5. Transfer the chicken thighs to a cutting board. Chop the chicken into bite-sized pieces and then return the chopped chicken to the pot. 6. Add the cauliflower rice, zucchini, turnips, parsley, celery, turmeric, marjoram, thyme, and oregano to the pot. Stir to combine. 7. Lock the lid. Select Manual mode and set cooking time for 3 minutes on High Pressure. 8. When cooking is complete, quick release the pressure. 9. Open the lid. Ladle the soup into serving bowls. Serve hot.

Tomato-Basil Parmesan Soup

Prep time: 5 minutes | Cook time: 12 minutes | Serves 12

- 2 tablespoons unsalted butter or coconut oil
- ½ cup finely diced onions
- Cloves squeezed from 1 head roasted garlic , or 2 cloves garlic, minced
- 1 tablespoon dried basil leaves
- 1 teaspoon dried oregano leaves
- 1 (8 ounces / 227 g) package cream cheese,
- softened
- 4 cups chicken broth
- 2 (14½ ounces / 411 g) cans diced tomatoes
- 1 cup shredded Parmesan cheese, plus more for garnish
- 1 teaspoon fine sea salt
- ¼ teaspoon ground black pepper
- Fresh basil leaves, for garnish

1. Begin by placing the butter in the Instant Pot and pressing the Sauté button. Once the butter has melted, add the onions, garlic, basil, and oregano, cooking while stirring often for about 4 minutes, or until the onions are soft. Press Cancel to stop the sautéing process. 2. Add the cream cheese to the pot and whisk it to loosen; using a whisk is essential to avoid clumps in the soup. Gradually whisk in the broth until well combined. Next, add the tomatoes, Parmesan cheese, salt, and pepper, stirring to combine all the ingredients. 3. Secure the lid on the Instant Pot, press the Manual button, and set the timer for 8 minutes. Once the cooking time is up, turn the valve to venting for a quick pressure release. 4. Carefully remove the lid and purée the soup using a stick blender until smooth. Alternatively, you can transfer the soup to a standard blender or food processor and blend until smooth. If using a regular blender, you may need to process the soup in batches to avoid overfilling the jar. 5. Adjust the seasoning with additional salt and pepper if desired. Ladle the soup into bowls and garnish with extra Parmesan cheese and basil leaves before serving. Enjoy your delicious soup!

Silky Spiced Carrot Soup with Pomegranate Drizzle

Prep time: 15 minutes | Cook time: 10 minutes | Serves 6 to 8

- 2 tablespoons extra-virgin olive oil
- 2 onions, chopped
- 1 teaspoon table salt
- 1 tablespoon grated fresh ginger
- 1 tablespoon ground coriander
- 1 tablespoon ground fennel
- 1 teaspoon ground cinnamon
- 4 cups vegetable or
- chicken broth
- 2 cups water
- 2 pounds (907 g) carrots, peeled and cut into 2-inch pieces
- ½ teaspoon baking soda
- 2 tablespoons pomegranate molasses
- ½ cup plain Greek yogurt
- ½ cup hazelnuts, toasted, skinned, and chopped
- ½ cup chopped fresh cilantro or mint

1. Using highest sauté function, heat oil in Instant Pot until shimmering. Add onions and salt and cook until onions are softened, about 5 minutes. Stir in ginger, coriander, fennel, and cinnamon and cook until fragrant, about 30 seconds. Stir in broth, water, carrots, and baking soda. 2. Lock lid in place and close pressure release valve. Select high pressure cook function and cook for 3 minutes. Turn off Instant Pot and quick-release pressure. Carefully remove lid, allowing steam to escape away from you. 3. Working in batches, process soup in blender until smooth, 1 to 2 minutes. Return processed soup to Instant Pot and bring to simmer using highest sauté function. Season with salt and pepper to taste. Drizzle individual portions with pomegranate molasses and top with yogurt, hazelnuts, and cilantro before serving.

Cauliflower Soup

Prep time: 10 minutes | Cook time: 6 minutes | Serves 4

- 2 cups chopped cauliflower
- 2 tablespoons fresh cilantro
- 1 cup coconut cream
- 2 cups beef broth
- 3 ounces (85 g) Provolone cheese, chopped

1. Begin by adding the cauliflower, cilantro, coconut cream, beef broth, and cheese to the Instant Pot. Stir everything together until well mixed. 2. Select Manual mode and set the cooking time for 6 minutes at High Pressure. 3. When the timer beeps, allow the pressure to release naturally for 4 minutes, then carefully release any remaining pressure before opening the lid. 4. Blend the soup until smooth, then ladle it into bowls for serving. Enjoy your delicious soup!

Gigante Bean Soup with Celery and Olives

Prep time: 30 minutes | Cook time: 12 minutes | Serves 6 to 8

- 1½ tablespoons table salt, for brining
- 1 pound (454 g) dried gigante beans, picked over and rinsed
- 2 tablespoons extra-virgin olive oil, plus extra for drizzling
- 5 celery ribs, cut into ½-inch pieces, plus ½ cup leaves, minced
- 1 onion, chopped
- ½ teaspoon table salt
- 4 garlic cloves, minced
- 4 cups vegetable or chicken broth
- 4 cups water
- 2 bay leaves
- ½ cup pitted kalamata olives, chopped
- 2 tablespoons minced fresh marjoram or oregano
- Lemon wedges

1. In a large container, dissolve 1½ tablespoons of salt in 2 quarts of cold water. Add the beans and soak them at room temperature for at least 8 hours, or up to 24 hours. After soaking, drain and rinse the beans thoroughly. 2. Set the Instant Pot to the highest sauté function and heat oil until it shimmers. Add the chopped celery, onion, and ½ teaspoon of salt, cooking until the vegetables are softened, about 5 minutes. Stir in the garlic and cook until fragrant, about 30 seconds. Then, add the broth, water, soaked beans, and bay leaves to the pot. 3. Secure the lid on the Instant Pot and close the pressure release valve. Select the high pressure cooking function and set the timer for 6 minutes. Once the cooking time is complete, turn off the Instant Pot and let the pressure release naturally for 15 minutes. After that, perform a quick release for any remaining pressure and carefully remove the lid, allowing the steam to escape away from you. 4. In a separate bowl, combine the celery leaves, olives, and marjoram. Discard the bay leaves from the soup. Season the soup with salt and pepper to taste. Serve individual portions topped with the celery-olive mixture and a drizzle of extra oil, alongside lemon wedges for added flavor. Enjoy your delicious soup!

Green Garden Vegetable Soup with Kale and Cauliflower

Prep time: 20 minutes | Cook time: 29 minutes | Serves 5

- 1 tablespoon olive oil
- 1 garlic clove, diced
- ½ cup cauliflower florets
- 1 cup kale, chopped
- 2 tablespoons chives, chopped
- 1 teaspoon sea salt
- 6 cups beef broth

1. Heat the olive oil in the Instant Pot on Sauté mode for 2 minutes and add the garlic. Sauté for 2 minutes or until fragrant. 2. Add cauliflower, kale, chives, sea salt, and beef broth. 3. Close the lid. Select Manual mode and set cooking time for 5 minutes on High Pressure. 4. When timer beeps, use a quick pressure release and open the lid. 5. Ladle the soup into the bowls. Serve warm.

Butternut Squash Soup

Prep time: 30 minutes | Cook time: 15 minutes | Serves 4

- 2 tablespoons margarine
- 1 large onion, chopped
- 2 cloves garlic, minced
- 1 teaspoon thyme
- ½ teaspoon sage
- Salt and pepper to taste
- 2 large butternut squash, peeled, seeded, and cubed (about 4 pounds)
- 4 cups low-sodium chicken stock

1. Start by melting the margarine in the inner pot of the Instant Pot using the Sauté function. 2. Once melted, add the onion and garlic, cooking until they become soft, about 3 to 5 minutes. 3. Next, add thyme and sage, cooking for an additional minute. Season with salt and pepper to taste. 4. Stir in the butternut squash and pour in the chicken stock. 5. Secure the lid, ensuring the vent is set to sealing. Using the Manual setting, cook the squash and seasonings at high pressure for 10 minutes. 6. When the cooking time is complete, perform a quick release of the pressure. 7. Puree the soup in a food processor or use an immersion blender directly in the pot. If the soup is too thick, add more stock to achieve your desired consistency. Adjust the seasoning with additional salt and pepper as needed. Enjoy your delicious soup!

Beef Oxtail Soup with White Beans, Tomatoes, and Aleppo Pepper

Prep time: 20 minutes | Cook time: 1 hour 10 minutes | Serves 6 to 8

- 4 pounds (1.8 kg) oxtails, trimmed
- 1 teaspoon table salt
- 1 tablespoon extra-virgin olive oil
- 1 onion, chopped fine
- 2 carrots, peeled and chopped fine
- ¼ cup ground dried Aleppo pepper
- 6 garlic cloves, minced
- 2 tablespoons tomato paste
- ¾ teaspoon dried oregano
- ½ teaspoon ground
- cinnamon
- ½ teaspoon ground cumin
- 6 cups water
- 1 (28-ounce / 794-g) can diced tomatoes, drained
- 1 (15-ounce / 425-g) can navy beans, rinsed
- 1 tablespoon sherry vinegar
- ¼ cup chopped fresh parsley
- ½ preserved lemon, pulp and white pith removed, rind rinsed and minced (2 tablespoons)

1. Begin by patting the oxtails dry with paper towels and sprinkling them generously with salt. Using the highest sauté function, heat oil in the Instant Pot for about 5 minutes, or until it is just smoking. Brown half of the oxtails for 4 to 6 minutes on each side, then transfer them to a plate. Set aside the uncooked oxtails. 2. In the remaining fat in the pot, add the chopped onion and carrots, cooking on the highest sauté setting until they soften, about 5 minutes. Stir in the Aleppo pepper, minced garlic, tomato paste, oregano, cinnamon, and cumin, cooking until fragrant for about 30 seconds. Pour in water, scraping up any browned bits from the bottom, then add the diced tomatoes. Nestle the uncooked oxtails back into the pot along with the browned oxtails and any accumulated juices. 3. Secure the lid in place and close the pressure release valve. Select the high pressure cooking function and set the timer for 45 minutes. Once the cooking time is complete, turn off the Instant Pot and perform a quick release of the pressure. Carefully open the lid, allowing steam to escape away from you. 4. Transfer the oxtails to a cutting board and let them cool slightly. Use two forks to shred the meat into bite-sized pieces, discarding the bones and excess fat. Strain the broth through a fine-mesh strainer into a large container, returning the solids to the now-empty pot. Use a wide, shallow spoon to skim off any excess fat from the surface of the liquid, then return the broth to the pot. 5. Stir the shredded oxtails along with any accumulated juices and beans back into the pot. Using the highest sauté function, cook until the soup is heated through, about 5 minutes. Stir in the vinegar and chopped parsley, then season with salt and pepper to taste. Serve the soup warm, passing preserved lemon separately for added flavor. Enjoy!

Creamy Button Mushroom Soup

Prep time: 10 minutes | Cook time: 10 minutes | Serves 4

- 1 pound (454 g) sliced button mushrooms
- 3 tablespoons butter
- 2 tablespoons diced onion
- 2 cloves garlic, minced
- 2 cups chicken broth
- ½ teaspoon salt
- ¼ teaspoon pepper
- ½ cup heavy cream
- ¼ teaspoon xanthan gum

1. Press the Sauté button and then press the Adjust button to set heat to Less. Add mushrooms, butter, and onion to pot. Sauté for 5 to 8 minutes or until onions and mushrooms begin to brown. Add garlic and sauté until fragrant. Press the Cancel button. 2. Add broth, salt, and pepper. Click lid closed. Press the Manual button and adjust time for 3 minutes. When timer beeps, quick-release the pressure. Stir in heavy cream and xanthan gum. Allow a few minutes to thicken and serve warm.

Summer Vegetable Soup

Prep time: 10 minutes | Cook time: 6 minutes | Serves 6

- 3 cups finely sliced leeks
- 6 cups chopped rainbow chard, stems and leaves separated
- 1 cup chopped celery
- 2 tablespoons minced garlic, divided
- 1 teaspoon dried oregano
- 1 teaspoon salt
- 2 teaspoons freshly ground black pepper
- 3 cups chicken broth, plus more as needed
- 2 cups sliced yellow summer squash, ½-inch slices
- ¼ cup chopped fresh parsley
- ¾ cup heavy (whipping) cream
- 4 to 6 tablespoons grated Parmesan cheese

1. Begin by adding the leeks, chard, celery, 1 tablespoon of garlic, oregano, salt, pepper, and broth to the inner pot of the Instant Pot. 2. Secure the lid in place. Select the Manual setting and adjust the pressure to High, then cook for 3 minutes. Once the cooking time is complete, quick-release the pressure and unlock the lid. 3. If necessary, add more broth to achieve your desired consistency. 4. Switch the pot to the Sauté function and increase the heat to high. Add the yellow squash, parsley, and the remaining 1 tablespoon of garlic. 5. Cook for 2 to 3 minutes, or until the squash is tender and fully cooked. 6. Stir in the cream, then ladle the soup into bowls. Top each serving with a sprinkle of Parmesan cheese before serving. Enjoy your delicious soup!

Pork and Daikon Stew

Prep time: 15 minutes | Cook time: 3 minutes | Serves 6

- 1 pound (454 g) pork tenderloin, chopped
- 1 ounce (28 g) green onions, chopped
- ½ cup daikon, chopped
- 1 lemon slice
- 1 tablespoon heavy cream
- 1 tablespoon butter
- 1 teaspoon ground black pepper
- 3 cups water

1. Add all ingredients to the Instant Pot and use a spatula to stir them together until well mixed. 2. Secure the lid on the pot. Set it to Manual mode and adjust the cooking time to 20 minutes at High Pressure. 3. Once the cooking is finished, allow for a natural pressure release for 15 minutes, then carefully release any remaining pressure before opening the lid. 4. Serve the dish warm and enjoy!

Savory Beef Stew with Mushrooms, Turnips, and Parsnips

Prep time: 0 minutes | Cook time: 55 minutes | Serves 6

- 1½ pounds beef stew meat
- ¾ teaspoon fine sea salt
- ¾ teaspoon freshly ground black pepper
- 1 tablespoon cold-pressed avocado oil
- 3 garlic cloves, minced
- 1 yellow onion, diced
- 2 celery stalks, diced
- 8 ounces cremini mushrooms, quartered
- 1 cup low-sodium roasted beef bone broth
- 2 tablespoons Worcestershire sauce
- 1 tablespoon Dijon mustard
- 1 teaspoon dried rosemary, crumbled
- 1 bay leaf
- 3 tablespoons tomato paste
- 8 ounces carrots, cut into 1-inch-thick rounds
- 1 pound turnips, cut into 1-inch pieces
- 1 pound parsnips, halved lengthwise, then cut crosswise into 1-inch pieces

1. Sprinkle the beef all over with the salt and pepper. 2. Select the Sauté setting on the Instant Pot and heat the oil and garlic for 2 minutes, until the garlic is bubbling but not browned. Add the onion, celery, and mushrooms and sauté for 5 minutes, until the onion begins to soften and the mushrooms are giving up their liquid. Stir in the broth, Worcestershire sauce, mustard, rosemary, and bay leaf. Stir in the beef. Add the tomato paste in a dollop on top. Do not stir it in. 3. Secure the lid and set the Pressure Release to Sealing. Press the Cancel button to reset the cooking program, then select the Meat/Stew, Pressure Cook, or Manual setting and set the cooking time for 20 minutes at high pressure. (The pot will take about 10 minutes to come up to pressure before the cooking program begins.) 4. When the cooking program ends, perform a quick pressure release by moving the Pressure Release to Venting, or let the pressure release naturally. Open the pot, remove and discard the bay leaf, and stir in the tomato paste. Place the carrots, turnips, and parsnips on top of the meat. 5. Secure the lid and set the Pressure Release to Sealing. Press the Cancel button to reset the cooking program, then select the Pressure Cook or Manual setting and set the cooking time for 3 minutes at low pressure. (The pot will take about 15 minutes to come up to pressure before the cooking program begins.) 6. When the cooking program ends, perform a quick pressure release by moving the Pressure Release to Venting. Open the pot and stir to combine all of the ingredients. 7. Ladle the stew into bowls and serve hot.

Hearty Garlic Beef Soup with Bacon and Avocado

Prep time: 12 minutes | Cook time: 42 minutes | Serves 8

- 10 strips bacon, chopped
- 1 medium white onion, chopped
- Cloves squeezed from 3 heads roasted garlic, or 6 cloves garlic, minced
- 1 to 2 jalapeño peppers, seeded and chopped (optional)
- 2 pounds (907 g) boneless beef chuck roast, cut into 4 equal-sized pieces
- 5 cups beef broth
- 1 cup chopped fresh cilantro, plus more for garnish
- 2 teaspoons fine sea salt
- 1 teaspoon ground black pepper
- For Garnish:
- 1 avocado, peeled, pitted, and diced
- 2 radishes, very thinly sliced
- 2 tablespoons chopped fresh chives

1. Place the bacon in the Instant Pot and press Sauté. Cook, stirring occasionally, for 4 minutes, or until the bacon is crisp. Remove the bacon with a slotted spoon, leaving the drippings in the pot. Set the bacon on a paper towel-lined plate to drain. 2. Add the onion, garlic, and jalapeños, if using, to the Instant Pot and sauté for 3 minutes, or until the onion is soft. Press Cancel to stop the Sauté. 3. Add the beef, broth, cilantro, salt, and pepper. Stir to combine. 4. Seal the lid, press Manual, and set the timer for 35 minutes. Once finished, let the pressure release naturally. 5. Remove the lid and shred the beef with two forks. Taste the liquid and add more salt, if needed. 6. Ladle the soup into bowls. Garnish with the reserved bacon, avocado, radishes, chives, and more cilantro.

Lamb and Broccoli Soup

Prep time: 10 minutes | Cook time: 25 minutes | Serves 4

- 7 ounces (198 g) lamb fillet, chopped
- 1 tablespoon avocado oil
- ½ cup broccoli, roughly chopped
- ¼ daikon, chopped
- 2 bell peppers, chopped
- ¼ teaspoon ground cumin
- 5 cups beef broth

1. In the Instant Pot, sauté the lamb fillet with avocado oil for about 5 minutes until browned. 2. Add the broccoli, daikon, bell peppers, ground cumin, and beef broth to the pot. 3. Secure the lid and select Manual mode, setting the cooking time for 20 minutes at High Pressure. 4. Once the timer beeps, allow for a natural pressure release for 10 minutes, then carefully release any remaining pressure before opening the lid. 5. Serve the dish warm and enjoy your meal!

Classic Hot and Sour Soup with Shiitake Mushrooms and Pork

Prep time: 0 minutes | Cook time: 30 minutes | Serves 6

- 4 cups boiling water
- 1 ounce dried shiitake mushrooms
- 2 tablespoons cold-pressed avocado oil
- 3 garlic cloves, chopped
- 4 ounces cremini or button mushrooms, sliced
- 1 pound boneless pork loin, sirloin, or tip, thinly sliced against the grain into ¼-inch-thick, ½-inch-wide, 2-inch-long strips
- 1 teaspoon ground ginger
- ½ teaspoon ground white pepper
- 2 cups low-sodium chicken broth or vegetable broth
- One 8-ounce can sliced bamboo shoots, drained and rinsed
- 2 tablespoons low-sodium soy sauce
- 1 tablespoon chile garlic sauce
- 1 teaspoon toasted sesame oil
- 2 teaspoons Lakanto Monkfruit Sweetener Classic
- 2 large eggs
- ¼ cup rice vinegar
- 2 tablespoons cornstarch
- 4 green onions, white and green parts, thinly sliced
- ¼ cup chopped fresh cilantro

1. In a large liquid measuring cup or heatproof bowl, pour the boiling water over the shiitake mushrooms. Cover and let soak for 30 minutes. Drain the mushrooms, reserving the soaking liquid. Remove and discard the stems and thinly slice the caps. 2. Select the Sauté setting on the Instant Pot and heat the avocado oil and garlic for 2 minutes, until the garlic is bubbling but not browned. Add the cremini and shiitake mushrooms and sauté for 3 minutes, until the mushrooms are beginning to wilt. Add the pork, ginger, and white pepper and sauté for about 5 minutes, until the pork is opaque and cooked through. 3. Pour the mushroom soaking liquid into the pot, being careful to leave behind any sediment at the bottom of the measuring cup or bowl. Using a wooden spoon, nudge any browned bits from the bottom of the pot. Stir in the broth, bamboo shoots, soy sauce, chile garlic sauce, sesame oil, and sweetener. 4. Secure the lid and set the Pressure Release to Sealing. Press the Cancel button to reset the cooking program, then select the Pressure Cook or Manual setting and set the cooking time for 5 minutes at high pressure. (The pot will take about 10 minutes to come up to pressure before the cooking program begins.) 5. While the soup is cooking, in a small bowl, beat the eggs until no streaks of yolk remain. 6. When the cooking program ends, let the pressure release naturally for at least 15 minutes, then move the Pressure Release to Venting to release any remaining steam. 7. In a small bowl, stir together the vinegar and cornstarch until the cornstarch dissolves. Open the pot and stir the vinegar mixture into the soup. Press the Cancel button to reset the cooking program, then select the Sauté setting. Bring the soup to a simmer and cook, stirring occasionally, for about 3 minutes, until slightly thickened. While stirring the soup constantly, pour in the beaten eggs in a thin stream. Press the Cancel button to turn off the pot and then stir in the green onions and cilantro. 8. Ladle the soup into bowls and serve hot.

Chicken and Kale Soup

Prep time: 5 minutes | Cook time: 5 minutes | Serves 4

- 2 cups chopped cooked chicken breast
- 12 ounces (340 g) frozen kale
- 1 onion, chopped
- 2 cups water
- 1 tablespoon powdered chicken broth base
- ½ teaspoon ground
- cinnamon
- Pinch ground cloves
- 2 teaspoons minced garlic
- 1 teaspoon freshly ground black pepper
- 1 teaspoon salt
- 2 cups full-fat coconut milk

1. Begin by placing the chicken, kale, onion, water, chicken broth base, cinnamon, cloves, garlic, pepper, and salt into the inner pot of the Instant Pot. 2. Secure the lid in place and select the Manual setting, adjusting the pressure to High. Set the cooking time for 5 minutes. Once the cooking is complete, allow the pressure to release naturally for 10 minutes, then perform a quick release for any remaining pressure. Carefully unlock the lid. 3. Stir in the coconut milk and taste the soup, adjusting any seasonings as needed before serving. Enjoy your flavorful dish!

Broccoli Brie Soup

Prep time: 5 minutes | Cook time: 14 minutes | Serves 6

- 1 tablespoon coconut oil or unsalted butter
- 1 cup finely diced onions
- 1 head broccoli, cut into small florets
- 2½ cups chicken broth or vegetable broth
- 8 ounces (227 g) Brie cheese, cut off rind and cut into chunks
- 1 cup unsweetened almond milk or heavy cream, plus more for drizzling
- Fine sea salt and ground black pepper, to taste
- Extra-virgin olive oil, for drizzling
- Coarse sea salt, for garnish

1. Begin by placing the coconut oil in the Instant Pot and selecting the Sauté function. Once the oil is hot, add the chopped onions and sauté for about 4 minutes, or until they are soft. Press Cancel to stop the sautéing process. 2. Add the broccoli and broth to the pot. Secure the lid, press Manual, and set the timer for 10 minutes. Once cooking is complete, allow the pressure to release naturally. 3. After removing the lid, add the Brie cheese and almond milk to the pot. Transfer the mixture to a food processor or blender and blend until smooth, or use a stick blender to purée the soup directly in the pot. 4. Season the soup with salt and pepper to taste. Ladle the soup into bowls and drizzle with additional almond milk and olive oil. Garnish with coarse sea salt and freshly ground pepper before serving. Enjoy!

Creamy Chicken and Wild Rice Comfort Soup

Prep time: 15 minutes | Cook time: 15 minutes | Serves 5

- 2 tablespoons margarine
- ½ cup yellow onion, diced
- ¾ cup carrots, diced
- ¾ cup sliced mushrooms (about 3–4 mushrooms)
- ½ pound chicken breast, diced into 1-inch cubes
- 6.2-ounce box Uncle Ben's Long Grain & Wild
- Rice Fast Cook
- 2 14-ounce cans low-sodium chicken broth
- 1 cup skim milk
- 1 cup evaporated skim milk
- 2 ounces fat-free cream cheese
- 2 tablespoons cornstarch

1. Select the Sauté feature and add the margarine, onion, carrots, and mushrooms to the inner pot. Sauté for about 5 minutes until onions are translucent and soft. 2. Add the cubed chicken and seasoning packet from the Uncle Ben's box and stir to combine. 3. Add the rice and chicken broth. Select Manual, high pressure, then lock the lid and make sure the vent is set to sealing. Set the time for 5 minutes.

4. After the cooking time ends, allow it to stay on Keep Warm for 5 minutes and then quick release the pressure. 5. Remove the lid; change the setting to the Sauté function again. 6. Add the skim milk, evaporated milk, and cream cheese. Stir to melt. 7. In a small bowl, mix the cornstarch with a little bit of water to dissolve, then add to the soup to thicken.

Quick and Easy Southern Brunswick Stew

Prep time: 20 minutes | Cook time: 8 minutes | Serves 12

- 2 pounds pork butt, visible fat removed
- 17-ounce can white corn
- 1¼ cups ketchup
- 2 cups diced, cooked potatoes
- 10-ounce package frozen
- peas
- 2 10¾-ounce cans reduced-sodium tomato soup
- Hot sauce to taste, optional

1. Place pork in the Instant Pot and secure the lid. 2. Press the Slow Cook setting and cook on low 6–8 hours. 3. When cook time is over, remove the meat from the bone and shred, removing and discarding all visible fat. 4. Combine all the meat and remaining ingredients (except the hot sauce) in the inner pot of the Instant Pot. 5. Secure the lid once more and cook in Slow Cook mode on low for 30 minutes more. Add hot sauce if you wish.

French Market Ham and Bean Soup

Prep time: 20 minutes | Cook time: 1 hour | Serves 8

- 2 cups mixed dry beans, washed with stones removed
- 7 cups water
- 1 ham hock, all visible fat removed
- 1 teaspoon salt
- ¼ teaspoon pepper
- 16-ounce can low-sodium tomatoes
- 1 large onion, chopped
- 1 garlic clove, minced
- 1 chile, chopped, or 1 teaspoon chili powder
- ¼ cup lemon juice

1. Combine all ingredients in the inner pot of the Instant Pot. 2. Secure the lid and make sure vent is set to sealing. Using Manual, set the Instant Pot to cook for 60 minutes. 3. When cooking time is over, let the pressure release naturally. When the Instant Pot is ready, unlock the lid, then remove the bone and any hard or fatty pieces. Pull the meat off the bone and chop into small pieces. Add the ham back into the Instant Pot.

Beef and Eggplant Tagine

Prep time: 15 minutes | Cook time: 25 minutes | Serves 6

- 1 pound (454 g) beef fillet, chopped
- 1 eggplant, chopped
- 6 ounces (170 g) scallions, chopped
- 4 cups beef broth
- 1 teaspoon ground allspices
- 1 teaspoon erythritol
- 1 teaspoon coconut oil

1. Add all the ingredients to the Instant Pot and stir well to combine. 2. Secure the lid and select Manual mode, setting the cooking time for 25 minutes at High Pressure. 3. Once the timer beeps, allow for a natural pressure release for 15 minutes before releasing any remaining pressure. Carefully open the lid. 4. Serve the dish warm and enjoy!

Thai Coconut Shrimp and Mushroom Soup

Prep time: 15 minutes | Cook time: 10 minutes | Serves 6

- 2 tablespoons unsalted butter, divided
- ½ pound (227 g) medium uncooked shrimp, shelled and deveined
- ½ medium yellow onion, diced
- 2 cloves garlic, minced
- 1 cup sliced fresh white mushrooms
- 1 tablespoon freshly grated ginger root
- 4 cups chicken broth
- 2 tablespoons fish sauce
- 2½ teaspoons red curry
- paste
- 2 tablespoons lime juice
- 1 stalk lemongrass, outer stalk removed, crushed, and finely chopped
- 2 tablespoons coconut aminos
- 1 teaspoon sea salt
- ½ teaspoon ground black pepper
- 13½ ounces (383 g) can unsweetened, full-fat coconut milk
- 3 tablespoons chopped fresh cilantro

1. Select the Instant Pot on Sauté mode. Add 1 tablespoon butter. 2. Once the butter is melted, add the shrimp and sauté for 3 minutes or until opaque. Transfer the shrimp to a medium bowl. Set aside. 3. Add the remaining butter to the pot. Once the butter is melted, add the onions and garlic and sauté for 2 minutes or until the garlic is fragrant and the onions are softened. 4. Add the mushrooms, ginger root, chicken broth, fish sauce, red curry paste, lime juice, lemongrass, coconut aminos, sea salt, and black pepper to the pot. Stir to combine. 5. Lock the lid. Select Manual mode and set cooking time for 5 minutes on High Pressure. 6. When cooking is complete, allow the pressure to release naturally for 5 minutes, then release the remaining pressure. 7. Open the lid. Stir in the cooked shrimp and coconut milk. 8. Select Sauté mode. Bring the soup to a boil and then press Keep Warm / Cancel. Let the soup rest in the pot for 2 minutes. 9. Ladle the soup into bowls and sprinkle the cilantro over top. Serve hot.

Turkey and Pinto Chili

Prep time: 0 minutes | Cook time: 60 minutes | Serves 8

- 2 tablespoons cold-pressed avocado oil
- 4 garlic cloves, diced
- 1 large yellow onion, diced
- 4 jalapeño chiles, seeded and diced
- 2 carrots, diced
- 4 celery stalks, diced
- 2 teaspoons fine sea salt
- 2 pounds 93 percent lean ground turkey
- Two 4-ounce cans fire-roasted diced green chiles
- 4 tablespoons chili powder
- 2 teaspoons ground cumin
- 2 teaspoons ground coriander
- 1 teaspoon dried oregano
- 1 teaspoon dried sage
- 1 cup low-sodium chicken broth
- 3 cups drained cooked pinto beans, or two 15-ounce cans pinto beans, drained and rinsed
- Two 14½-ounce cans no-salt petite diced tomatoes and their liquid
- ¼ cup tomato paste

1. Start by selecting the Sauté setting on the Instant Pot. Heat the oil and garlic for about 3 minutes until the garlic is bubbling but not browned. Then, add the onion, jalapeños, carrots, celery, and salt, sautéing for 5 minutes until the onion begins to soften. Next, add the turkey, using a wooden spoon or spatula to break up the meat as it cooks, and sauté for 6 minutes until it's cooked through with no pink remaining. Stir in the green chiles, chili powder, cumin, coriander, oregano, sage, and broth, scraping up any browned bits from the bottom of the pot. 2. Layer the beans on top of the turkey, followed by the tomatoes and their juices. Add the tomato paste in a dollop on top without stirring in the beans, tomatoes, or paste. 3. Secure the lid and set the Pressure Release to Sealing. Press the Cancel button to reset the cooking program, then select the Pressure Cook or Manual setting, adjusting the cooking time to 15 minutes at high pressure. (The pot will take about 15 minutes to come to pressure before the cooking program begins.) 4. Once the cooking program ends, allow the pressure to release naturally for at least 20 minutes, then switch the Pressure Release to Venting to release any remaining steam. Carefully open the pot and stir the chili to combine all the ingredients. 5. Press the Cancel button again to reset the cooking program, then select the Sauté setting and set the cooking time for 10 minutes. Allow the chili to reduce and thicken, but do not stir while it cooks to prevent sputtering. 6. When the cooking program ends, the pot will turn off. Using heat-resistant mitts, carefully remove the inner pot from the housing. Wait for about 2 minutes to let the chili stop simmering, then give it a final stir. 7. Ladle the chili into bowls and serve hot. Enjoy your delicious meal!

Creamy Bacon Curry Soup

Prep time: 10 minutes | Cook time: 20 minutes | Serves 4

- 3 ounces (85 g) bacon, chopped
- 1 tablespoon chopped scallions
- 1 teaspoon curry powder
- 1 cup coconut milk
- 3 cups beef broth
- 1 cup Cheddar cheese, shredded

1. Heat the the Instant Pot on Sauté mode for 3 minutes and add bacon. Cook for 5 minutes. Flip constantly. 2. Add the scallions and curry powder. Sauté for 5 minutes more. 3. Pour in the coconut milk and beef broth. Add the Cheddar cheese and stir to mix well. 4. Select Manual mode and set cooking time for 10 minutes on High Pressure. 5. When timer beeps, use a quick pressure release. Open the lid. 6. Blend the soup with an immersion blender until smooth. Serve warm.

Hearty Pasta e Fagioli with Beef and Veggies

Prep time: 0 minutes | Cook time: 30 minutes | Serves 8

- 2 tablespoons extra-virgin olive oil
- 4 garlic cloves, minced
- 1 yellow onion, diced
- 2 large carrots, diced
- 4 celery stalks, diced
- 1½ pounds 95 percent extra-lean ground beef
- 4 cups low-sodium vegetable broth
- 2 teaspoons Italian seasoning
- ½ teaspoon freshly
- ground black pepper
- 1¼ cups chickpea-based elbow pasta or whole-wheat elbow pasta
- 1½ cups drained cooked kidney beans, or one 15-ounce can kidney beans, rinsed and drained
- One 28-ounce can whole San Marzano tomatoes and their liquid
- 2 tablespoons chopped fresh flat-leaf parsley

1. Select the Sauté setting on the Instant Pot and heat the oil and garlic for 2 minutes, until the garlic is bubbling but not browned. Add the onion, carrots, and celery and sauté for 5 minutes, until the onion begins to soften. Add the beef and sauté, using a wooden spoon or spatula to break up the meat as it cooks, for 5 minutes; it's fine if some streaks of pink remain, the beef does not need to be cooked through. 2. Stir in the broth, Italian seasoning, pepper, and pasta, making sure all of the pasta is submerged in the liquid. Add the beans and stir to mix. Add the tomatoes and their liquid, crushing the tomatoes with your hands as you add them to the pot. Do not stir them in. 3. Secure the lid and set the Pressure Release to Sealing. Press the Cancel button to reset the cooking program, then select the Pressure Cook or Manual setting and set the cooking time for 2 minutes at low pressure. (The pot will take about 15 minutes to come up to pressure before the cooking program begins.) 4. When the cooking program ends, let the pressure release naturally for 10 minutes, then move the Pressure Release to Venting to release any remaining steam. Open the pot and stir the soup to mix all of the ingredients. 5. Ladle the soup into bowls, sprinkle with the parsley, and serve right away.

Parmesan Zucchini Soup

Prep time: 10 minutes | Cook time: 1 minute | Serves 2

- 1 zucchini, grated
- 1 teaspoon ground paprika
- ½ teaspoon cayenne pepper
- ½ cup coconut milk
- 1 cup beef broth
- 1 tablespoon dried cilantro
- 1 ounce (28 g) Parmesan, grated

1. Place the grated zucchini, paprika, cayenne pepper, coconut milk, beef broth, and dried cilantro into the Instant Pot. 2. Secure and seal the lid. 3. Cook the soup on Manual (High Pressure) for 1 minute, then perform a quick pressure release. 4. Ladle the soup into serving bowls and top with Parmesan cheese. Enjoy your delicious soup!

Curried Chicken Soup

Prep time: 10 minutes | Cook time: 10 minutes | Serves 6

- 1 pound (454 g) boneless, skinless chicken thighs
- 1½ cups unsweetened coconut milk
- ½ onion, finely diced
- 3 or 4 garlic cloves, crushed
- 1 (2-inch) piece ginger, finely chopped
- 1 cup sliced mushrooms, such as cremini and
- shiitake
- 4 ounces (113 g) baby spinach
- 1 teaspoon salt
- ½ teaspoon ground turmeric
- ½ teaspoon cayenne
- 1 teaspoon garam masala
- ¼ cup chopped fresh cilantro

1. In the inner pot of your Instant Pot, combine the chicken, coconut milk, onion, garlic, ginger, mushrooms, spinach, salt, turmeric, cayenne, garam masala, and cilantro. 2. Secure the lid in place, select the Manual setting, and adjust the pressure to High. Set the cooking time for 10 minutes. Once the cooking is complete, allow the pressure to release naturally before unlocking the lid. 3. Using tongs, transfer the chicken to a bowl and shred it. Stir the shredded chicken back into the soup. 4. Serve the soup and enjoy your delicious meal!

Beef and Spinach Stew

Prep time: 20 minutes | Cook time: 30 minutes | Serves 4

- 1 pound (454 g) beef sirloin, chopped
- 2 cups spinach, chopped
- 3 cups chicken broth
- 1 cup coconut milk
- 1 teaspoon allspices
- 1 teaspoon coconut aminos

1. Add all ingredients to the Instant Pot and stir to combine thoroughly. 2. Secure the lid and set the Instant Pot to Manual mode, adjusting the cooking time to 30 minutes at High Pressure. 3. Once the timer beeps, allow for a natural pressure release for 10 minutes before releasing any remaining pressure. Carefully open the lid. 4. Use an immersion blender to blend the mixture until smooth. 5. Serve the soup warm and enjoy!

Creamy Broccoli Cheddar Delight

Prep time: 5 minutes | Cook time: 10 minutes | Serves 4

- 2 tablespoons butter
- ⅛ cup onion, diced
- ½ teaspoon garlic powder
- ½ teaspoon salt
- ¼ teaspoon pepper
- 2 cups chicken broth
- 1 cup chopped broccoli
- 1 tablespoon cream cheese, softened
- ¼ cup heavy cream
- 1 cup shredded Cheddar cheese

1. Press the Sauté button and add butter to Instant Pot. Add onion and sauté until translucent. Press the Cancel button and add garlic powder, salt, pepper, broth, and broccoli to pot. 2. Click lid closed. Press the Soup button and set time for 5 minutes. When timer beeps, stir in heavy cream, cream cheese, and Cheddar.

Beef and Mushroom Stew

Prep time: 15 minutes | Cook time: 30 minutes | Serves 4

- 2 tablespoons coconut oil
- 1 pound (454 g) cubed chuck roast
- 1 cup sliced button mushrooms
- ½ medium onion, chopped
- 2 cups beef broth
- ½ cup chopped celery
- 1 tablespoon sugar-free tomato paste
- 1 teaspoon thyme
- 2 garlic cloves, minced
- ½ teaspoon xanthan gum

1. Begin by pressing the Sauté button on the Instant Pot and adding coconut oil. Brown the cubes of chuck roast until they are golden, working in batches if necessary to avoid overcrowding the pan, which can prevent proper browning. Once browned, set the meat aside. 2. Next, add the mushrooms and onions to the pot. Sauté until the mushrooms start to brown and the onions become translucent. Then, press the Cancel button to stop the sautéing process. 3. Pour the broth into the Instant Pot, using a wooden spoon to scrape up any browned bits from the bottom if needed. Add the celery, tomato paste, thyme, and garlic. Secure the lid and close it. Press the Manual button and set the cooking time for 35 minutes. When the timer beeps, allow for a natural pressure release. 4. Once the pressure valve drops, stir in the xanthan gum to thicken the soup. Serve warm and enjoy!

Provençal Chicken Fennel Soup

Prep time: 20 minutes | Cook time: 30 minutes | Serves 6 to 8

- 1 tablespoon extra-virgin olive oil
- 2 fennel bulbs, 2 tablespoons fronds minced, stalks discarded, bulbs halved, cored, and cut into ½-inch pieces
- 1 onion, chopped
- 1¾ teaspoons table salt
- 2 tablespoons tomato paste
- 4 garlic cloves, minced
- 1 tablespoon minced fresh thyme or 1 teaspoon dried
- 2 anchovy fillets, minced
- 7 cups water, divided
- 1 (14½-ounce / 411-g) can diced tomatoes, drained
- 2 carrots, peeled, halved lengthwise, and sliced ½ inch thick
- 2 (12-ounce / 340-g) bone-in split chicken breasts, trimmed
- 4 (5- to 7-ounce / 142- to 198-g) bone-in chicken thighs, trimmed
- ½ cup pitted brine-cured green olives, chopped
- 1 teaspoon grated orange zest

1. Using highest sauté function, heat oil in Instant Pot until shimmering. Add fennel pieces, onion, and salt and cook until vegetables are softened, about 5 minutes. Stir in tomato paste, garlic, thyme, and anchovies and cook until fragrant, about 30 seconds. Stir in 5 cups water, scraping up any browned bits, then stir in tomatoes and carrots. Nestle chicken breasts and thighs in pot. 2. Lock lid in place and close pressure release valve. Select high pressure cook function and cook for 20 minutes. Turn off Instant Pot and quick-release pressure. Carefully remove lid, allowing steam to escape away from you. 3. Transfer chicken to cutting board, let cool slightly, then shred into bite-size pieces using 2 forks; discard skin and bones. 4. Using wide, shallow spoon, skim excess fat from surface of soup. Stir chicken and any accumulated juices, olives, and remaining 2 cups water into soup and let sit until heated through, about 3 minutes. Stir in fennel fronds and orange zest, and season with salt and pepper to taste. Serve.

Chicken Cauliflower Rice Soup

Prep time: 5 minutes | Cook time: 20 minutes | Serves 4

- 4 tablespoons butter
- ¼ cup diced onion
- 2 stalks celery, chopped
- ½ cup fresh spinach
- ½ teaspoon salt
- ¼ teaspoon pepper
- ¼ teaspoon dried thyme
- ¼ teaspoon dried parsley
- 1 bay leaf
- 2 cups chicken broth
- 2 cups diced cooked chicken
- ¾ cup uncooked cauliflower rice
- ½ teaspoon xanthan gum (optional)

1. Start by pressing the Sauté button on the Instant Pot and adding butter. Once melted, add the onions and sauté until they become translucent. Then, add the celery and spinach, continuing to sauté for 2 to 3 minutes until the spinach wilts. Press the Cancel button to stop the sautéing process. 2. Next, sprinkle the seasoning into the pot, and add the bay leaf, broth, and cooked chicken. Secure the lid and close it. Press the Soup button and adjust the cooking time to 10 minutes. 3. When the timer beeps, perform a quick release of the pressure and stir in the cauliflower rice. Keep the Instant Pot on the Keep Warm setting for an additional 10 minutes to finish cooking the cauliflower rice. Serve warm. 4. If you prefer a thicker soup, stir in xanthan gum to achieve your desired consistency. Enjoy your meal!

Hearty Ground Turkey Chili Stew

Prep time: 5 minutes | Cook time: 25 minutes | Serves 5

- 1 tablespoon olive oil
- 1 onion, chopped
- 1 pound ground turkey
- ½ teaspoon garlic powder
- 1 teaspoon chili powder
- ¾ teaspoon cumin
- 2 teaspoons coriander
- 1 teaspoon dried oregano
- ½ teaspoon salt
- 1 green pepper, chopped
- 1 red pepper, chopped
- 1 tomato, chopped
- 1½ cups reduced-sodium tomato sauce
- 1 tablespoon low-sodium soy sauce
- 1 cup water
- 2 handfuls cilantro, chopped
- 15-ounce can reduced-salt black beans

1. Press the Sauté function on the control panel of the Instant Pot. 2. Add the olive oil to the inner pot and let it get hot. Add onion and sauté for a few minutes, or until light golden. 3. Add ground turkey. Break the ground meat using a wooden spoon to avoid formation of lumps. Sauté for a few minutes, until the pink color has faded. 4. Add garlic powder, chili powder, cumin, coriander, dried oregano, and salt. Combine well. Add green pepper, red pepper, and chopped tomato. Combine well. 5. Add tomato sauce, soy sauce, and water; combine well. 6. Close and secure the lid. Click on the Cancel key to cancel the Sauté mode. Make sure the pressure release valve on the lid is in the sealing position. 7. Click on Manual function first and then select high pressure. Click the + button and set the time to 15 minutes. 8. You can either have the steam release naturally (it will take around 20 minutes) or, after 10 minutes, turn the pressure release valve on the lid to venting and release steam. Be careful as the steam is very hot. After the pressure has released completely, open the lid. 9. If the stew is watery, turn on the Sauté function and let it cook for a few more minutes with the lid off. 10. Add cilantro and can of black beans, combine well, and let cook for a few minutes.

Creamy Kale and Chicken Curry Soup

Prep time: 10 minutes | Cook time: 15 minutes | Serves 3

- 2 cups kale
- 1 teaspoon almond butter
- 1 tablespoon fresh cilantro
- ½ cup ground chicken
- 1 teaspoon curry paste
- ½ cup heavy cream
- 1 cup chicken stock
- ½ teaspoon salt

1. Put the kale in the Instant Pot. 2. Add the almond butter, cilantro, and ground chicken. Sauté the mixture for 5 minutes. 3. Meanwhile, mix the curry paste and heavy cream in the Instant Pot until creamy. 4. Add chicken stock and salt, and close the lid. 5. Select Manual mode and set cooking time for 10 minutes on High Pressure. 6. When timer beeps, make a quick pressure release. Open the lid. 7. Serve warm.

Nancy's Vegetable Beef Soup

Prep time: 25 minutes | Cook time: 8 hours | Serves 8

- 2 pounds roast, cubed, or 2 pounds stewing meat
- 15 ounces can corn
- 15 ounces can green beans
- 1 pound bag frozen peas
- 40 ounces can no-added-salt stewed tomatoes
- 5 teaspoons salt-free beef bouillon powder
- Tabasco, to taste
- ½ teaspoons salt

1. Add all ingredients to the Instant Pot, ensuring not to drain the vegetables. 2. Pour in water until it reaches the fill line in the inner pot. 3. Secure the lid, or if using a glass lid, set the Instant Pot to Slow Cook mode on Low for 8 hours, or until the meat is tender and the vegetables are soft. Enjoy your meal!

Sicilian Swordfish Stew with Pine Nuts and Mint

Prep time: 10 minutes | Cook time: 10 minutes | Serves 4 to 6

- 2 tablespoons extra-virgin olive oil
- 2 onions, chopped fine
- 1 teaspoon table salt
- ½ teaspoon pepper
- 1 teaspoon minced fresh thyme or ¼ teaspoon dried
- Pinch red pepper flakes
- 4 garlic cloves, minced, divided
- 1 (28-ounce / 794-g) can whole peeled tomatoes, drained with juice reserved, chopped coarse
- 1 (8-ounce / 227-g) bottle clam juice
- ¼ cup dry white wine
- ¼ cup golden raisins
- 2 tablespoons capers, rinsed
- 1½ pounds (680 g) skinless swordfish steak, 1 to 1½ inches thick, cut into 1-inch pieces
- ¼ cup pine nuts, toasted
- ¼ cup minced fresh mint
- 1 teaspoon grated orange zest

1. Using highest sauté function, heat oil in Instant Pot until shimmering. Add onions, salt, and pepper and cook until onions are softened, about 5 minutes. Stir in thyme, pepper flakes, and three-quarters of garlic and cook until fragrant, about 30 seconds. Stir in tomatoes and reserved juice, clam juice, wine, raisins, and capers. Nestle swordfish into pot and spoon some cooking liquid over top. 2. Lock lid in place and close pressure release valve. Select high pressure cook function and cook for 1 minute. Turn off Instant Pot and quick-release pressure. Carefully remove lid, allowing steam to escape away from you. 3. Combine pine nuts, mint, orange zest, and remaining garlic in bowl. Season stew with salt and pepper to taste. Sprinkle individual portions with pine nut mixture before serving.

Favorite Chili

Prep time: 10 minutes | Cook time: 35 minutes | Serves 5

- 1 pound extra-lean ground beef
- 1 teaspoon salt
- ½ teaspoons black pepper
- 1 tablespoon olive oil
- 1 small onion, chopped
- 2 cloves garlic, minced
- 1 green pepper, chopped
- 2 tablespoons chili powder
- ½ teaspoons cumin
- 1 cup water
- 16-ounce can chili beans
- 15-ounce can low-sodium crushed tomatoes

1. Begin by pressing the Sauté button and adjusting it to the Sauté More function. Wait until the display indicates that it is "hot." 2. Season the ground beef generously with salt and black pepper. 3. Add olive oil to the inner pot, ensuring the entire bottom is coated with the oil. 4. Once the oil is hot, add the ground beef to the pot. Allow it to release its moisture and brown slightly, stirring occasionally to break it up. Taste and adjust the seasoning with additional salt and black pepper as needed. 5. Incorporate the diced onion, minced garlic, chopped pepper, chili powder, and cumin into the pot. Sauté for about 5 minutes until the spices begin to release their fragrance, stirring frequently. 6. Add water and one can of chili beans (undrained), mixing thoroughly. Pour in the can of crushed tomatoes and combine well. 7. Close and secure the lid, ensuring that the vent is set to sealing. Pressure cook on Manual at high pressure for 10 minutes. 8. Once the cooking time is complete, allow the pressure to release naturally. Carefully open the lid and enjoy your dish!

Creamy Chicken and Asparagus Curry Soup

Prep time: 7 minutes | Cook time: 11 minutes | Serves 8

- 1 tablespoon unsalted butter (or coconut oil for dairy-free)
- ¼ cup finely chopped onions
- 2 cloves garlic, minced
- 1 (14-ounce / 397-g) can full-fat coconut milk
- 1 (14-ounce / 397-g) can sugar-free tomato sauce
- 1 cup chicken broth
- 1 tablespoon red curry paste
- 1 teaspoon fine sea salt
- ½ teaspoon ground black pepper
- 2 pounds (907 g) boneless, skinless chicken breasts, cut into ½-inch chunks
- 2 cups asparagus, trimmed and cut into 2-inch pieces
- Fresh cilantro leaves, for garnish
- Lime wedges, for garnish

1. Place the butter in the Instant Pot and press Sauté. Once melted, add the onions and garlic and sauté for 4 minutes, or until the onions are soft. Press Cancel to stop the Sauté. 2. Add the coconut milk, tomato sauce, broth, curry paste, salt, and pepper and whisk to combine well. Stir in the chicken and asparagus. 3. Seal the lid, press Manual, and set the timer for 7 minutes. Once finished, turn the valve to venting for a quick release. 4. Remove the lid and stir well. Taste and adjust the seasoning to your liking. Ladle the soup into bowls and garnish with cilantro. Serve with lime wedges or a squirt of lime juice.

Appendix
1

Instant Pot Cooking Timetable

Dried Beans, Legumes and Lentils

Dried Beans and Legume	Dry (Minutes)	Soaked (Minutes)
Soy beans	25 – 30	20 – 25
Scarlet runner	20 – 25	10 – 15
Pinto beans	25 – 30	20 – 25
Peas	15 – 20	10 – 15
Navy beans	25 – 30	20 – 25
Lima beans	20 – 25	10 – 15
Lentils, split, yellow (moong dal)	15 – 18	N/A
Lentils, split, red	15 – 18	N/A
Lentils, mini, green (brown)	15 – 20	N/A
Lentils, French green	15 – 20	N/A
Kidney white beans	35 – 40	20 – 25
Kidney red beans	25 – 30	20 – 25
Great Northern beans	25 – 30	20 – 25
Pigeon peas	20 – 25	15 – 20
Chickpeas (garbanzo bean chickpeas)	35 – 40	20 – 25
Cannellini beans	35 – 40	20 – 25
Black-eyed peas	20 – 25	10 – 15
Black beans	20 – 25	10 – 15

Fish and Seafood

Fish and Seafood	Fresh (minutes)	Frozen (minutes)
Shrimp or Prawn	1 to 2	2 to 3
Seafood soup or stock	6 to 7	7 to 9
Mussels	2 to 3	4 to 6
Lobster	3 to 4	4 to 6
Fish, whole (snapper, trout, etc.)	5 to 6	7 to 10
Fish steak	3 to 4	4 to 6
Fish fillet,	2 to 3	3 to 4
Crab	3 to 4	5 to 6

Fruits

Fruits	Fresh (in Minutes)	Dried (in Minutes)
Raisins	N/A	4 to 5
Prunes	2 to 3	4 to 5
Pears, whole	3 to 4	4 to 6
Pears, slices or halves	2 to 3	4 to 5
Peaches	2 to 3	4 to 5
Apricots, whole or halves	2 to 3	3 to 4
Apples, whole	3 to 4	4 to 6
Apples, in slices or pieces	2 to 3	3 to 4

Meat

Meat and Cuts	Cooking Time (minutes)	Meat and Cuts	Cooking Time (minutes)
Veal, roast	35 to 45	Duck, with bones, cut up	10 to 12
Veal, chops	5 to 8	Cornish Hen, whole	10 to 15
Turkey, drumsticks (leg)	15 to 20	Chicken, whole	20 to 25
Turkey, breast, whole, with bones	25 to 30	Chicken, legs, drumsticks, or thighs	10 to 15
Turkey, breast, boneless	15 to 20	Chicken, with bones, cut up	10 to 15
Quail, whole	8 to 10	Chicken, breasts	8 to 10
Pork, ribs	20 to 25	Beef, stew	15 to 20
Pork, loin roast	55 to 60	Beef, shanks	25 to 30
Pork, butt roast	45 to 50	Beef, ribs	25 to 30
Pheasant	20 to 25	Beef, steak, pot roast, round, rump, brisket or blade, small chunks, chuck,	25 to 30
Lamb, stew meat	10 to 15		
Lamb, leg	35 to 45	Beef, pot roast, steak, rump, round, chuck, blade or brisket, large	35 to 40
Lamb, cubes,	10 t0 15		
Ham slice	9 to 12	Beef, ox-tail	40 to 50
Ham picnic shoulder	25 to 30	Beef, meatball	10 to 15
Duck, whole	25 to 30	Beef, dressed	20 to 25

Appendix 2

Index

Made in the USA
Monee, IL
28 December 2024